Galileans under Jerusalem and Roman Rule

Galileans under Jerusalem and Roman Rule

RICHARD A. HORSLEY

EDITED BY
K. C. Hanson

CASCADE *Books* · Eugene, Oregon

GALILEANS UNDER JERUSALEM AND ROMAN RULE

Copyright © 2024 Richard A. Horsley. All rights reserved. Except for brief quotations in critical publications or reviews, no part of this book may be reproduced in any manner without prior written permission from the publisher. Write: Permissions, Wipf and Stock Publishers, 199 W. 8th Ave., Suite 3, Eugene, OR 97401.

Cascade Books
An Imprint of Wipf and Stock Publishers
199 W. 8th Ave., Suite 3
Eugene, OR 97401

www.wipfandstock.com

PAPERBACK ISBN: 979-8-3852-2020-5
HARDCOVER ISBN: 979-8-3852-2021-2
EBOOK ISBN: 979-8-3852-2022-9

Cataloguing-in-Publication data:

Names: Horsley, Richard A., author. | Hanson, K. C. (Kenneth Charles), 1951–, editor.

Title: Galileans under Jerusalem and Roman rule / Richard A. Horsley ; edited by K. C. Hanson.

Description: Eugene, OR: Cascade Books, 2024. | Includes bibliographical references and index.

Identifiers: ISBN 979-8-3852-2020-5 (paperback). | ISBN 979-8-3852-2021-2 (hardcover). | ISBN 979-8-3852-2022-9 (ebook).

Subjects: LCSH: Galilee (Israel)—History. | Jews—History—Rebellion, 66–73. | Hasmoneans. | Maccabees. | Josephus, Flavius. | Jews—History—586 B.C.–210 A.D.

Classification: DS110.G2 H64 2024 (print). | DS110.G2 (epub).

09/10/24

Contents

	List of Abbreviations	vii
	Introduction	1
1	The Expansion of Hasmonean Rule	27
2	Conquest and Social Conflict in Galilee	61
3	Power Vacuum and Power Struggle in 66–67 CE	101
4	Bandits, Messiahs, and Longshoremen: Popular Unrest in Galilee around the Time of Jesus	127
5	Archaeology and the Villages of Upper Galilee: A Dialogue with Archaeologists	151
6	Archaeology of Galilee and the Historical Context of Jesus	173
	Acknowledgments	193
	Bibliography	195
	Index	205

Abbreviations

ANRW	*Aufstieg und Niedergang der romischen Welt*
Ant.	Josephus, *Antiquities of the Judeans*
b.	Babylonian Talmud (Babli)
BA	*Biblical Archaeologist*
BASOR	*Bulletin of the American Schools of Oriental Research*
Bik.	Bikkurim
CBQ	*Catholic Biblical Quarterly*
JJS	*Journal of Jewish Studies*
JSJ	*Journal for the Study of Judaism*
m.	Mishnah
Ned.	Nedarim
NovT	*Novum Testamentum*
NTS	*New Testament Studies*
SBL	Society of Biblical Literature
SJLA	Studies in Judaism in Late Antiquity
SNTSMS	Society for New Testament Studies Monograph Series
SPB	Studia Post-Biblica
t.	Tosefta
Ta'an.	Ta'anit
War	Josephus, *Judean War*
y.	Jerusalem Talmud (Yerushalmi)

Introduction

IN GRADUATE SCHOOL IN the 1960s it became clear that we could not trust the standard scholarly constructs and even standard procedures in the fields of ancient Jewish history and biblical studies. Training in these fields meant learning how our mentors focused on often small fragments of ancient texts to attest to or to illustrate basic concepts, symbols, and doctrines. Coming from undergraduate training in history, I wondered why biblical scholars did not read more widely in their texts and try to understand them in historical context. And why didn't they recognize that some people had power over other people? For example, other academic fields had long since discovered the existence of peasants, villagers subject to overlords, who comprised the vast majority in any preindustrial society in almost any area of the world. Meanwhile in the 1960s, European countries in which the fields of biblical studies and ancient Jewish history developed were dealing with anti-colonial movements of peoples they had subjugated.

It did not take long in graduate school to recognize that most of the extant written texts that were our sources (with the exception of the Gospels) were the products of the cultural and political elite. In many articles and a few books in the 1970s and 1980s I sought a broader and more contextual understanding of historical figures and movements mentioned in our sources.[1] It had become clear, for example, that the synthetic construct of "the Zealots" had lumped together what our sources indicated were a diversity of popular movements of renewal and resistance along with some

---

1. See, for example, the series of articles now collected and republished in Horsley, *Politics, Conflict, and Movements in First-Century Palestine*; Horsley with J. S. Hanson, *Bandits, Prophets, and Messiahs*, which is based on the research in those articles; and Horsley, *Jesus and the Spiral of Violence*.

scribal movements of protest and resistance, and that there was no standard "Jewish expectation" of "the Messiah."[2]

My reading of whole texts and sustained narratives, the histories of Josephus for example, soon led to questioning the fundamental controlling modern scholarly constructs in the fields of biblical studies and ancient Jewish history. In the late 1980s and early 1990s several developments in these and other fields were leading to troubling further questions about the standard assumptions as well as the standard scholarly constructs of our training. For example, it was standard in New Testament studies to refer to the high priests as "Jewish leaders." I had already pointed out that in the first century the high priests almost always were complicit with the Romans who kept them in power, which meant that they did not represent the Judean people in their seemingly legitimate protests of Roman abuses.[3]

Reading more extensively in Josephus' histories meant learning that long before the Roman conquest the Hasmonean high priests had not only exploited and abused the Judean people, but had conquered nearby peoples with the mercenary troops they hired, becoming imitators of the Hellenistic kings who had previously conquered the Judeans. This meant that the Judean high priesthood had gone from ruling only the tiny territory and population in the environs of Jerusalem to conquering and controlling most of Palestine. Josephus' accounts also indicated that the inhabitants of Galilee, who had been assumed to be "Jews" like the people in Judea itself, had come under Jerusalem rule only about a century before the lifetime of Jesus. After the regional revolts against Jerusalem and Roman rule in 4 BCE, moreover, the Romans installed Herod's son Antipas as Tetrarch in Galilee, so that Galileans were no longer under Jerusalem rule at the time of Jesus' mission. It was puzzling to me that others in these fields, including friends, continued in what had become the standard constructs, concepts, and approaches, either not reading more widely in Josephus' histories or glossing over what he was recounting. This was all the more puzzling because it was becoming evident that we did not know what we previously thought we knew about Galilee and that because of the gap in our sources for early first century and second century, we knew little about Galilee at the time of Jesus and about Galilee during early development of rabbinic schools.

2. See Horsley, "Popular Messianic Movements;" and the collections of articles by biblical scholars and Jewish historians who were awakening in the 1980s to the limited and fragmentary evidence for Jewish expectations of the Messiah, Neusner, et al., *Judaisms and Their Messiahs*; and Charlesworth, ed., *The Messiah*.

3. In Horsley, "High Priests and the Politics of Roman Palestine."

Meanwhile some of my graduate school contemporaries were launching archeological explorations of key sites in Galilee. The findings of their digs were of potential importance to my intensified interest in Galilee because of the paucity of sources for people and events in Galilee during the lifetime of Jesus and the developments toward emergence of the Mishnah and Tosefta. I had great respect for these archaeological pioneers because they were, in effect, creating a new subfield and developing appropriate questions and techniques as they went. Having engaged in a major investigation and (revisionist) construction of the historical Jesus in the wider historical context of social and political conflict, I was eager to learn from the findings of their digs about the historical context "on the ground" in Galilee.

The first four articles collected in this volume are some of my early attempts to research and construct a more critical, precise, and comprehensive understanding of the complex history of late second-temple Judea and the other areas of Palestine that became subject to Jerusalem rule. It was important to understand this history for a grasp of the dynamics and conflicts between the high priestly and Herodian rulers in Jerusalem and the people under their control. But it was also important to have a better grounded understanding of this history as the watershed leading to Jesus' mission and the rapid expansion of Jesus-movements and leading to the Great Revolt[4] and the Roman re-conquest that left a political vacuum in the areas of Palestine in which rabbinic circles could form and develop. The other two articles were some of my early attempts to engage archaeologists in discussions aimed at more complete understanding of the historical context of Jesus' mission and movements and of the later work of rabbinic circles in Galilee.

GALILEANS COME UNDER HASMONEAN, ROMAN, AND HERODIAN RULE

The first article/chapter is an expanded form of a paper delivered in the "Sociology of the Second Temple" section of the SBL. I had read extensively in sociology, particularly historical sociology, while in graduate

---

4. I am using "Great Revolt" (in caps) here and throughout this collection to indicate how widespread and prolonged the revolt against Roman, high priestly, and Herodian rule was in 66–70 CE. What have become the standard terms, "the Jewish Revolt" and "the Jewish War," were influenced by the Flavian propaganda in Rome following their destruction of Jerusalem and Judea, as explained on pp. 16–18 below.

school and had become critical of what seemed like uncritical borrowing of structural-functional sociology that had already been largely abandoned by sociologists by the 1970s.[5] Some New Testament scholars were summarizing sociological models, such as the scheme of multiple "classes" of Gerhard Lenski's discussion of advanced agrarian societies,[6] then applying that model directly to biblical texts and/or illustrating the model from text-fragments taken at face value from New Testament texts. Some Hebrew Bible/Old Testament scholars had a more subtle understanding of how Lenski's comparative studies might be more carefully adapted.[7] A likely factor in the formation of the Sociology of the Second Temple section in the SBL was the slowness of scholars of Second-Temple texts and history to engage in serious learning of and adaptation of historical sociology. Having already witnessed the uneasiness of more tradition-oriented colleagues about the direct application of sociological models to texts, I had moved toward demonstrating how the social structure and dynamics of Judea ruled by the temple-state under the rule of Hellenistic imperial regimes could be discerned by careful examination of texts, Ben Sira's instructional discourses in particular.[8]

Lenski's model of horizontal "classes," one on top of another, was helpful in discerning how learned scribes such as Ben Sira functioned as advisers and representatives ("retainers") of "the rulers" and "governing class." But direct application of multiple horizontal "classes" distracted attention from the dominant divide between the rulers and the villagers they ruled. Moreover, Ben Sira's instructional discourses indicated that learned scribes

---

5. My sharp critique did not reach publication until the late 1980s, in Horsley, *Sociology and the Jesus Movement*; see the similar critique in Elliott, "Social Scientific Criticism of the New Testament."

6. Lenski, *Power and Privilege*.

7. Marvin Chaney exhibited a far more profound understanding of Lenski and how his model required appropriate adaptation to illuminate the historical context and messages of Israelite prophets; see Chaney, *Peasants, Prophets, and Political Economy*, esp. chaps. 1, 4, 6, 7.

8. To ensure that my reading of Ben Sira's discourses was sound, it was fortunate that Patrick Tiller, whose knowledge of Hebrew and Greek was far better than mine, was eager to co-author the presentation and its expansion, "Ben Sira and the Sociology of the Second Temple," presented in the Sociology of the Second Temple Section of SBL in 1993, but which was not published until 2002. Republished in Horsley and Tiller, *After Apocalyptic and Wisdom*, chap 1. See further Tiller, "The Social Settings of the Components of *1 Enoch*." Fuller discussion of the historical context in Horsley, *Scribes, Visionaries, and the Politics of Second Temple Judea*, chaps. 2–4.

serving the high priestly rulers had their own authorization from the Most High, so that they were not solely dependent on the high priests' authorization. Learned scribes had their own sense of how the temple-state should operate. And that became abundantly evident when the dominant faction of high priests maneuvered to transform the traditional Judean covenantal "constitution" of temple-state into a *polis* patterned after the imperial Hellenistic political ideology and practice. As can be seen clearly in the Animal Vision in 1 Enoch 85–90 and the parallel historical vision in Daniel 10–12, "Enoch" scribes and the *maskilim* could not only disagree with their high priestly patrons, but mount active resistance.[9] Critical reflection on the history of factions in the high priestly aristocracy that was closely connected with the rivalry between the Ptolemies and the Seleucids and the subsequent demise of the Seleucid Empire into rival ruling factions, moreover, led to the recognition of vertical divisions between imperial rulers, between high priestly factions in Jerusalem, and divisions among circles of scribes.

In chapter 1 below, this more nuanced analysis, derived from close reading of texts such as Ben Sira's speeches and historical visions such as the Animal Vision, informed my analysis and reconstruction of the history of the Hasmonean conquest of the Idumeans and take-over and rule of the Galileans. This required a more critical reading of Josephus' histories, particularly reading Josephus' sustained treatment of events and institutions and historical contingencies, in contrast to previous treatments that focused narrowly on brief accounts and text-fragments extracted from broader narrative context. The Hasmonean conquest and treatment of the Idumeans is important for understanding subsequent Judean history. But it is also important insofar as how we read Josephus' cursory account of the Hasmonean take-over of Galilee depends heavily on his more extensive accounts of the conquest of the Idumeans and his subsequent accounts of Idumeans. Uncritical and even careless reading of Josephus' accounts that does not notice the conflict between them requires detailed discussion and correction. The failure to recognize that the conflictual history of the relation between a subject people and the Hasmonean high priesthood cannot be understood in terms of religion separate from political power relations. The projection of modern concepts such as religious conversion (forced or voluntary) simply oversimplifies and distorts the history of relations

---

9. My careful analysis of these so-called "apocalyptic" texts was eventually published in Horsley, *Scribes, Visionaries, and the Politics of Second Temple Judea*, chaps. 7–9 and Conclusion.

between the Idumeans and the Hasmoneans. The Idumeans evidently retained much of their culture and evidently their tribal social structure. Idumeans from prominent families became high-ranking officers in the Hasmonean and Herodian administrations while still cultivating their traditional religion. Generations later ordinary Idumeans, far from becoming defenders of the Jerusalem temple-state, sided with Judean peasant forces in the great revolt against Roman and high priestly rule.

Sources for what happened to the Galileans as a result of the Hasmonean take-over of the territory only a century before the lifetime of Jesus are few and far-between. Much of the history of who the Galileans were and their life under the later Hasmoneans and then the Romans and Herod depends on the implications of indirect sources and historical reasoning from much earlier sources. The section of the article focused on the Hasmonean take-over of Galilee is my first attempt to probe the fragmentary evidence and clues from earlier sources and to reason carefully toward what seems like the most likely reconstruction of who the residents of Galilee were and the imperial arrangements for rule of Galilee that was significantly different from the rule of the Judeans by the temple-state.

Earlier and continuing discussion of the Galileans had generally failed to take into account that the vast majority were peasants living in villages in the countryside, same as the vast majority of the Judeans. Whereas Judean villagers had lived for centuries under the temple-state in Jerusalem, however, Galileans who came under Jerusalem rule only in 104 BCE were ruled and taxed by Judean garrisons in several fortified towns. To recognize this requires noting those occasional brief references to such garrisons and fortresses in Josephus accounts. In this chapter I was still entertaining the possibility that the Pharisees might have been involved in Galilee as representatives of the temple-state, while indicating the problems with this hypothesis.[10] In subsequent research I backed away further from this possibility. The shifting political situation, often chaotic, of the later Hasmoneans, Roman conquest, and the rise of Herod meant that there was never a period during which they could have mounted a campaign of "resocialization" of

---

10. In subsequent research on the Pharisees in their service in the temple-state I continued to entertain this possibility, while pointing out the difficulties, as in some of the articles collected in Horsley, *The Pharisees and the Temple-State of Judea*. The chaotic circumstances in the temple-state under the later Hasmoneans and the chaotic situation of Palestine under Roman rule and the Pharisees preoccupation with carefully resisting the tyranny of Herod, however, make this hypothesis extremely unlikely, as argued in Horsley, *The Pharisees and the Politics of Roman Palestine* (forthcoming).

the Galileans in their village communities. What we can ferret out of the sources, particularly the accounts of Josephus, indicates that neither in Idumea nor Galilee did the Jerusalem rulers plan, much less implement, a program to transform local village community life. That the Hasmoneans forced the Galileans, like the Idumeans, to live according to "the laws of the Judeans" did not mean that they required them to live according to all the laws in the books of the Pentateuch intended to regulate the operations of the priests in the temple (e.g., the Holiness Code in Leviticus). Rather, they forced them to live under the rule of the Judean temple-state, that is to submit to the laws of the Hasmonean state.

In the section of chapter 1 on "The Inhabitants of Galilee Prior to Hasmonean Takeover" (pp. 48–53), I explained how all of the three views of who the inhabitants of Galilee were before the Hasmoneans took over rule of Galilee were problematic and unsupported by the fragmentary evidence available. In that section, however, I did not include a fourth view that had only recently been floated particularly by archaeologists beginning excavations in certain sites in Galilee.[11] Evidently aware that the inhabitants of Galilee at the Hasmonean take-over were not predominantly "Gentiles," some or many of whom were supposedly "converted" to Judaism, and that only some of them were already Jews/Judeans, these archaeologists asserted that after the Hasmonean take-over large numbers of Jews/Judeans migrated north to become settlers in Galilee. Mark Chancey may have picked up this view from one of the pioneers of Galilean archaeology, his mentor Eric Meyers. Chancey's welcome dissertation and first book, *The Myth of a Gentile Galilee,* surely helped lay to rest that problematic "myth." His follow-up second book helped refute another "myth," of the "cosmopolitan" Hellenistic Lower Galilee as the context of Jesus' mission, which ironically was based on archaeologists estimates of the size of the newly built cities that in turn were based on passing literary references to the Hellenistic-Roman urban institutions in Sepphoris or Tiberias. Chancey's subsequent article, "The Ethnicities of Galileans," offers concise summaries of material from his own two books and other archaeological reports, but includes no solid evidence for the assertion that large numbers of Jews/Judeans migrated north to become settlers in Galilee during the hundred years of Hasmonean and Herodian rule.

11. Chapters 5 and 6 below are my earliest attempts at dialogue and mutual learning with some of these archaeologists a few years after researching and writing what are chapters 1 and 2.

The surmise about Judeans' migrating northward after the Hasmonean "annexation" of Galilee is evidently an explanation of how it supposedly happened "that Galileans by and large *were* Judeans in terms of identity, ancestry, and cultural orientation."[12] Chancey begins his presentation with an argument by some archaeologists, based on large-scale surface surveys, that, "with many sites abandoned," Lower Galilee was "significantly deserted" in late Iron Age.[13] This presumably explains why the later Galileans could not have been descendants of the northern Israelites, as I had contended. As other archaeologists pointed out, however, such surface surveys are notoriously unreliable. In any case, Galilee was by no means totally depopulated. In Upper Galilee the survey found twenty-eight sites in Iron II.[14] In the eighth century BCE the Assyrians deported mainly the ruling elite in Samaria and their trained military and artisans who would have been useful in the administration of the empire, as did the neo-Babylonian armies in Jerusalem at the beginning of the sixth century. Both imperial armies left on the land whatever Israelite peasants had not been killed in their invasions. The depopulation was serious in Judah in the sixth century as well as in Galilee in the eighth. Archaeological estimates of the population of Yehud after the ancestors of the exiled Jerusalemites were sent back to colonize the area at only about 30,000, including "the people left on the land." In Galilee the Persian period saw considerable recovery, with an expansion of the number of sites evident. And with no further imperial conquest in the shift to the Hellenistic period, village sites further expanded, ruled and taxed by "Greek" officers and soldiers in fortified towns.

Given archaeologists' acknowledgment that their periodization is very general and inexact ("Hellenistic II" supposedly runs 152–37 BCE), we may doubt the claim that "it is precisely" at the time of the Hasmonean takeover (i.e. from 104 BCE, right in the middle of that period) that marked changes become noticeable in Galilean material culture.[15] Chancey immediately cites the coins of Alexander Jannaeus as evidence of this change. But of what change? If most of those coins were found in fortified sites, they indicate a change of officers and soldiers in those sites, not in a supposed change to a Judean cultural orientation of the villages of Galilee in general.

---

12. Chancey, "The Ethnicities of Galileans," 118.
13. Chancey, "The Ethnicities of Galileans," 113.
14. Chancey, "The Ethnicities of Galileans," 114.
15. Chancey, "The Ethnicities of Galileans," 116.

INTRODUCTION

When he comes to "Gentiles in Galilee," Chancey recognizes that "their ancestors could have been Persian, Ptolemaic, or Seleucid administrators and soldiers stationed in Galilee."[16] Somehow it did not occur to him that the Hasmoneans/Judeans ruled Galilee in somewhat the same way. Josephus' accounts make clear: that after their take-over the Hasmoneans (followed by Herod) ruled Galilee through the garrisons they stationed in fortresses there, such as Sepphoris, Gush Halav, and Yodfat. Unaware of—or discounting—Josephus' accounts, Chancey instead affirms archaeologists' surmise of Judeans migrating north. He confidently asserts that these settlements of Judeans are "facts," but cites no solid evidence for them. In lieu of good evidence for migration of Judeans into Galilee, he walks through various kinds of "shared material culture" that supposedly illustrate "the Jewishness of Galileans." But the principal sites in which he mentions that *mikva'ot* were found were fortress towns in which (Judean) officers of the Hasmoneans had been stationed (118).[17] In order to critically evaluate what artifacts such as "stoneware vessels" and oil lamps made in Jerusalem may indicate we would need to know at what kind of sites and in what sort of buildings they were found (in "small residences" as well as "the mansions of the wealthy"?).[18] Ritual baths and stoneware vessels found mainly in fortress sites prpobably indicate that there were Judean descendants of Hasmonean officers in Galilee and that some of them were figures Josephus refers to as *dynatoi*, such as the ones "the Galileans" drowned in the Lake in their resistance to Herod's conquest. But do artifacts found mainly in sites that were fortresses staffed by Hasmonean officers and their descendants indicate that "most of the region's population" were Jews/Judeans? That seems highly doubtful.[19]

16. Chancey, "The Ethnicities of Galileans," 122.

17. Chancey, "The Ethnicities of Galileans," 118. In an article written about the same time, "Purity and Politics in Galilee," 16–19, Morten Hørning Jensen includes the welcome perspective of a survey of *miqva'ot* found in Judah as well as Galilee, including theories of their function(s). Of 850 "ritual baths" 430 were in Judea, not including another 170 in Jerusalem, with 40 immediately around the temple (suggesting a ritual purity function). Of a hundred in Galilee, 41 were in Sepphoris. Others were found in the fortress town of Yodfat and the Judean fortress town of Gamla in the Golan.

18. Chancey, "The Ethnicities of Galileans," 119. As explained in chapters 1 and 2 above and several other publications, "synagogues" in the Gospels refer not to Jewish religious buildings but to village *assemblies*, and synagogue buildings in Galilee were rare until late antiquity (and then, says Chancey, "reflect the artistic trends of the larger Greco-Roman world" ("The Ethnicities of Galileans," 121).

19. In the articles reprinted as chapters 1 and 2 below, I argued that the most likely

GALILEANS UNDER JERUSALEM AND ROMAN RULE

THE COMPLEXITIES OF JERUSALEM RULE OF THE GALILEANS

The investigations in chapter 2 closely related to and building on those in chapter 1, are addressed to these generalizations. This article was prepared for a conference on "Recruitment, Conquest, and Conflict," subjects rarely addressed in biblical studies and ancient Jewish history, suggesting that at least some scholars were beginning to probe the history that the sources attest. Because so little attention had been paid to Galilee and Galileans, the 1980 book *Galilee* by Sean Freyne presented a handy reference point that confirmed what was a standard assumption, that Galileans were (already) Jews steadfastly loyal to temple and Torah.[20] Following standard practice in biblical studies, Freyne (like others) often took text-fragments from books such as 1 Maccabees at face value, without considering the narrative context or making comparisons with the often parallel accounts in 2 Maccabees, and making claims that repeated the assumptions on which they were based. The field was only beginning to recognize that texts must be read critically, even suspiciously. First Maccabees, for example, was being recognized to have been Hasmonean propaganda that glorified Judas and the Maccabeans as a revival of ancient Israelite heroes and their victories. Josephus was following 1 Maccabees for the history of Maccabean exploits, but his more detailed or somewhat different accounts sometimes provide clarification, and indications that text-fragments from 1 Maccabees cannot be taken at face value. Critical examination of the text-fragments adduced to attest Freyne's and others' generalizations and claims in broader literary and historical context,

---

reconstruction from limited and fragmentary textual evidence is that the Galileans taken over by the Hasmoneans were descendants of northern Israelites. But I did *not* argue that Galileans considered themselves as a "very different *ethnos* from the Judeans to the south" as Chancey asserts ("The Ethnicities of Galileans," 127). If the residents (of many? most?) of the villages in Galilee were descendants of the northern tribes of Israel, then they were Israelites, just as the villagers of Judea were Israelites as the descendants of the tribes of Judah and Benjamin. From the Hasmonean takeover of Galilee to the death of Herod, the Galilean Israelites as well as the Judean Israelites were subject to the Judean high priests, who then no longer had jurisdiction once Herod Antipas was installed as ruler over Galilee. In some official decrees the Romans referred to the Judeans as an *ethnos*, but the inclusive "insider" term used both in the Gospels and in later rabbinic texts was *Israel*.

20. Sean Freyne and I had become good friends with common interests and parallel projects on ancient Galilee and the historical Jesus, so I was proceeding carefully, often reluctantly coming to critical conclusions. Of course, he was articulating standard views, and I was (and am still) the skeptical "revisionist."

however, suggested that they are not good evidence for Galilee and Galileans having been Jewish, loyal to the temple and torah already prior to the Hasmonean take-over.[21] One important reason to have this article republished and more accessible is that it includes critical probes that support but may not be included in my alternative construction of pre-Hasmonean history in the subsequent book, *Galilee: History, Politics, People*.

To understand who the Galileans may have been before and during Hasmonean rule it is helpful to review the ostensible history of the northern Israelite tribes and their relation to the Davidic monarchy and then the probable history of the Assyrian conquest. This history indicates a tradition of resistance, not loyalty to Jerusalem rule, on the one hand, and a continuation of early Israelite tradition in the villages that later were the Galileans, on the other. A review of the conflicts and virtual political chaos of later Hasmonean times, Roman conquest and early rule, and the rise of Herod suggests that it is highly unlikely that the Hasmoneans would have mounted a campaign to transform Galilean village culture, for example, by sending the Pharisees to work in the villages.

In earlier accounts of Hasmonean expansion one finds the effects on the conquered peoples termed as "Judaization." This is a vague term that begs rather than suggests what it may have meant. This appears to be a scholarly projection onto a history that is poorly attested in mid-second century and then increasingly complex, with the Hasmonean conquests followed by the Roman conquest and chaotic early rule of Palestine. Perhaps

---

21. It is puzzling that Jensen, in a 2014 article ("Political History in Galilee," 54–55), reverts to taking selected text-fragments in 1 Maccabees at face value, as had Freyne in 1980, as "a number of written sources" that suggest a growing Judean presence in Galilee before the takeover of Galilee by Aristobulus. The passages, however, especially if 1 Maccabees is read critically, do not attest Jensen's claim. He then cites "a growing amount of archeological data" to indicate "a clear rise in Judean material culture in Galilee," and cites surface surveys, that indicate "a sudden increase in settlement activity around the beginning of the first century CE. As archaeologists themselves admit, surface surveys are notoriously unreliable evidence (as noted above; an increase from 82 settlements in the Persian period to 106 in the Hellenistic period in Upper Galilee is hardly either a "sudden" or an appreciable increase). Jensen then (p. 56) admits that "none of the arguments presented above drives home a solid conclusion" about the Galilean population on the eve of the Hasmonean take-over. As noted just above, there were surely some Judeans in Galilee in the early first century CE insofar as the Hasmoneans ruled through the garrisons in fortresses such as at Sepphoris. But there is no solid evidence of "a large influx of settlers," presumably "Judeans," following the Hasmonean take-over. Elsewhere in his article Jensen takes other text-fragments at face-value, for example, not probing what Josephus may be indicating in the statement that when Herod arrived back in Galilee to conquer his subjects, "all Galilee went over to him" (p. 60).

"Judaization" refers simply to whatever effects may have occurred from political subjection to the Judean temple-state. In any case, a more complete and critical reading of sources such as Josephus indicates that the effects cannot be described as not loyalty to the temple. The effects were rather a reversion to the historical structural divide between rulers and ruled, enforced by the Hasmoneans with their mercenary troops, followed by the overwhelming military forces of the Romans and Herod's systematically repressive regime But the structural division was occasionally interrupted by outbreaks of resistance and rebellion against the temple-state. This happened under John Hyrcanus in the late second century, then against Alexander Jannaeus in the early first century. Then after the complex wars between rival Hasmonean claimants compounded by the Roman empire-wide civil war, the Galileans mounted sustained resistance to Herod's conquest of the people he was appointed to rule. At Herod's death widespread revolt erupted in Galilee and Judea, and after protests in mid-first century CE, Galileans and later Idumeans joined Judean villagers in the great revolt against high priestly as well as Roman rule.

The second half of chapter 2 focuses on the question of the supposed Judaization of Galileans and other people who were subjected to the Jerusalem temple-state and on the more specific claims of Freyne that Galileans were solidly "Jewish" in steadfastly loyalty to both temple and Torah. Standard Christian theological construction of this history, still assuming that the main conflict was between Jews and Gentiles, between Judaism and the surrounding Hellenistic world, was not yet cognizant of the structural division between high priestly rulers and Judean and Galilean villagers. When Freyne and I were in graduate school in the 1960s, Christian theological biblical scholars were eager to find Galileans eagerly participating in Judaism. With inflated estimates of the numbers of the faithful, they imagined hundreds of thousands of pilgrims, including Galileans, faithfully travelling to the pilgrimage festivals in the temple. Freyne simply assumes and follows this view, for example, of unsubstantiated numbers of pilgrims to festivals, also assuming that their motivation was faithful loyalty to the temple. Critical examination of Josephus' accounts understood in historical and geographical context, indicate a far more complex situation and motivation. Even if the Galileans were descendants of the northern tribes of Israel, then a review of Israelite tradition indicates that there was no basis in history or tradition for the claim that Galileans were loyal to the Jerusalem temple as their "cultic center."

Introduction

With regard to the Galileans and their supposed loyalty to the Torah, there is no point in framing the issue as an argument against Freyne's presentation. His research and discussion in the 1980 *Galilee* book predates more recent research that called into question older standard assumptions in the fields of Christian biblical studies and ancient Jewish history. The sources for the relations between the high priestly rulers and the Galileans do not refer to "the Law/Torah, but rather to particular laws and customs. Even in the 1980s and 1990s, well before the assumption-shattering research into scribal training[22] and the publication of the results of text-critical examination of manuscripts of the "books" of the Torah found at Qumran,[23] it had become necessary to distinguish between what appears in a book of Torah proper and what the sources refer to. The latter may include particular laws or customs that are similar to or refer to something also found in a Torah scroll, or to "regulations" from "the tradition of the elders/ancestors" of the Pharisees, and time-honored local customs of Israelite villagers.

The appropriate procedure here would be a critical examination of incidents and events recounted by Josephus in which particular laws, customs, or covenantal commandments play a key role. Josephus describes several of these incidents in his first-hand accounts of Galileans' actions during the time he was trying to keep a lid on the revolt in Galilee, in 66–67 CE. These several incidents indicate that the Galileans were motivated by adherence to Mosaic covenantal commandments. But there is no suggestion that the insistence of adherence to particular commandments were somehow derived from scrolls of Torah. In the one incident of a fellow in Tarichaeae waving a scroll of torah in the air, it appears to have been a symbol of independence of the rulers, not of loyalty to them, and of course it was rare that such a scroll would be available even in a Galilean city. It seems that we have to reckon with the Galileans being insistent on keeping the commandments of the Mosaic covenant that they knew from time-honored Israelite tradition but that this did not involve knowledge of or obedience to (a scroll of a "book" of) the Torah proper.[24]

---

22. See now the important study of scribal training by David Carr, *Writing on the Tablet of the Heart*, and my own continuation of such investigation focusing on Ben Sira's instructional "wisdom" in *Scribes, Visionaries, and the Politics of Second Temple Judea*, chaps. 3–5.

23. See especially Ulrich, *Dead Sea Scrolls and the Origins of the Bible*.

24. This conclusion has been borne out by the lines of more recent research into ancient communications media. I have attempted to pull together the implications of these lines of research in several publications, the most comprehensive being the lengthy

The final section of chapter 2 focuses on the Pharisees and whether they had a role in Galilee during the hundred years of Jerusalem rule there. In both study of ancient Judaism and Christian theological New Testament studies, the Pharisees were still understood as the precursors of the later rabbis, the leaders of Judaism, and the most prominent interpreters of the Torah. They were also closely associated with the synagogues (understood as religious buildings), that were assumed to have been functioning in Galilee as well as Judea[25] and that became *the* basic religious institutions after the Roman destruction of the temple. The Pharisees were also assumed to have been the leaders of the synagogues after and even before the destruction of the temple. The latter assumption appeared to have been confirmed by some prominent Jewish scholars who argued from Josephus' supposed change of his portrayal of the Pharisees from the earlier *War* to the later *Antiquities* that Romans were placing the Pharisees in charge of Judaism in Palestine after the destruction of the temple.[26] Prominent Christian scholars of Jesus and the Gospels seized on the hypothesis that the Romans had placed the Pharisees in charge of Judaism in the vacuum left by the destruction of the temple to mean that they were already prominent in leadership of the synagogues at the time the Gospels were "written."[27] This became their basis for arguing that the Pharisees were the rivals or competitors of Jesus and his followers.

All of these interrelated components presented several pieces of a puzzle of life in Galilee every one of which seemed questionable, hence required critical reexamination. The questionable bases for some of these puzzling pieces had begun to be addressed. What remained to be investigated more critically were the only sources for the supposed presence of the Pharisees in Galilee, the Gospels. More circumspect and suspicious investigation of key Gospel passages suggest the possibility but the historically unlikely probability of the physical presence of Pharisees in Galilee.

---

article, Horsley, "Can Study of the Historical Jesus Escape Its Typographical Captivity?"

25. The continuing assertion that the Pharisees were active, even resident in Galilee, like some of the other assertions in this composite picture had resulted from taking text fragments in the sources at face value, This was true even of Saldarini's innovative investigation that explained how the Pharisees' position in the temple-state resembled that of "retainers" in Lenski's cross-cultural sociological analysis of advanced agrarian societies, in Saldarini, *Pharisees, Sadducees, and Scribes*.

26. For example, Cohen, *Josephus in Galilee and Rome*. This argument about the change in Josephus' representations of the Pharisees is more fully addressed in chapter 3 below.

27. For example, Kee, "Transformation of the Synagogue"; Mack, *The Myth of Innocence*.

More circumspect analysis of key Gospel passages shows that the clauses on which Christian theological interpretation bases the stereotype of the Pharisees as legalists obsessed with ritual law, especially purity, are rhetorical flourishes, while the Gospels' Jesus is concerned about the effects on the people of their role in the Jerusalem temple-state.

THE IMPLICATIONS OF GALILEANS' RESISTANCE TO THE REASSERTION OF TEMPLE-STATE RULE

In retrospect the conflicts at multiple levels in the history of the Judeans, Samaritans, Galileans, Idumeans and others subject to Judean high priestly and Herodian rule can be understood as moving inexorably toward the breakdown of social-political order and the eruption of the great revolt in 66 CE. The incompetence of and rivalry between Hasmonean high priests, compounded by the conquest by and "civil war' between Roman warlords imposed chaotic, devastating, and oppressive conditions for the Judean and Galilean people. These repeated devastations would have left sustained collective trauma among the villagers. Systematic repression by the military strongman appointed "king of the Judeans" by the Roman warlords imposed order for a few decades. But sustained repression left a restive populace in Jerusalem, Judea, and Galilee. Pent-up popular resentment burst forth at Herod's death in 4 BCE. Massive protests by the people of Jerusalem, which was only intensified by Archelaus' violent reprisals, touched off revolts by villagers in Galilee, northwestern Judea, and the Transjordan.

The brutal suppression by Roman legions seemingly "restored order," but only on the surface. The Romans installed Herod Antipas as ruler over Galilee and Perea, who built new capital cities in Galilee, at the cost of heavy extraction from his peasant economic base. A decade later the Romans placed an expanded but weakened high priestly aristocracy in charge of Judea, subject to Roman governors and dependent on the Romans to maintain their position of power and privilege.

The imperial political order seemed restored, but the structural conflict remained and resistance was building among the people in the countryside, among the people of Jerusalem, and even in scribal circles. People protested arrogant intrusions by the Roman governors. The prophet John led a covenant-renewal movement focused on a "baptism of repentance" that attracted widespread participation. Jesus of Nazareth led another movement focused on renewal of the Mosaic covenant in the villages of

Galilee that spread rapidly, especially after his martyrdom at the hands of the Roman governor in Judea. In mid-century a sequence of popular prophets led their Judean peasant followers out into the wilderness to experience new divine acts of deliverance. Among scribal circles trained to serve in the temple-state, a prominent group called the "fourth philosophy" by Josephus, led by the Pharisee Zaddok and the teacher Judas from Gamla, organized a refusal to pay the tribute to Caesar (an act the Romans viewed as tantamount to rebellion). In mid-century another circle of scribal teachers called the "dagger-men" (*sicarioi*) began assassinating high priestly figures who had been collaborating closely in Roman rule. Meanwhile, banditry was becoming epidemic in the countryside while leading high priestly figures were becoming increasingly predatory on the people. Clearly social order was breaking down. And the provocative actions by Roman governors exacerbated the deteriorating situation, until a revolt erupted in Jerusalem that touched off widespread revolt in the countryside.

With few exceptions, scholars in the fields of ancient Jewish history and biblical studies seemed uninterested. They were paying little attention to the histories of Josephus, uniquely extensive sources for this period of history that is of singular importance, especially for Galilee since it was the context of the mission of Jesus and then of formative deliberations in rabbinic circles.

Meanwhile, in the world outside the libraries and studies of scholars in these fields many colonized peoples were mounting anti-colonial movements, some of which took the form of peasant revolts. Inside theological circles in Latin America "liberation theologians" were calling attention to the conditions that led to popular organizing and revolt. While some teachers in North America and Europe warned their students against *individual overt acts* of violence, Dom Helder Camara, a bishop in northeast Brazil, explained the spiral of violence that was unfolding in many countries: *systemic structural violence* of political-economic oppression led to people's *resistance* that in turn evoked systemic *repression* by colonial and client governments. I finally found time to lay out how there had been a similar sequence of steps in ancient Judean and Galilean history under Roman imperial rule.[28] Under Roman rule and for centuries before, the Judean and Galilean villagers had been subject to the systemic violence of imperial conquest and oppression compounded by the client high priestly rulers in Jerusalem. The people had mounted resistance for several generations and

---

28. Horsley, *Jesus and the Spiral of Violence*, chaps. 1–4.

continued, as the Romans, through Herod in particular but then the Herodian and high priestly rulers, attempted to suppress resistance by degrees of repression. At Herod's death and then again much more extensively in Judea and Galilee, however, this spiral of violence eventually led to a fourth stage, that of popular *revolt*.

In the aftermath of its "glorious" victory over the coalition of ragtag peasant forces in the great revolt who resisted the Roman re-conquest of Jerusalem, the Flavian regime headed by the emperor Vespasian and his son and successor Titus launched an intensive propaganda campaign. They staged their massive Triumph in the imperial capitol depicting the siege and eventual victory over the Judeans, and rebuilt the Forum in Rome to include the central monument, the Arch of Titus—still a featured tourist attraction in Rome. Flavian propaganda presented their triumph as a victory over the whole Judean people. And the wealthy elite Jerusalem priest who had staged his surrender to Titus at Yodfat (Jotapata) in Galilee in 67, took the name Flavius Josephus and settled into enjoyment of imperial patronage in Rome. Some Josephus scholars think that in writing the *War* he fully supported the Flavian propaganda that the priestly aristocracy had led "the Jewish War" against Roman rule. Curiously the view of the Great Revolt in the Flavian propaganda has been adopted in modern presentations of the war. Suggesting a lack of scholarly interest, there were few serious treatments in the 1970s and 1980s. Among these, Shaye Cohen's was particularly interested in the supposed change in Josephus' view of the revolt from the writing of the *War* to the more extensive *Antiquities* and its "appendix" in the *Life*.[29] In *The Ruling Class of Judea*, on the other hand, Martin Goodman was fully aware that the high priestly aristocracy was "the ruling class" and that their incompetence and predatory behavior was a major factor leading to the revolt.[30] But he still assumed that once the revolt was erupting, high priestly figures and others of the ruling class stepped up to lead the revolt. He seems to assume that the war must have been led by figures of the ruling class since, he supposes, the common people were incapable of such leadership.

If Josephus' *War* is read carefully and critically, however, it becomes evident that he presents a complex account of the events in which he was a participant. I found several Josephus scholars who agreed with my reading that there is no serious difference between his accounts in the *War* and in

---

29. Cohen, *Josephus in Galilee and Rome*.
30. Goodman, *The Ruling Class of Judaea*.

the *Life*. Most important for our use of those accounts as historical sources, in both accounts he admits that he and leading high priests who had not already fled Jerusalem who formed a "provisional ruling council" were only pretending to prepare for war but were really trying to delay and control the revolt until they could negotiate with the Romans. From my repeated reading of Josephus' histories I had come to believe that the "Jewish War" was really more of a peasant revolt. All of the insurgents in Jerusalem and the temple fighting the Roman siege had come into the city from the countryside, many of them fleeing the Romans' "scorched earth" destruction of their villages and slaughter of the people. Few of them, however, had come from Galilee, where the Romans had suppressed the revolt by the summer of 67. The conference on "The Jewish Revolt" at Macalester and the University of Minnesota in 1999 provided a welcome opportunity to carefully comb through the accounts of Josephus about the revolt in Galilee in 66–67 that Josephus himself had been sent by the Jerusalem "junta" to control.

What I found, laid out in chapter 3, is a remarkable variety of conflicts, mainly between the pro-Roman ruling cities of Sepphoris and Tiberias and villagers whom Josephus calls "the Galileans." Although we may want to take his self-serving accounts "with a grain of salt," it is remarkable how he could manipulate Galilean peasants into paying brigand bands in a "protection racket" that he controlled. He also manipulated the prominent wealthy men of Tarichaeae into helping him trick and suppress the insurrectionary "riff-raff" of Tiberias. Comparison with how the revolt in Judea that steadily escalated and became centralized in Jerusalem makes the decentralized and effectively mitigated actions in Galilee look like a revolt that happened mainly in local conflicts and skirmishes. In retrospect, this exposition of local conflicts and incidents in this chapter indicates much about the instability of the Roman imperial order in Galilee. With certain local variations, the regime of Agrippa II in Tiberias and the city of Sepphoris that had been exploiting "the Galileans" had become the targets peasant discontent. The resulting economic pressures on the people had resulted in many large bands of brigands on the frontiers that became significant forces in the breakdown of political order that led to the revolt.

Introduction

FOCUS ON THE PEOPLE OF GALILEE: EXAMPLES OF RESISTANCE AND REVOLT

Chapter 4, which originated as an SBL Seminar paper years earlier when some of us were trying to generate more attention to Galilee and Galileans, explores the bands of brigands mainly on the frontiers of Galilee and the one known "messianic" movement in Galilee that arose from the repeatedly intensified economic pressures on the villagers. The chapter also explores the actions of the urban poor in the great revolt in Tiberias that had been established as a second capital in Galilee only two generations earlier. In contrast to New Testament scholars' usual focus on the Pharisees, Sadducees, and Qumran community who, as the scribal elite comprised only a small fraction of the Judeans, this chapter focuses on the some of the principal groups of ordinary people in Galilee known because they made trouble for the rulers. Such an exploration beings us closer to the ordinary people among whom Jesus pursued his mission of renewal and resistance.

It was not surprising that there was considerable resistance to my attempt at a critical and more complete reading of Josephus' accounts of an often epidemic surge of social banditry and of resistance movements led by popularly acclaimed "kings" and popular prophets. While initially interested, Sean Freyne still worked under the shadow of the older scholarly construct of "the Zealots" and soon reverted to the standard older view that *lēstai* in Josephus accounts referred to insurrectionists. He claimed that the *lēstai* in Galilee were not bands of brigands, but the remaining Hasmoneans and their partisans still battling against Herod's consolidation of power. To lay this often mixed-up reading of text-fragments from Josephus required careful scrutiny of his accounts of the struggles between rival Hasmonean claimants (and their officers) and between some of them and Herod (and their officers, who sometimes changed sides). The first section in chapter 4 reaffirms that the *lēstai* in Josephus' accounts were indeed *lēstai*, that is brigands, and explores again what I had laid out in 1979: how epidemic banditry emerges from the difficult social-economic conditions resulting from continued and/or destructive warfare, intensified exploitation, and/or drought and famine.[31] And, as Hobsbawm explained from his cross-cultural historical studies, social banditry was/is "pre-political" and even as it might lead into more serious peasant revolt, is even then not necessarily politically "revolutionary."

---

31. Horsley, "Josephus and the Bandits."

Galileans under Jerusalem and Roman Rule

Well-known brigands, however, become legendary folk-heroes. The Galilean brigand-chieftain Ezekias, whom the arrogant young Herod murdered, for which he was brought to trial before a formal high priestly council in Jerusalem, became a legend among Galilean villagers. So it is not surprising that in the revolt in Galilee after Herod's death in 4 BCE the Galileans acclaimed his son Judas as their "king," acting out the popular Israelite legends of the "messiahing" of the young David and/or the Elisha's anointing of Jehu to lead their struggles against unwanted rulers. Again because of the previous scholarly con-fusion of the popular king Judas son of Ezechias in 4 BCE in Galilee and Judas from Gamla (Gaulanitis), the scribal teacher who co-led the "Fourth Philosophy" in Judea ten years later, in 6 CE, it seems appropriate to probe Josephus accounts of the popular king in Galilee. This should further illuminate the discontent of Galilean villagers under Jerusalem and Roman rule and the rich cultural heritage of Israelite popular tradition upon which they drew in generating this movement that has a distinctively Israelite social form. This review also just happens to provide further evidence that the Galileans were the descendants of former northern Israelites.

The third section of chapter 4, focused on the urban poor of Tiberias, the second capital founded by Herod Antipas only about fifty years previously. In his *Life* Josephus provides a considerable amount of information about (a) the conflicts and turmoil in this city that were interrelated with conflicts elsewhere in Galilee and (b) the conflicts between the Roman client "King" Agrippa II and his officers ruling Tiberias and the provisional council attempting to reassert control of Galilee and the revolt. More specifically, Josephus offers a highly informative picture of what could only be called the overt "class struggle" between the urban poor, some of whose ancestors had been villagers forced into the city by Antipas, and the Herodian officers attempting to control affairs, as he manipulates one side against the other. Josephus' account of this conflict in 66–67 indicates the concrete dynamics of mid-first century Tiberias. The first-hand accounts of Josephus, read critically, are a dramatic contrast to the speculative accounts by some archaeologists about the early "urbanization" of Galilee or claims of how essentially "Jewish" or "Hellenistic" the cities of Galilee were. The conflict in Tiberias, interrelated with the conflict between the ruling cities and the Galilean villagers in general, also expose the naïve romanticism of arguments that there was a confluence of interests between the villages and

INTRODUCTION

cities of Galilee, with supposed mutually beneficial urban-rural trade and villagers going into the cities for "entertainment" in the theater.

CAN HISTORICAL JESUS SCHOLARS & ARCHAEOLOGISTS OF GALILEE LEARN FROM EACH OTHER?

Chapters 5 and 6 were and are parts of my attempt to engage with archaeologists involved in excavating sites in Galilee. Insofar as the Gospels, the sources for the historical Jesus, portrayed his mission as focused on Galilean villages, it seemed that scholars should pay special attention to Galilee as central in Jesus' historical context. Historical Jesus studies, however, caught up in narrow individualistic focus on his individual sayings, were paying little attention to the historical context, much less to Galilee in particular. New Testament scholarship in general, in fact, had paid little attention to Galilee. Sean Freyne's book broke new ground in its focus on this area of Roman Palestine, but in many respects was not critical history, as noted in chapters 1 and 2 above.

I remembered that some of my contemporaries in graduate school were pioneering archaeological explorations in villages and later in cities in Galilee. Hoping to find important information, I began gathering and reading everything published on archaeology of Galilee. Still on the steering committee of the "Historical Jesus Section" in the Society of Biblical Literature, with Andrew Overman, who had become involved in archaeological explorations, I planned a joint session with archaeologists and historical Jesus scholars. For that session in 1994 I wrote a long paper, summarizing recent historical Jesus studies and mainly exploring how historical Jesus scholars and archaeologists focused on Galilee could learn from each other: about political-economic relations in early Roman Galilee and about culture and cultural relations, in the cities, in villages, and in urban-rural relations. The articles reprinted in chapters 5–6 were based on the extensive research and reflections behind that long paper written for serious exchange between archaeologists and Jesus-scholars focused on literary remains.

In preparation for the exchange with archaeologists I had read recent critical reflections of the general field of archaeology by leading figures such as Colin Renfrew and Bruce Trigger.[32] Earlier work in largely separate and largely uncritical "biblical archaeology" provided limited help for

---

32. Renfrew and Bahn, *Archaeology: Theories, Methods, and Practice*; Trigger, *A History of Archaeological Thought*.

those who launched the unprecedented excavations in Galilee. "Biblical archaeology" had not been in serious dialogue with the more general field of archaeology.[33] The innovative scholars who launched the new sub-field, particularly Eric Meyers and James Strange, were formulating strategies and drawing conclusions with each new exploration, just as I was seeking understanding of the general historical situation in Galilee and circumstances among the Galileans with whom Jesus had interacted. So it seemed that Jesus-scholars and Galilean archaeologists might learn from one another in exploration of circumstances in Galilee.

Both historical Jesus studies and the archaeology of Galilee were subfields of the larger fields of ancient Jewish history and New Testament studies. Scholars in both sub-fields were proceeding in the deeply ingrained habit of focusing on text-fragments taken out of literary context (whether in the Gospels or in Josephus' histories) and/or by excavating in supposedly representative "squares" in which they found fragmentary evidence of buildings and various artifacts. Scholars in both subfields then classified text-fragments or material artifacts according to the broad essentialist constructs that controlled interpretation in both fields. The symbols or buildings or cities or figures mentioned in text-fragments or the artifacts or buildings or the cities in which the squares were excavated were classified as either "Jewish" or "Hellenistic," or as either "Jewish" or "Christian." Jesus-scholars classified individual Jesus-sayings as "apocalyptic" or "sapiential." Some of the latter were found to resemble the sayings of vagabond Cynic philosophers, that is, "Hellenistic" philosophers active in "Hellenistic cities." Archaeologists classified buildings mentioned in text-fragments from Josephus or found in excavations as typical of "Hellenistic cities," or classified artifacts found as "Jewish." Scholars in both fields jumped from particular text-fragments or particular material evidence found in their squares to broad generalizations about Jesus or about Galilean cities. A statement that a city had a "council" (*boulē*) or a dig that found evidence of a theater meant the city was a "Hellenistic *polis*." Estimates (grossly exaggerated) of size and population meant that the ethos of the Hellenistic city was "cosmopolitan." A comment in passing by Eric Meyers that "the great urban centers" had mediated a "cosmopolitan atmosphere" to the villages of Lower Galilee, and an SBL "seminar paper" by a young scholar learning

---

33. Neil Asher Silberman (who a few years later sought me out as a coauthor) had written a fascinating history of the early development of biblical archaeology, *Digging for God and Country*; and a review of the recent practice of archaeology in countries such as Egypt, Greece, Turkey, and esp. Israel, in Silberman, *Between Past and Present*.

archaeology from Meyers and Strange[34] provided the basis for John Dominic Crossan and Burton Mack to assert that Jesus had to be understood in that cosmopolitan atmosphere.[35]

To their credit, archaeologists excavating in Galilee soon realized that those estimates of city populations were grossly exaggerated and that the cultural situation was more complex, although they continued to apply essentialist concepts. It took historical Jesus studies decades longer to begin questioning their narrow focus on individual sayings and their broad essentialist categorization and their leaps from text-fragments to essentialist worldviews. Neither sub-field had exhibited much interest in the distinctive history of Galilee before it was taken over by Hasmonean rule and what may have been the effects of Hasmonean rule, Herod's rule, and then the imposition of two newly constructed capital cities in the relatively small territory of Lower Galilee. Neither field has been interested in what can be learned about Galilee from Josephus' accounts, particularly from his relatively detailed first-hand account of the complex interaction of many different groups early in the great revolt in 66–67 CE.

My two books on Galilee were attempts to provide a critical investigation of the often fragmentary evidence for the history of Galilee and constructive analysis of the political-economic relations, institutional political-economic forms, indigenous social-cultural forms and traditions, and social dynamics of Galilee in early Roman times.[36] The second book attempted explicitly to learn from and critically respond to archaeological explorations in Galilee (as of 1996) in the complex historical political-economic and intercultural context. Chapter 5 in this volume works more explicitly from the reports on the innovative regional archaeological excavations in Meiron and nearby villages than the section in the book on the villages of Upper Galilee. Chapter 6 is a partial summary of my earlier long paper for interchange between archaeologists and Jesus-scholars and is a far more concise summary of the resulting 1996 book based on that paper.[37]

---

34. E. M. Meyers, "The Cultural Setting of Galilee," 697–98; Overman, "Who Were the First Urban Christians?"

35. Crossan, *The Historical Jesus*, 18–19; Mack, *A Myth of Innocence*, 53–78.

36. Horsley, *Galilee: History, Politics, People*; Horsley, *Archaeology, History, and Society in Galilee*.

37. Chapter 6 was a paper delivered to the New Testament Department at UNISA (University of South Africa) in Pretoria in 1995, just at the end of apartheid. South African scholars, having been cut off from interaction and direct conversation with international scholars, had been reading extensively in scholarly journals and books. They were

I think it would be fair to say that the American archaeologists who had launched the excavations in various sites in Galilee were not all that interested in the conversations I was attempting to inaugurate and in how we might learn from each other. No more than biblical scholars focused on text-interpretation were they interested in how we might become critical of the "models" we were following or borrowing, or in how we might learn from the more recently critical wider field of archaeology in general with which earlier "biblical archeology" had not been engaged. Eric Meyers in particular, reacting to my attempted engagement in the *BASOR* article reprinted below as chapter 5, appealed to a just-published book insisting that, in contrast with the rest of the Roman Empire, the economy in Jewish Palestine was basically a market economy (like what Meyers had imagined for the villages in Upper Galilee).

Thus it was a relief and gratifying that over decade later, when we were two or the three speakers at the fiftieth anniversary celebration of the general journal *Archaeology,* we agreed over lunch that a principal aspect of both of our agendas was to lay to rest the view that Lower Galilee was the cosmopolitan Hellenistic culture that John Dominic Crossan and Burton Mack had made the basis of their presentation of Jesus as an individualist countercultural Jewish cynic.

Another welcome indication that there were notes to be shared with archaeologists came in polemical session of the Q Section of the Society of Biblical Literature: The presentations by several younger Q-scholars all took aim at my Galilee books mainly on the basis of archaeological surface surveys. When they had finished—and half the audience had left—the veteran Galilean archaeological respondent (who had no knowledge of my books) turned to face the presenters and lectured them on how their use of archaeological explorations, especially surface surveys, was off-base and unacceptable. There are still plenty of discussions to be held from which historically oriented biblical scholars and Galilean archaeologists can learn from one another.

Taken together these articles provide a discussion of the distinctive history of Galilee that is both more comprehensive and precise than can be

---

much less stuck in the narrow specialized research "trenches" and more interested, for example, in adapting social-scientific approaches than (for example) were historical Jesus specialists in North America.

found in handbooks of the late second temple period focused on Judea and "Judaism." Far from the newly (re-)built cities imposed on Galilee having a symbiosis with the surrounding villages it is clear mainly from Josephus' accounts that the villagers, whom he calls "the Galileans," were resentful of exploitation by their rulers and their tax-collectors nicely housed in Sepphoris and Tiberias and, later, Tarichaeae. Given the limited and fragmentary evidence, the most likely hypothesis for who the residents of Galilee were when the Hasmoneans took control of the area is the descendants of the most northerly Israelites who had lived under imperial administrations but with no aristocracy of their own. Their culture would have been Israelite, but different from what had developed in the scribal circles of the Judean temple-state, some of which we know as the books of the Hebrew Bible. The Hasmoneans required the Galileans to submit to rule by the Jerusalem temple-state, and ruled and taxed the people through garrisons in fortresses such as Sepphoris. Given the political chaos of the first decades of Jerusalem rule and then the tyrannical rule of Herod, it is unlikely that the Galileans were forced or induced to conform their village community life to scribal Judean culture, laws, and customs. The resentment and hostility of the Galileans to Herodian, high priestly, and Roman rule evident in the great revolt would hardly have originated in the immediately preceding decades. This complex historical political-economic and mixed cultural situation was the historical context of the mission of Jesus in the villages of Galilee and the context to which some Judean scribes and sages migrated northward and formed nascent rabbinic "academies."

I

The Expansion of Hasmonean Rule

"SOCIOLOGY OF THE SECOND Temple" must mean something very different when we move from the beginning of the Hasmonean regime to its climax under Alexander Jannaeus. The territory controlled by the Hasmoneans changed from a tiny area of a day's walk in any direction from Jerusalem to all of Palestine. Jerusalem went from an out-of-the-way town in the Judean hills to the capital of one of the largest kingdoms that arose in the decline of the Seleucid empire. The Hasmoneans Judas, Jonathan, and Simon had been local leaders of bands of brigands and guerrillas, whereas John Hyrcanus and his sons conquered extensive territory and beat down domestic opposition with their professional armies. The populace went from the 100,000 to 200,000 Judeans ruled by their hereditary high priests to perhaps a million people of diverse ethnic-cultural backgrounds, many of whom were supposedly Judaized by order of priest-kings whose administration consisted of a number of Palestinian strongmen of various ethnic-cultural backgrounds. This is a historical transformation as dramatic as that in eastern North America between 1720 and 1820 or that in German-speaking territory between 1770 and 1870. To use the term "Judaism" with reference to both social-religious phenomena in tiny Judea in the first half of the second century BCE and social-religious phenomena in wider areas of Palestine in the early first century BCE would only perpetuate hopelessly vague or even false knowledge. In order to appreciate the dramatic historical changes we must generate far greater precision in our conceptual apparatus, research and historical constructions.

We tend to approach the history of late Second Temple Palestine out of a certain naivete, somewhat oblivious to the hard realities of the structural tensions and outright conflicts that dominate our literary sources. Despite the volume of recent scholarship documenting the extreme diversity of late Second Temple Palestine, we continue to use the vague conceptual apparatus of earlier theologically based constructions. For example, we use the term "Jews" in reference both to Ben Sira, the pious sage of pre-Hasmonean Jerusalem, and to the Galileans who followed Jesus of Nazareth barely one hundred years after the Hasmonean takeover of Galilee. We assume that both the Jerusalem scribe and those Galilean peasants and fisher-folk were involved in something called "Judaism" which was focused on the twin redemptive media of temple and Torah. And we refer to the events of 66–70 CE as "the Jewish revolt" (or the Great Revolt) in the sense that a somewhat unified Jewish people rebelled against Roman rule, or at least that a widespread "Zealot" (or "politics of holiness") movement devoted to temple and Torah fought persistently for their faith.

But in what sense could Galileans at the time of Jesus be called Jews? Is there any evidence that those Galileans understood themselves as involved in "Judaism" and/or were familiar with or loyal to temple and Torah? Or, with regard to events of 66–70, were the parallel insurrections by peasants in different regions of Palestine driven by loyalty to or protest against the Temple and high priesthood? Did the temple and high priesthood have legitimacy among the peasantry?

The application of sociological questions, methods and models to the history of late Second Temple Palestine is timely and should begin to make a difference in our historical constructions. The increasing diversity of literary and archaeological evidence generated by burgeoning recent studies can simply no longer be accommodated by the vague general received conceptual apparatus with which we have been working. Indeed, much of our literary and archaeological evidence becomes more intelligible only as we adjust our conceptual apparatus to the recognition of ancient social structural realities. Moreover, historical-sociological analysis can be pursued not simply to describe social structures for their own sake, but to elucidate the dynamics of the virtually continuous social conflicts that characterize Palestine in this period.

The Expansion of Hasmonean Rule

The extension of Hasmonean rule over Idumea and Galilee has been variously understood as a fanatical national-religious crusade, a (forced or voluntary) "conversion" to "Judaism," a military conquest, or a reunion of peoples previously cut off with their longstanding cultic and cultural center in Jerusalem. Each of these constructions either projects an inappropriate concept onto political-economic-religious events in the second century BCE and/or provides only a partial explanation. A more adequate and comprehensive approach entails, among other things, recognition that social phenomena and relations we designate as "religious" were inseparable from those we call "ethnic" and "political-economic" (including imperial and military!), that the Hasmonean high-priestly "state" was different from the Judean people and other peoples they ruled, and that nearly all of our literary sources focus on relations between the ruling elites of ancient societies. The historical-sociological analysis below focuses on events of the late second century. Yet it has important implications for our continuing attempts to understand both the origins of early Christian movements and the emergence of rabbinic circles in Galilee and their relationship with the people of Galilee.

FROM THE ONIADS TO THE HASMONEANS: CONTINUITY IN FUNDAMENTAL STRUCTURE, CHANGE IN BASIS OF POWER

Judea on the Eve of the Reform

From the proverbial wisdom of Ben Sira we can discern that the fundamental political-economic-religious structure of the Judean society headed by the temple-state was similar to what the sociologist Lenski studied as traditional agrarian societies. The structure consisted basically of two classes, the rulers based in Jerusalem along with the scribal "retainers" and artisans who were their staff and dependents, on the one hand, and the peasantry located in the surrounding villages, on the other. Because the "state" and the ruling aristocracy were sacerdotal and the ordinary priests held higher social status than the common peasants, some of Lenski's categories must be collapsed or adjusted.[1] As the paean of praise that Ben Sira hymns to the high priest Simon II illustrates, high-priestly rule of Judean society

---

1. Lenski, *Power and Privilege*. See the essay by Horsley and Tiller, "Ben Sira and the Sociology of the Second Temple."

was elaborately grounded in the mystified epic traditions of the great office holders of Israel's hoary antiquity (Sir 44–50).[2]

The Judean temple-state, however, was also an integral part of the larger Seleucid (and previously Ptolemaic and Persian) imperial system, which shared most of the principal features of the political–economic structure of "aristocratic empires," as delineated by John Kautsky.[3] As the machinations of Ptolemaic and Seleucid politics make clear, the concrete political-economic power of the high priesthood was dependent on the favor and fiscal desires of the imperial regime. Because of the latter, vertical divisions could and did emerge within the ruling Judean aristocracy as factions competing for imperial patronage and domestic power. Broadly speaking, it was when the dominant faction relied overly much on imperial favor and neglected the importance of the traditional sacred legitimation that the Judean temple-state system disintegrated.

The Rise and Consolidation of Hasmonean Rule

What was missing in the Judean temple-state system under imperial sponsorship was precisely what brought that system back into operation: a Judean military force. The "Maccabees" were apparently not so much leaders of a holy war of resistance to religious persecution and of divinely inspired "national liberation," as the later Hasmonean propaganda would have it, as local strongmen who exploited the situation of extreme political-religious turmoil to expand their militarily based political power in rural Judea.[4] It is increasingly clear that, once we cut through the rhetoric and agenda of 1 Maccabees and 2 Maccabees, the leadership of a revolt by Judas the Maccabee began in local raids and harassment by insurgents based in the Gophna mountain and never commanded a wide-spread following throughout the Judean population. The central Seleucid government had far more important matters demanding their attention. Judas' first victories were merely guerrilla strikes against small forces led by low-ranking Seleucid officers, the routing of Seron taking place at Beth Horon, an optimal site for an ambush by local insurgents familiar with the terrain, as the Roman

---

2. See Mack, *Wisdom and Hebrew Epic*.

3. Kautsky, *The Politics of Aristocratic Empires*. See also Horsley and Tiller, "Ben Sira and the Sociology of the Second Temple."

4. So, with appropriate sensitivity to the social-historical situation, Schwartz, "Josephus in Galilee."

The Expansion of Hasmonean Rule

army found out in the summer of 66 CE (1 Macc 3:10-26). The withdrawal of the invasionary force led by Lysias in 165 (1 Macc 4:28-35) was almost certainly due to attempts at negotiation (see the letters cited in 2 Macc 11:16-33). Other Judean groups, those described as "Hasideans,"[5] had long since become active, and were pursuing negotiation and compromise with the Seleucid regime.

Apparently the Seleucid forces mounted no new invasion from the fall of 165 to the spring of 163. Judas and his band, however, took the occasion of the interlude to seize at least partial control of Jerusalem and besieged the Seleucid garrison in the Akra (1 Macc 4:36-41). If we read between the lines of 1 Macc 4:42-58, the narrative does not claim either that Judas and his brothers purified the temple or that the priests who did purify the temple at that point were under the command of Judas. Apparently the priests were somewhat independent and only allied with him in some way. Ensuing events—the continuing struggles led by brothers Jonathan and Simon-indicate that by no means had Judas led and won a "war of national liberation." But he had generated a sizeable and experienced fighting force to be reckoned with, and set a precedent both of persistent opposition to Seleucid rule and of unwillingness to compromise with rival groups of Judeans, even those with whom he was ostensibly in alliance. When other important groups settled for the high priesthood of Alcimus, despite the reconciliation by the scribes of the "Hasideans," Judas' s forces persisted in their agitations until defeated (temporarily) by Seleucid forces.

After Alcimus died in 160 CE, Judas's brother Jonathan emerged in the ensuing power vacuum as leader of one of the rival forces seeking dominance in Judea (do the origins of the Qumran community lie in one of those rival groups that lost in the struggle for control of the temple government in Jerusalem?). Opportunities that Jonathan could exploit in his maneuvering for power presented themselves in the emergence of rival factions among the Seleucids, from 153 BCE onwards. By playing one rival badly in need of allies off against another, Jonathan achieved Seleucid blessings on his army and finally recognition of himself as the new high priest and of his jurisdiction over three districts of Samaria just north of Judea (1 Macc 9-10). There was still serious opposition to his rule within Judea, however, and the way in which he maintained power in Judea and by which he eventually lost his life—by maneuvering between rival Seleucid

---

5. See Davies, "Hasidim in the Maccabean Period."

factions—reveals that his authority was that of a regent dependent on recognition by a Seleucid regime (1 Macc 11–12).

The third brother, Simon, finally consolidated Hasmonean power in Jerusalem, apparently by making accommodations with some of his Judean opponents. The decree of the great assembly and stela erected in the temple in Simon's third year (1 Macc 14:28–49) provide revealing indications of the bases of Simon's power and of the rival power blocks in Judean society with whom some accommodation must have been reached. Such an unprecedented "great assembly" and grant of powers—well into his reign—would be unnecessary for a ruler already firmly and legitimately in control of the ruling institutions. His original and ultimate base of power was apparently the substantial military force that he and his brothers had built up over the previous decades. With the extensive wealth (t)he(y) had acquired, for instance from spoils,[6] he had even created a professional army (14:32). His initial recognition as "ruler and high priest" by "the people" was related to, and perhaps even the same as. the army, for in 1 Maccabees the term "people" seems almost coextensive with the ordinary people and/or those fighting with the Hasmoneans (and exclusive both of priests and of their opponents; 14:35; cf. 5:30; 7:6; 12:44; 13:2, 7; and note that "people" is not differentiated from "the soldiers" by 12:32).[7] The circumstances by which Simon obtained Seleucid recognition of his high-priestly authority indicates that he was now quite blatantly playing the Romans off against the Seleucids, on the one hand, but was still dependent on Seleucid approval on the other (14:38–40).

The "great assembly" was necessary, however, to formalize compromises with other power blocks and royal leadership. That it was necessary to prohibit meetings without Simon or speaking against him indicates that there had been active opposition (14:41–45). Previous high-priestly office holders (the *archontes tou ethnous*), (different factions among) the ordinary priests, and prominent "elders from the countryside," had to be appeased and neutralized (14:28). Some of the opposition, such as the priestly-scribal faction that withdrew to Qumran, was not so easily placated. That Simon was given authorization to make appointments of officials in charge of fortresses, armories, and the countryside, as well as of the temple itself, indicates that he had not previously consolidated these powers in his regime.

---

6. On Hasmonean economic consolidation, see Applebaum, "The Hasmoneans," 10–11, 15.

7. Contrary to Sievers, *The Hasmoneans and Their Supporters*, 125.

The decree and stela cited in 1 Macc 14 also thus indicate that, despite the Maccabean revolt, the fundamental social structure of Judea remained much the same as it had been at the time of Ben Sira. "The people" lived in larger or smaller villages scattered throughout "the countryside," with certain more powerful men having prominence as "elders." But political-economic power was concentrated in Jerusalem, legitimated as a temple-state staffed by ordinary priests, but dominated by a priestly aristocracy (the *archontes tou ethnous*), with the whole headed by a high priest. Whereas the Zadokite high priesthood had the legitimacy of a lineage of hoary antiquity, however, the principal base of power for the nascent Hasmonean high priests was their own, increasingly professional army. From that base Simon could now consolidate his power by placing his own men in crucial administrative as well as military positions. This consolidation of powers in the hands of Simon amid the wider context of the decline of Seleucid power set the stage for the expansion of Hasmonean rule over the rest of Palestine in the next two generations.

FROM THE EARLY TO THE LATER HASMONEANS: CONTINUITY IN BASIS OF POWER, DRAMATIC CHANGE IN SCOPE

Scope and Structure of Hasmonean Rule in Early First Century BCE

By the time Alexander Jannaeus completed his conquests, the territory under Hasmonean rule equaled or exceeded the scope of the Davidic–Solomonic empire (*Ant.* 13.395–397). Hasmonean control in the conquered areas was consolidated under Alexandra Salome, who also enlarged the army despite the fact that no more expansionist wars were being conducted. Before I explore the dramatic extension of Hasmonean rule to most of Palestine, however, I should note that the fundamental structure of political-economic relations did not change, nor did the basis of Hasmonean power, the Hasmonean military. To appreciate the structure and character of the relationship between Hasmonean rulers and subject populations I shall look briefly at two bits of evidence, that of the confirmation of Hasmonean rule once the regime became subject to Roman imperial control, and that of the extensive network of fortresses and garrisons by which the regime maintained its rule. Josephus cites a series of decrees by which Julius Caesar had confirmed the power and prerogatives of the Hasmonean regime over its principal Judean and other subjects even after the conquered Hellenistic cities had been restored to their freedom (under Roman rule).[8]

> It is my wish that Hyrcanus, son of Alexander, and his children shall be Ethnarchs of the Judeans and shall hold the office of High Priests of the Judeans for all time in in accordance with their ancestral customs (*ta patria ethē*); . . . and whatever high-priestly rights or other [pecuniary] privileges exist in accordance with their laws (*tous idious nomous*), these he and his children shall possess by my command . . . That his children shall rule over the Judean people and enjoy the fruits of the places given them . . . That both Hyrcanus and his sons shall be High Priest and Priests of Jerusalem and of their people with/by the same rights and laws/regulations (*epi dikaiois kai nomimois*) as those with/by which their forefathers uninterruptedly held the priesthood . . . These men shall receive and fortify the city of Jerusalem . . . That [the Judeans] in the second year shall pay the tribute at Sidon, consisting of one-fourth of the produce sown, and in addition, they shall also pay tithes to Hyrcanus and his sons, just as they paid to their forefathers . . . For the city of Joppa, Hyrcanus and his sons shall pay tribute, collected from those who inhabit the territory . . . As for the villages in the Great Plain, which Hyrcanus and his forefathers before him possessed, it is the pleasure of the Senate that Hyrcanus and the Judeans shall retain them with the same rights (*epi tois dikaiois*) as they formerly had. Also the ancient rights (*dikaia*) which the Judeans and the high priests and the priests had in relation to each other should continue, and also the [pecuniary] privileges which they received by vote of the people and the Senate. As for the places, lands (*chōras*), and farms, the fruits of which the kings of Syria and Phoenicia, as allies of the Romans, were permitted to enjoy by their gift, these the Senate decrees that the ethnarch Hyrcanus and the Judeans shall have (*Ant.* 14.194-196, 199-200, 203, 205-209).

The traditional "rights and privileges" that the Romans here confirm to the Hasmonean regime are those of ruler over and taxation of the people under their jurisdiction. It is not necessary to determine whether "the Judeans" in the phrases "High Priest of the Judeans" and "Judean people" are ethnically or geographically precise or limited to a particular area/populace. The

---

8. On these decrees, see Rajak, *Josephus*. Freyne (*Galilee*, 62) takes these Roman decrees as evidence that Galileans could claim the rights of Jews.

reference to the Great Plain makes clear that the Hasmonean dynasty is here being confirmed in control of its wider territory (excepting the Hellenistic cities). However vague the phrase "Hyrcanus and the Judeans" (in *Ant.* 14.207, 209) may seem, it is clear from the rest of these decrees that the vast majority of "Judeans" were politically-economically-religiously subject to the Hasmonean regime. Especially noteworthy for consideration of the relations between Hasmonean regime and Galileans below is the function of "their own / traditional laws (or customs or regulations)" in this connection. That is, all of the three times the decrees refer to "the laws" are understood as legitimating or regulating the "rights and (economic) privileges" of the high-priestly rulers of the Judeans (*Ant.* 14.194, 195, 199).

It seems clear from information which Josephus provides almost in passing, but which is confirmed by numerous archaeological digs, that the means by which the Hasmoneans maintained their rule over the vastly expanded territories was the (increasingly mercenary) army. Josephus reports that Aristobulus II, unhappy that his brother Hyrcanus II was to succeed their mother in power, moved quickly to take control of the military fortresses. In fifteen days, says Josephus, he had gained control of twenty-two fortresses (already commanded by his father's "friends"). Since this did not include the major royal fortresses of Alexandrium, Hyrcania, Machaerus, and the Jerusalem citadel, it suggests that the Hasmonean regime had upwards of thirty fortresses around the various districts that they used to control and administer the local areas as well as, along the frontiers, to protect against attack.[9] We should attend to evidence of fortresses again below insofar as they may be relevant to relations between the Hasmonean regime and Galilee.

WAS HASMONEAN EXPANSION A RELIGIOUS CRUSADE OR BY "CONVERSION TO JUDAISM"?

In reconstructing the history of Second Temple Judea it is important precisely not to move too quickly and directly from literary text to historical context and precisely not to formulate a broad general picture of affairs on the basis of a synthesis of accounts from various sources (without taking adequately into account the ideology of those sources).

---

9. See the evidence and analysis in Schatzman, *Armies of the Hasmoneans and Herod*, 44, 95–96.

Previous constructions of Hasmonean history as a religious crusade by the Maccabean people's armies destroying idols in its territory and forcibly Judaizing neighboring peoples depends heavily on certain passages in 1 Maccabees as read through a conceptual apparatus developed by modern Christian biblical studies. The construct of "Judaism" as a religion is something projected back into Second Temple times by modern Europeans. That this was an especially exclusive and "national" religion in late second-century Palestine is a further extension of this modern conceptualization developed without attention to ancient social and political forms.[10] That 1 Maccabees has its own particular political-religious ideology is, of course, now clearly recognized, enabling us to avoid imposing that ideology uncritically onto the events of Hasmonean expansion.

With regard to the Idumeans to the south and the inhabitants of Galilee to the north, the expansion of Hasmonean rule is (often) imagined as some sort of religious "conversion" to "Judaism." Such a conceptualization would appear problematic simply on the surface of the matter. The concept "conversion" usually implies a deep sense of change in one's religious conviction by an individual,[11] not the shift in political-religious (even ethnic) status of a whole people. And "Judaism," as just noted, is used to refer to a religion, whereas no religion separable from the political-economic-ethnic forms of communal life had yet been differentiated in Second Temple Judea.

More substantively, moreover, recent presentations of Hasmonean expansion in terms of "conversion" to "Judaism," whether "forcible" or "voluntary," are based on a broadly synthetic reading of the sources. The intricate arguments for a gradual and "voluntary conversion" offered recently by Kasher[12] are problematic and unconvincing.[13] While accepting some of Kasher's arguments for Galilee, Grabbe has recently argued with regard to

---

10. The peculiar modern concept of "Judaism" as a religion determines the construction of the history of Hasmonean expansion and other ancient Judean history as can be seen clearly in Hengel, *Judaism and Hellenism*, 305-7.

11. As in the classic study of ancient Mediterranean materials (Nock, *Conversion*), who defined conversion as "the reorientation of the soul of an individual, his deliberate turning from indifference or from an earlier form of piety to another, a turning which implies a consciousness that a great change is involved, that the old was wrong and the new is right" (p. 7). A quick check of the entries on "conversion" in standard dictionaries and encyclopedias whether in biblical studies and religion or general) will further indicate how problematic the concept is for Second Temple history.

12. Kasher, *Jews, Idumaeans, and Ancient Arabs*, chap. 3.

13. See the critique in Shatzman, *The Armies of the Hasmoneans and Herod*, 58-59n90.

the Idumeans that, however problematic the hypothesis of forced conversion, it is plausible in this case.[14] Grabbe comments:

> [T]he effects of the conversion ... lasted. Forced conversion does not usually represent a change of mind, and, if possible, those compelled carry on their original religion covertly and revert to it openly as soon as they can. This did not happen with the Idumeans. Although we know of the occasional individual who intended to return to the ancestral religion (e.g., Costobarus [*Ant.* 15.7.9 §§253-255]), the Idumeans as a whole supported the Jews in their later wars with the Romans. For example, in the 'war of Varus' (ca. 4 B.C.E.) Idumea revolted along with Jerusalem (*War* 2.5.2-3 §§72-79). Attested in even greater detail is the participation of several thousand Idumeans in the defense of Jerusalem during the 66-70 war.[15]

As long as we are working with the broad general categories "Judaism" and "Jews" and "Idumeans" (reading references to whatever groups or incidents in highly synthetic fashion as implying "Jews" or "Judaism" generally) such conclusions may seem warranted. Once we ask questions of political-economic structure and historical dynamics, however, such a synthetic picture begins to disintegrate. With these more precise questions in mind, a closer look at Josephus's reports of incidents involving Idumeans reveals a very different situation.

To claim that "Idumea revolted along with Jerusalem" after the death of Herod is to go far beyond what Josephus's reports suggest. First of all, the widespread insurrections in 4 BCE were not centered in or led from Jerusalem. The protest of the Jerusalemites to Varus, according to Josephus's accounts (*War* 2.73; *Ant.* 17.293), that they had not been involved in the revolt, has some credibility, for Josephus makes clear here as well as earlier in his accounts that those besieging the Romans in Jerusalem were from the countryside. The insurrections put down by Varus were themselves based in the countryside in Galilee and Perea as well as Judea itself, even though

---

14. Grabbe, *Judaism*, 2:329; similarly Sievers, *Hasmoneans and Their Supporters*, 143.

15. Kasher (*Jews, Idumaeans, and Ancient Arabs*, 63, 65) makes even more of Josephus's accounts of Idumeans' actions in the Great Revolt: "The sincerity of the Idumeans' conversion and their considerable integration into Jewish life may also indirectly be seen by their activist stand during the Great Revolt against the Romans. They proved themselves faithful sons to the Jewish nation and fought with uncompromising devotion, a fact which may serve to show the depth of their national and religious integration ... This demonstrates once more the degree of their integration into Jewish society and the fervor of their Jewish nationalism ..."

the former two had attacked royal armories to obtain weapons and supplies (*War* 2.56–65; *Ant.* 17.271–284). Josephus also mentions 2,000 veterans of Herod in Idumea (*War* 2.55; had they been settled there?) assembled in Judea fighting against Herod's troops under Achiab, a cousin of Herod (*Ant.* 17.270). Then, after Varos had suppressed the insurrections in Galilee, Perea and Judea, 10,000 more rebels surrendered to Varus on the advice of Achiab. Josephus calls the latter *Ioudaioi* in one report (*Ant.* 17.297) and locates them in Idumea in the other (*War* 2.76). Perhaps these last holdouts were fugitives from Varus's suppression of widespread insurrection in the Judean countryside. If they were Idumeans, they were acting parallel to the peasantry in the other districts of Herod's realm, not revolting "along with Jerusalem."

Moreover, whether or not those 10,000 were Idumeans involved in outright rebellion, the motives of the rebels from the various districts of Palestine may be indicated in Josephus's reports of the massive demonstration in Jerusalem at Pentecost. Panicking at the insistent demands by the crowds at Passover, Archelaus had already turned his troops loose against the demonstrators in the temple courtyard, who had included many peasants from the countryside. Further angered by the high-handed actions and harassment of Caesar's *epitropos* of Syria sent in to handle Herod's estate, huge crowds gathered in Jerusalem at Pentecost (late May), predominantly from Judea, but also from Galilee, Idumea and Perea. In both accounts Josephus states explicitly that they came more out of indignation at the actions of Sabinus and the Roman troops than for the customary ritual (*War* 2.39–44; *Ant.* 17.250–255). Thus according to our principal source for such events, the insurrections in 4 BCE were popular outbursts of long pent-up resentment of Herodian tyranny touched off by Archelaus's and Sabinus's repressive measures. There is nothing in Josephus's accounts to suggest that these rebellions were somehow motivated by "Judaism," much less that Idumeans protesting at Pentecost were making common cause with "Jerusalem."

The second argument offered for the solid conversion of the Idumeans to "Judaism" is the participation of several thousand in the defense of Jerusalem in 69–70. The Great Revolt of 66–70, however, cannot be understood simply as a two-sided conflict between "the Jews" and the Romans. Josephus's accounts make it clear repeatedly that the revolt was also a civil war, indeed a class conflict between the priestly aristocracy and Herodian nobility, on the one side, and the ordinary people, on the other. Moreover, the principal fighting forces who continued resistance to the Roman siege of Jerusalem had originated from among the peasantry in different districts of Palestine, and battled among themselves even during the siege. The Idumeans, furthermore, appear as distinctive among those rival groups, with their own indigenous social structure, apparently a traditional tribal structure headed by chieftains (Josephus's *archontes*; *War* 4.228-235, 517-520). We cannot take the speeches by Jesus the chief priest and Simon the Idumean chieftain as good evidence for the Idumeans' views of Jerusalem and the temple since they are written from the point of view of the wealthy and powerful Judean priest, Josephus—the very historian who claimed that from the time of Hyrcanus the Idumeans had continued to be Judeans.[16] According to Josephus's accounts, finally, the Idumeans were invited into Jerusalem by "the Zealots" (a coalition of peasants fleeing the Roman reconquest in northwest Judea) to aid them in their struggle against the priestly aristocracy. Tiring of the purge of the nobility, most of the Idumeans withdrew from the city, some remaining with the party of John of Gischala. Later, after Simon bar Giora took control of Idumea by treachery, against the resistance by the tribal militia, some Idumeans joined his army. But when they attempted to surrender to the Romans, Simon bar Giora thwarted their plan (*War* 4.228-235, 326-333, 345-353, 517-526, 566-572). It would be difficult to claim that the Idumeans were fighting faithfully for the temple and Torah of "Judaism" in the events of 68-70, or that the spasmodic involvement of some contingents of Idumeans is evidence of the permanent conversion of Idumeans generally to Judaism.

Not only are Josephus's reports of events in 4 BCE and 68-70 CE not susceptible of interpretation in terms of religious conversion, but he also provides evidence that some Idumeans were not effectively "converted" at all. The case of Costobar provides evidence that indigenous Idumean traditions were still being cultivated and Judean traditions resisted nearly a century after Hyrcanus supposedly effectively converted the Idumeans to "Judaism." Grabbe dismisses Costobar as an "occasional individual who intended to return to the ancestral religion," and Kasher, while recognizing this evidence that conversion had not been imposed on all the Idumeans collectively, claims "there is reason to believe this was just a small group

---

16. For some reason, Stern (*Greek and Latin Authors on Jews and Judaism*, vol. 1, 356) fails to consider that the very text he cites as evidence that "at the end of the period of the Second Temple the Idumeans felt themselves to be Jews in every respect," *War* 4.270-275 is a speech written in good Hellenistic historiographic fashion by Josephus himself and hardly a valid source for Idumeans' own feelings.

... and something of an exception," but offers none.[17] Costobar, however, was not simply "an occasional individual." He was a scion from one of the most distinguished among the Idumean aristocratic families, whose ancestors had been priests of the Idumean god Koze, and he possessed his own ancestral estates in Idumea (*Ant.* 15.253, 264). His family was thus parallel to another high ranking and most powerful Idumean family, that of Antipater, Herod's father. Thus it may not be surprising to find that Costobar had cast his lot with Herod in the struggle for the domination of Palestine and that Herod rewarded him for his loyalty by appointing him governor of Idumea and Gaza and by giving Costobar his sister Salome in marriage. According to Josephus's report, Costobar, from one of the most powerful families in Idumea and descendant of the priests of the Idumean god, did not think it right that the Idumeans should be adopting the customs of the Judeans or be ruled by them. But this was nearly a century after Hyrcanus had supposedly successfully insisted that the Idumeans observe "the law of the Judeans." Moreover, Costobar was dismissed and eliminated by Herod, not for failing to enforce the laws and customs of the Judeans in Idumea, but for his questionable loyalty to Herod in having protected the sons of Baba, prominent figures of great popularity in Jerusalem who had been supporters of Antigonus, Herod's last remaining Hasmonean rival. Clearly Palestinian politics were a matter of shifting coalitions and loyalties among prominent Judean and Idumean families and their power and influence (see further *Ant.* 14.8-10).[18] Observance of the laws of the Judeans was of secondary importance at most. With regard to how complete the "conversion" of the Idumeans was, if a prominent figure such as Costobar, already assimilated into the world of Hellenistic power politics, was still surreptitiously loyal to Idumean traditions, can it not be surmised that Idumean villagers were equally or even more so?

The available historiographical evidence of relations between Judea and the Idumeans is thus not susceptible of interpretation in terms of conversion. Indeed, the very concept of conversion (to a religion or way of life) seems inapplicable to a situation in which the religious dimension was inseparable from the political and economic dimensions of life.

In a series of recent studies, Shaye Cohen has been struggling with similar difficulties in the use of the concept "conversion" in relation to the

---

17. Grabbe, *Judaism*, 2:329; Kasher, *Jews, Idumaeans, and Ancient Arabs*, 62-63.

18. Contra Kasher, *Jews, Idumaeans, and Ancient Arabs*, such links between powerful Idumean families do not suggest integration into Jewish society.

different meanings and nuances of the term *Ioudaios/oi* and *ethnos*, among others. His observations may be helpful in clarifying the issues. In consideration of material primarily from Diaspora situations he argues that "conversion to Judaism" (as distinct from some more partial demonstration or respect for Judaism) involved three components: "practice of the Jewish laws; exclusive devotion to the god of the Jews; and integration into the Jewish community."[19] As should be clear from the preceding discussion of Josephus's accounts of the relations between the Idumeans and the Judeans, however, the Idumeans apparently did not meet any of the three criteria: although they supposedly agreed to live according to the laws of the Judeans, at least some, as illustrated by the family of Costobar, resisted for generations. Again, as illustrated by the prominent priestly family of Costobar, at least some Idumeans continued to worship their own traditional god(s). And they were clearly not integrated into the Jewish community, having remained a separate ethnos with its traditional social structure. Thus the Idumeans did not become ethnic *Ioudaioi*, but retained their own ethnic identity. In the case of the Idumeans (and surely of the inhabitants of Galilee as well) the question of the degree of change of religion or way of life is inseparably bound up with the way in which they became subject to a state that operated according to the traditional "laws of the Judeans." It is necessary to re-examine the evidence and re-reconstruct the history.

Hasmonean Expansion in the Vacuum of Imperial Power

While the most dramatic expansion of Hasmonean rule over most of Palestine happened under John Hyrcanus and his sons, Hasmonean expansion into districts bordering the tiny area ruled by the temple-state prior to the Maccabean revolt had begun under Jonathan and Simon. The Seleucid ruler Demetrius had transferred the three districts just north of Judea—Aphairema, Lydda, and Rathamin—from Samarian jurisdiction to Jerusalem high-priestly rule (1 Macc 10:30, 38; 11:34). To the west toward the Sea, Simon had taken and fortified Joppa and Gazara, and settled Judeans there (1 Macc 13:43–48; 14:3–7, 34).

Extensive expansion began under John Hyrcanus, but not until after one last effort by the declining Seleucids to resubject Judea to its control. During the lengthy siege, Hyrcanus ejected from Jerusalem all but the able-bodied defenders, which could not have endeared him to ordinary

---

19. Cohen, *From the Maccabees to the Mishnah*, 26.

Jerusalemites and the Judean populace at large. Hyrcanus also plundered David's tomb of three thousand talents, using three hundred to buy off Antiochus VII Sidetes, and the remainder to hire mercenaries, which Josephus claims was unprecedented (*War* 1.61; *Ant.* 13.249; at least since the Jewish Persian governors such as Nehemiah! Cf. Neh 2:9). Josephus also reports that Hyrcanus amassed great wealth by his exploitation of Judea, thus providing a secure economic basis for the expansion of his rule into new territory (*Ant.* 13.273).[20]

While Josephus places Hyrcanus's destruction of Shechem and the temple on Mt. Gerizim early in his reign, the excavators of the site date the destruction of Shechem after 112 BCE.[21] This date would be much closer to the subsequent year-long siege and destruction of Samaria toward the end of his reign. Judging from the severity of the devastation in both cases (according to Josephus's accounts, *War* 1.65; *Ant.* 13.281), Hyrcanus was apparently eliminating any possibility that a rival center of political-religious power could remerge in Samaria or Gerizim. It is even credible that Hyrcanus had the inhabitants of Samaria enslaved, for there is no reference to *protoi* of the Samaritans active in political affairs until well after the city was restored following the Roman takeover in Palestine (*War* 1.166, 213, 229, 302–303; *Ant.* 18.88–89; 20.118–136). With the destruction of both temple and capital city, Hyrcanus apparently intended to rule the whole district up to Scythopolis and Mt. Carmel directly from Jerusalem. The effects of this conquest, however, was finally to create an irreconcilable alienation between Judeans and Samaritans that erupts occasionally into the historical record in incidents such as the Samaritans' strewing bones in the temple courtyard and armed attacks which eventually implicated even the respective aristocracies under Cumanus in mid-first century CE (*Ant.* 18.30; 20.118–136). That popular traditions continued among the people in Samaria is dramatically evident in the movement led by the prophet who promised his followers he would find the sacred vessels Moses had deposited on Mt. Gerizim (*Ant.* 18.85–87).

The Hasmonean expansion that has been inappropriately dealt with in terms of conversion was over the Idumeans and Galileans. Because of their implications for subsequent developments, including the ministry of Jesus,

---

20. See further Applebaum, "The Hasmoneans," 18–22.

21. Wright, *Shechem*, 172; Bull and Wright, "New Discovered Temples on Mt. Gerizim."

THE EXPANSION OF HASMONEAN RULE

the Great Revolt, and the emergence of rabbinic leadership in Galilee, these cases require closer scrutiny and analysis.

RELATIONS BETWEEN THE HASMONEANS AND THE IDUMEANS

The Idumeans appear still to have retained a traditional tribal structure into the second century BCE.[22] Significantly, in contrast to the temple-state of Judea, no central capital city ruled over the whole area. Rather, regional towns, principally Hebron, Adora and Marisa, held prominence in relations to the surrounding villages, with a certain degree of Hellenistic influence evident in Marisa. It is interesting to speculate that Idumean villagers may have developed "an identity of interest" with their Judean counterparts as "oppressed native village populations,"[23] but we have little or no evidence to that effect.

The accounts of Judas's attacks into Idumea in 1 Macc 5 and 2 Macc 10 and 12 should be evaluated critically and in close comparison.[24] The accounts of raids into Idumea in 1 Macc 5:3, 65-67 do not fit the stated agenda of the series of attacks led by Judas and Simon to rescue kindred/"Israelites" (Judeans) under attack by hostile neighboring nations (5:1-2, 9-17). The accounts in 2 Macc 10-12, which have Seleucid officials rather than the neighboring peoples as the principal instigators of the conflicts, stand in a parallel sequence of several expeditions into neighboring lands, suggesting that a common source lies behind 1 Macc 5 and 2 Macc 10-12. That 2 Macc 10:15, in the account where the principal agenda is not such harassment by the Gentiles, mentions Idumeans "besieging" Judeans makes such harassment credible. Judas's attack against the strongholds of Idumea was not a rescue mission of fellow Jews under attack, however, but a punitive strike against the neighbors to the south who were also apparently harboring Judean opponents of Judas (refugees from Jerusalem?). First Maccabees 5:65-67 and 2 Macc 12:32-38 must then refer to a second attack

---

22. See Rappaport, "Hellenistic Cities and the Judaization of Palestine," 222.

23. Kasher, *Jews, Idumaeans, and Ancient Arabs*, 27, 46-47.

24. Kasher (*Jews, Idumaeans, and Ancient Arabs*, 25-33), after seemingly subjecting 1 Macc 5 to critical analysis, but without comparisons with 2 Macc 10-12, then trusts the narrative as basically historical record. Sievers (*Hasmoneans and Their Supporters*, 49-57) charts the parallel accounts that must depend on a common source, and notes some of the factors that account for the differences. Schwartz ("Israel and the Nations Roundabout") provides the most critical assessment of the ideology and rhetoric of 1 Maccabees.

into Idumea. Both accounts save Judas from any responsibility for what must have been a serious defeat, but they do so differently. First Maccabees has Judas conveniently absent on the expedition into Gilead, returning to retaliate against the Idumeans, while 2 Maccabees blames the defeat on idolatry (12:39–45). However serious the damage done behind the account in 1 Macc 5:65–66, these were not conquests but punitive or preemptive strikes at Hebron and Marisa, although it is conceivable that Hebron and its villages were from this point periodically under effective Hasmonean domination. In any case, the initial relations between the Hasmoneans and the Idumeans involved sharp hostilities, apparently from both sides.

Josephus has three brief accounts of John Hyrcanus's treatment of the Idumeans.

> He further took numerous cities in Idumea, including Adoreon and Marisa. (*War* 1.63)

> Hyrcanus also captured the Idumean cities of Adora and Marisa, and after subduing all the Idumeans, permitted them to remain in their country so long as they had themselves circumcised and were willing to observe the laws of the Judeans. And so, out of attachment to the land of their fathers, they submitted to circumcision and to making their manner of life conform in all other respects to that of the Judeans. And from that time on they have continued to be Judeans. (*Ant.* 13.257–258)

> Now Hyrcanus had altered their constitution/form of government (*politeia*) and made them adopt the customs and the laws of the Judeans. (*Ant.* 15.254)

To these should be compared to two other references to the Idumeans:

> Judeans and Idumeans differ, as Ptolemy states in the first book of the History of King Herod. For Judeans are those who are so naturally from origin, whereas the Idumeans . . . were not Judeans by origin, but Phoenicians and Syrians, having been subjugated by the Judeans and having been forced to undergo circumcision, so as to be counted among the nation [or, to contribute to the nation, *syntelein eis to ethnos*] and keep the same customs/laws (*nomima*), they were called Judeans. (Ptolemy the Historian)[25]

---

25. Stern, *Greek and Latin Authors on Jews and Judaism*, vol. 1, 146; trans. adapted.

The Expansion of Hasmonean Rule

> As for Judea, its western extremities ... are occupied by the Idumeans and by the lake. The Idumeans are Nabateans, but owing to a sedition they were banished from there, joined the Judeans and shared in the same customs/laws (*nomima*) with them. (Strabo, *Geographica* 16.2.34)[26]

Those who argue for "voluntary conversion" of the Idumeans to "Judaism" rely on the second sentence cited from the Strabo passage over against all the other texts. To do so they must take it out of literary context, for the latter testifies to the extremely mixed background of the peoples of "Judea." But there are two other major problems for their preferred reading of this sentence. Strabo has the first part wrong—the Idumeans were not Nabateans banished due to a sedition, but were descendants of the Edomites displaced (north-westward into what had been southern Judah) by the invading Nabateans (Arabs)—giving us reason to doubt the reliability of the second part. Moreover, the second part is vague, not specifying precisely how they came to "join" the Judeans. Insofar as the citation from "Ptolemy" is said explicitly to come from a history of Herod, it indicates observers still aware of the striking difference between the Idumeans and the Judeans over a century after the supposed "Judaization" of the former, according to Josephus.

Both of Josephus's principal accounts about John Hyrcanus's treatment of the Idumeans come in the midst of his summary reports of Hyrcanus's expansionist military expeditions against Shechem and Gerizim to the north, cities and their territories across the Jordan to the east, and eventually the city of Samaria. There seems no reason to doubt that military action was involved as John Hyrcanus took control of Idumea. Hyrcanus's actions, moreover, followed upon the earlier strikes against Hebron and Marisa by Judas. It is worth noting the marked increase in the numbers of Idumeans mentioned in Egyptian papyri in the late second century BCE, possibly a reference to refugees.[27] That the Idumeans were subjugated by Hyrcanus is independently suggested by the book of Jubilees (especially 36:1—38:6).[28] On the other hand, the relatively gentle treatment of the Idumeans stands in stark contrast with the utter destruction of Samaria by Hyrcanus and his sons. It may be surmised that the reason for the punitive destructive

---

26. Stern, *Greek and Latin Authors on Jews and Judaism*, vol. 1, 115.

27. Rappaport, "Les Idumens en Egypte."

28. That Jubilees pertains to the subjugation of the Idumeans in the 120s by Hyrcanus rather than to Judas the Maccabees' attacks in the 160s has been persuasively argued by Mendels (*The Land of Israel as a Political Concept*, 75–88).

measures against Samaria was to eliminate the principal historical rival of Jerusalem for power and influence in Palestine. Since no corresponding center of power had emerged in Idumea, there was no need of such extreme measures.

That the Idumeans remained in their territory, were circumcised or observant of the laws of the Judeans, is not susceptible of reduction to a religious dimension. It is abundantly clear from a story Josephus tells about the tense situation in Galilee in 66–67 CE that circumcision held broad social-political significance, and was not simply a religious and/or ethnic matter. Indeed the political and religious dimensions were inseparable (see *Life* 112–113, 149–154). It is likely that the Idumeans (and the Galileans and/or Itureans to be discussed below) already practiced circumcision.[29] Understanding circumcision simply as a cultural/religious practice leads to the hypothesis that Hyrcanus was demanding circumcision primarily of Hellenized Idumeans, primarily in the "city" of Marisa, who had not previously undergone circumcision. If, on the other hand, we recognize that circumcision was likely an important symbol of membership in a religious-political group or community, then the point of having the already circumcised Idumeans submit to circumcision (again, by the Judeans) was likely a symbol of their incorporation into the social-political community (i.e. the social-political "covenant")[30] based in the Jerusalem temple and ruled by/ subject to the Hasmonean high priesthood.

Moreover, Josephus uses "the laws (or customs) of the Judeans" in a comprehensive sense, traditional regulations of all aspects of social life, political-economic-religious-familial. If the account in *Ant.* 15.254 were our only source available, we would conclude simply that Hyrcanus had forced a change of polity on the Idumeans. This is a pattern familiar from some ancient empire-building. The Persian imperial regime had encouraged the revival of local laws among its subject peoples. But other ancient kingships imposed their own polity or laws on subjected peoples. This appears to be what Hyrcanus did with the Idumeans. Whatever else it may have meant for the Idumeans, observing "the laws of the Judeans" would have included the political-economic-religious relations of subordination

---

29. See Kasher, *Jews, Idumaeans, and Ancient Arabs*, 56 n35; Tcherikover, Fuks, and Stern, *Corpus Papyrorum Judaicarum*, vol. 1, 4; Stern, *Greek and Latin Authors on Jews and Judaism*, vol. 1, 2–4; vol. 2, 620–25.

30. Note that Barn. 9:6, precisely in a context of pointing out that other non-Judeans were also circumcised, refers to circumcision as the symbol of being part of the covenant/ community/polity.

to the Hasmonean high priesthood in Jerusalem, as indicated in the language of Caesar's decrees cited above.

If we have eyes to see, Josephus offers us glimpses of how the Hasmonean regime, and later the Herodian as well, actually governed the Idumeans. Herod's father Antipater was not the first powerful Idumean figure to become prominent in the Hasmonean regime. Alexander Jannaeus appointed his father Antipas as *stratēgos* of all Idumea, including Gaza; and we know from comments about Antipater elsewhere that these men were not only "Idumean by birth (*genos*)," but "in the front rank of the people (*ethnos*) by ancestry, wealth, and other advantages" (*Ant.* 14.10; *War* 1.123). Two generations later, once (the Idumean) Herod had become the Romans' client king, he in turn appointed Costobar, scion of another powerful, aristocratic Idumean (priestly!) family, as the governor of Idumea. That is, the Hasmonean rulers in Jerusalem made political alliances with powerful Idumean families, through which the district was then controlled. Insofar as Idumean society still maintained a certain patriarchal tribal structure, the rest of the society could be expected to follow the lead, or be subject to the power, of the most prominent families. As mentioned above, one receives the impression of a tribal structure still somewhat intact in Josephus's reports about the Idumeans in 68–69 CE. Josephus characterizes them as "a turbulent and disorderly people (*ethnos*)" whose multiple "chieftains" (*archontes*; Thackeray's translation is appropriate) can muster a popular militia "hastily from the countryside (*chōra*)," whether to respond to the call of Judean fellow peasants for help against the dominant aristocracy in Jerusalem or to defend their own territory against the ambitious popular Judean king-on-the-rise, Simon bar Giora (*War* 4.230–233). It is surely significant that throughout his treatment of Idumeans, whether of leading figures from prominent families or of the ordinary folk, Josephus refers to them as a people (*ethnos*) distinct from the Judeans (e.g. *War* 1.123). In the latter account, all the Judean peasants-turned-Zealots have to do to solicit an army of Idumeans is to appeal to their chieftains!

RELATIONS BETWEEN THE HASMONEANS AND THE GALILEANS

Since both the "Jesus movement" and Gospel tradition behind emergent Christianity and the emergence and consolidation of the rabbinic movement took place in Galilee, the watershed constituted by the Hasmonean takeover of the area is of great importance for subsequent history. Most scholarship in recent generations has simply assumed that Galilee in the first century CE was Jewish even though their "Judaism" was not as rigorous as the Pharisees and early rabbis would have liked. When one probes for evidence, however, there turn out to be precious few indicators. It would appear that many of our assumptions about the Galilee of the Jesus movement and early rabbis are rooted in the theologically influenced conceptual apparatus with which we are accustomed to dealing with the rise of "Christianity" out of "Judaism." But that is precisely what has been thrown into question by recent recognition both that religion is inseparable from political-economic life in traditional societies such as those in ancient Palestine and that there was a considerable diversity of social-religious phenomena in ancient Palestine. How the importance of the Hasmonean takeover of Galilee is understood and estimated depends heavily, first, on who the inhabitants of Galilee were at the time and, second, on what the structure and dynamics of Hasmonean rule in Galilee were.

The Inhabitants of Galilee Prior to Hasmonean Takeover

There are three different views on who were the inhabitants of Galilee prior to the expansion of Hasmonean rule to the area. One is that they were Gentile, either since the Assyrian conquest and deportation of Israelites or by gradual shifts in population over the centuries of Assyrian, Persian and Hellenistic rule, or at least since the Itureans controlled the area just prior to the Hasmonean takeover. The hypothesis that the inhabitants were (forcibly) converted to Judaism often accompanies this first view, so that Galilee then became "Jewish" in late Second Temple times (a view popularized by Emil Schürer's influential work).[31] The alternative longstanding view is that Galilee had become heavily if not predominantly Jewish over the centuries prior to the Hasmonean "annexation." With this view goes the hypothesis that those "Judaized" by the Hasmoneans were only the Itureans or other non-Jewish inhabitants at the time.[32]

These longstanding alternative views have been based on the same texts, albeit in different readings based on different presuppositions. For example, the report of Simon's expedition to Galilee to rescue several

---

31. Schürer, *Geschichte des jüdischen Volkes*; Schürer, *History of the Jewish People*.
32. The view now adopted in Kasher, *Jews, Idumaeans, and Ancient Arabs*; Grabbe, *Judaism*.

thousand Jews (1 Macc 5:21–23) is read by some to mean that Galilee was already Jewish, but read by others to indicate that there were only a few Jews in Galilee, concentrated in the west toward Ptolemais and Arbatta. The key passage in Josephus, where he is dependent on Timagenes as quoted by Strabo, is *Ant.* 13.318–319:

> [Aristobulus] made war on the Itureans and acquired a good part of their territory (*chōra*) for Judea and compelled the inhabitants (*tous enoikountas*), if they wished to remain in the country, to be circumcised and to live in accordance with the laws of the Judeans (*tous ioudaiōn nomous*) . . . (Strabo, quoting Timagenes) "he acquired additional territory for [the Judeans] and brought over to them a portion of the nation of Itureans whom he joined to them by a bond of circumcision."

If one either trusts the Timagenes statement or does not differentiate between the Itureans and the inhabitants of the country, then it appears that the Itureans themselves were being Judaized. Those who believe that Galilee was already heavily Jewish then read this passage as referring basically to Upper Galilee, since the Itureans were then apparently based in Lebanon just to the north. If one considers that Josephus is intentionally differentiating between the Itureans and the inhabitants of the country, then the inhabitants here being Judaized must have been other Gentiles of some sort. Since this is the key text for the Hasmonean expansion into Galilee, I must return to it below.

In yet a third view of the inhabitants of Galilee, Freyne has claimed recently that Galilee had, in effect, always been Jewish since earliest times, that in the centuries prior to the Hasmoneans Galilee's "religious and ethnic loyalties [had] transcend[ed] administrative and political boundaries," and that it was eagerly awaiting the opportune moment to be reunited with Jerusalem which had always been its "cultural and cultic center" or matrix.[33] On this view, the Hasmonean takeover was relatively insignificant, merely providing that "opportune moment" for Galileans to become reunited with Jerusalem.[34]

However, in the earlier history of Israel, the Israelite tribes in Galilee were Naphtali, Issachar and Zebulun; the tribes of Judah and Benjamin, which later formed the kingdom of Judah, being in the southernmost area.

---

33. Freyne, *Galilee*, 26, 38.

34. But see the qualification in Freyne: "Galilee was unmistakably Jewish, at least by the time of Pompey's intervention." Freyne, "Hellenistic/Roman Galilee," 898.

After David set up his capital over all Israel in the non-Israelite (Jebusite) stronghold of Jerusalem, the Israelite tribes rebelled twice against Davidic rule from Jerusalem (2 Sam 15-19; 20). After being resubjugated by David's professional army and acquiescing in Solomon's rule and forced labor needed to build the temple, the ten northern Israelite tribes rebelled again, successfully, against the Davidic monarchy in Jerusalem. Thereafter for two hundred years under their own kings, then for several hundred more years under foreign empires, the northern Israelite tribes and/or their ancestors, lived under quite separate political jurisdiction. It is difficult to discern how Galilee would have become Jewish at some point or how it would have formed an attachment to Jerusalem as its cultural and cultic matrix.

Moreover, texts and other "evidence" offered by Freyne and others that Galilee was "Jewish" in Hellenistic times, even supportive of the early Hasmoneans, appear to be read through the eyes of the view to be proven. In particular, the reading of several texts adduced in support of this view appear to be problematic.

The account of Simon's military mission to rescue "brothers" under attack in Galilee cannot be taken at face value.[35] This highly schematic account has been patterned after biblical passages such as Josh 9:12; Ezra 4:1; Neh 2:10, 19; 3:33; 4:1-2 ("the nations roundabout") and Deut 20:13-15 (Judas's treatment of towns in Gilead). The parallel sequence of places named indicates that 1 Macc 5 and 2 Macc 10-12 are following a common source. But 2 Maccabees (12:2; 10:14) represents as Seleucid officials' repression what 1 Maccabees portrays as Gentile persecution, and given the patterning of 1 Macc 5 after traditional Deuteronomistic patterns, it must be at least as tendentious as 2 Maccabees in this case. Furthermore, and most telling, 2 Maccabees lacks the reference to an expedition to Galilee. Little wonder that 1 Maccabees' account of a rescue mission to Galilee, with its lack of detail uncharacteristic of 1 Maccabees generally and its similarity to Judas's expedition into Gilead, has long since evoked scholarly suspicions.[36] Even if such an expedition into Galilee took place, the account still suggests that there were only a few thousand Jews in Galilee, and that in the extreme southwestern corner near Ptolemais and Arbatta.

---

35. See Sievers, *Hasmoneans and Their Supporters*, 49-57; Schwartz, "Israel and the Nations Roundabout," esp. 21-27.

36. See Wellhausen, "Über den geschichtlichen Wert des zweiten Makkabäerbuches im Verhältnis zum ersten."

The letter from Demetrius to the Judeans in 1 Macc 10 mentions "three districts added [to Judea] from Samaria and Galilee" (10:30), but subsequently clarifies that these three toparchies, Aphairema, Lydda, and Ramathairn, are "from the *chōra* of Samaria" (10:38; 11:34). This hardly supports a contention that Galilee was "essentially Jewish" at this time.[37]

Freyne argues that the report of the Seleucid general Bacchides marching into Judea via the road to Galgala and encamping at *maisalōth tēn en arbeois* and capturing it in 1 Macc 9:2 suggests that "the Galilean peasants of the region had given some sign of their support for their Judean brothers."[38] Only by reading this passage through Josephus's paraphrase of it in *Ant.* 12.421, however, can it be taken as a reference to Galilee. But what Josephus has done is transparent: assuming that "Judea" was the territory claimed by Jerusalem rulers in his own time (cf. his similar insertion of "Judea" at *Ant.* 13.174 for "his own country" in 1 Macc 12:35), he read Galgala as Galilee (thus generating the extremely awkward juxtaposition of "coming to Judea" and "encamping in Galilee") and read the dative plural *arbelois* as a reference to Arbela. (Josephus then embellished the brief reference in 1 Macc 9:2 with a bit of "local color" from the famous later exploits of Herod in ferreting out the brigands holed up in the caves near Arbela, *War* 1.304–313; *Ant.* 14.415–430). Bar-Kochva has recently offered both a telling critique of alternative suggestions and a convincing explanation for this problematic passage in 1 Macc 9:2 (*arbela* in the text could have resulted from the original Hebrew *har-bet-el*, the hill country of Bethel, cf. 1 Sam 13:2; Josh 16:1).[39] This suggestion locates Bacchides's encampment and military action just to the north of Jerusalem in Judea proper, precisely where he was headed to confront Judas.

Along with criticism of our sources in such texts, caution is necessary in drawing inferences from certain passing references. For example, the report in 1 Macc 12:47–51 that when Jonathan advanced on Ptolemais he left two-thirds of his troops in Galilee who subsequently stood their ground against Seleucid troops suggests nothing about Jonathan having "support" from Galileans. And Josephus's comment (*Ant.* 13.154) that Demetrius's generals believed that Jonathan was an "ally" of Galilee and

---

37. Freyne, *Galilee*, 40.
38. Freyne, *Galilee*, 39.
39. Bar-Kochva, *Judas Maccabaeus*, 552–59.

that "the Galileans" were "his own" (people) is not good evidence for the Galileans' longstanding political-religious loyalties.[40]

Ironically, some of the passages mentioned as evidence for Galileans being Jews turn out on closer inspection to illustrate the basic structure of political-economic-religious domination that the Hasmoneans were reassembling over Judea and beginning to extend into other areas of Palestine. In *Ant.* 12.138–144 Josephus cites a letter from Antiochus III to the governor of Coele-Syria and Phoenicia including the provision: *politeuesthōsan de pantes hoi ek tou ethnous kata taus patrious nomous*. Freyne takes this to mean that the right to live according to the Jewish law was confirmed to all the Jews under Ptolemy the governor, and this must have included Galilean Jews also.[41] Throughout the letter, however, the focus is on the Judeans in and around Jerusalem and the temple. Especially noteworthy, however, is that here, in an official Seleucid communication parallel to the later decrees of Caesar regarding Hyrcanus and his predecessors and successors, *hoi patrioi nomoi* pertains to how the nation is governed. Moreover, immediately following that key clause is another provision remitting taxes precisely to the imperial regime's client rulers in Jerusalem and their immediate retainers and dependents: *he gerousia kai hoi hiereis kai hoi grammateis tou hierou kai hoi hieropsaltai*. The early Hasmoneans Jonathan and Simon successfully inserted themselves at the head of exactly that state structure, which was soon to be free of imperial oversight. Furthermore the beginning steps of expansion of their rule over territory beyond Judea is indicated in the letter of Demetrius cited in 1 Macc 10: the three toparchies from the Samaritan *chōra* annexed to Judea are to "obey no other authority than the high priest" (10:38). The various texts cited as indications that Galilee was Jewish prior to the Hasmonean takeover turn out to provide no solid evidence for such a hypothesis. But some of them do indicate the political-economic-religious apparatus of the temple-state that the Hasmoneans had taken over prior to expansion of their rule into districts such as Galilee.

In the debate over the inhabitants of Galilee at the time of the Hasmonean takeover, especially considering the lack of textual or archaeological evidence for much of a distinctively "Jewish" presence there, there would seem to be another possibility: perhaps much of the population of Galilee was neither Gentile nor Judean, but descended from the ancient Israelites. Although there is precious little evidence for Galilean history from the

---

40. Freyne, *Galilee*, 41.
41. Freyne, *Galilee*, 36.

The Expansion of Hasmonean Rule

Assyrian conquest to the Hasmonean takeover, the continuation of former Israelites on the land would appear to be inherently probable given what is known of the policies and behavior of ancient imperial regimes and subject peoples. The ancient Assyrian and neo-Babylonian imperial rulers deported and replaced the governing and administrative elite of conquered peoples, but left the masses of peasants intact on the land. Such a practice by the Babylonians is clear from the account about Jerusalem/Judea in 2 Kgs 24–25. Apparently we should read the accounts of the Assyrian conquest of Galilee in 2 Kgs 15:29 and of Samaria itself in 2 Kgs 17 similarly. This is confirmed by Assyrian imperial records mentioning 27,290 deportees from Samaria, a figure which would correspond roughly to the ruling elite and its religious-political-military governing apparatus (i.e. perhaps 5 per cent but not likely more than 10 per cent of the total population). While the Assyrians pointedly replaced the governing class in Samaria itself, there is no evidence that they would have brought anything more than an administrative apparatus into Galilee. Since the Persian imperial regime even restored previously deported native elites to power, as in the case of Judea, it is unlikely to have settled Galilee with non-Israelites. Further, while the Hellenistic emperors founded cities in the areas surrounding Galilee, they did not interfere much with local village life and no foundations were made in Galilee itself. In the absence of any evidence for the transplantation of foreign peoples into Galilee during these many centuries of successive imperial overlords, it seems appropriate to conclude that most of the inhabitants of Galilee were descendants of ancient Israelites-probably what was left of the tribes of Naphtali and Zebulun.

The hypothesis that the inhabitants of Galilee were basically the descendants of Israelites also helps clarify the situation in Galilee just prior to the Hasmonean takeover, in particular Josephus's report, dependent on Strabo's citation of Timagenes, that the Itureans dominated the area. The Itureans, based in southern Lebanon, will have come to dominate Galilee in the vacuum left by the demise of Seleucid imperial power in Palestine—somewhat parallel to the way in which the Hasmoneans had consolidated and expanded their sway from Judea into Samaria and Idumea. Thus Josephus's report that Aristobulus battled against and took *chōra* from the Itureans, but imposed "the laws of the Judeans" on the inhabitants of the *chōra* would be an appropriate clarification of Timagenes's ambiguous report that he had acquired additional territory and brought over "a portion of the Iturean nation" (*Ant.* 13.318–319). Military action was surely involved. But this was neither a conquest nor a conversion of the Itureans, but a displacement and replacement of their domination of Galilee by the Hasmoneans. As John Hyrcanus had done with the Idumeans, Aristobulus then did with the inhabitants of Galilee: he incorporated them into the Hasmonean/Judean state, in which they were required to live in accordance with "the laws of the Judeans," if they wanted to remain in their ancestral homes in the Galilean *chōra*.

The Structure and Dynamics of Hasmonean Rule in Galilee

The Galileans, however, must have been different from the Idumeans in an important respect. Whereas the Idumeans' ancestors had not been part of early Israel, hence probably did not share Israelite cultural traditions, the Galileans, if they were descendants of Israelites, surely did share Israelite cultural traditions with the Judeans. It is clear that Israelite traditions such as the exodus and Mosaic covenantal principles were operative as popular traditions for many generations after the rise of the Jerusalem and Samaritan monarchies. Much has been made of the Israelite prophets drawing on those traditions, whether in the resistance movement led by Elijah and Elisha or in the oracles of an Amos. I have argued elsewhere that precisely such popular traditions, what anthropologists label "little traditions" as opposed to official, and often written, "great traditions," informed the emergence of both the popular messianic movements and the two types of popular prophets in late Second Temple times.[42] Thus the Galileans subjected to the Hasmonean high-priestly rule will have found some of "the laws/customs of the Judeans" somewhat familiar. On the other hand, precisely because there is a difference between the "little" and the "great" traditions, including the political power that accompanies the latter, and because in this case the "great" tradition came to the Galileans after centuries of separate shaping as the official state "laws of the Judeans," there will have been some serious differences.[43] Indeed, insofar as "the laws of the Judeans" were the articulation of the political-economic-religious structure of the relations

---

42. For a suggestive treatment of the relationship between the "little" and the "great" traditions in agrarian societies that has considerable relevance to late-Second Temple Palestine, see Scott, "Protest and Profanation." See further, Horsley, "Messianic Movements"; Horsley, "Like One of the Prophets of Old"; and Horsley, "Popular Prophetic Movements." These essays are now available in Horsley, *Politics, Conflict, and Movements in First-Century Palestine*.

43. See further Shatzman, *The Armies of the Hasmoneans and Herod*, 83-87, 94-97. And see further, Horsley, "Contesting Authority."

The Expansion of Hasmonean Rule

of domination between rulers and ruled, they will have been strange to the Galilean descendants of Israelites.

Again social-structural questions need to be kept in the forefront in analyzing the fragmentary evidence for Galilee under Hasmonean rule. In Judea itself there would have been a fundamental structural division in society between the village communities in which the vast majority of people lived, on the one hand, and the capital temple-city supposedly representing the community of the whole of Judea, but headed by the ruling priestly aristocracy, on the other. The subjection of Galileans (or Idumeans) to Hasmonean rule compounded the class difference with a historically deep-rooted historical-regional difference as well. Both levels must be considered in analyzing the structure and dynamics of Hasmonean rule in Galilee.

Minimal attention to ensuing historic.al events in Palestine reveals a general sense of the principal Hasmonean agenda. In the decades after Aristobulus took control of Galilee, Alexander Jannaeus was engaged in almost continuous wars of conquest, including areas on the frontiers of Galilee. Thus even if one assumed an utterly docile population in Galilee itself, the Hasmoneans would have established and maintained fortresses and garrisons in Galilee. This is exactly what the sources indicate. That Sepphoris was garrisoned (and as later probably already the principal administrative town) is suggested by Josephus's report that Ptolemy Lathyrus attacked but did not take the town (*Ant.* 13.338). In the later struggles between the Romans and the last of the Hasmoneans for control, particularly between Herod and Antigonus, Josephus assumes that there were a number of strongholds, including Sepphoris, that served as the basis for control of the area (see esp. *Ant.* 14.413-414). In the midst of these struggles, Marion, whom Cassius had installed as ruler of Tyre, captured three fortresses, presumably along the Galilean frontier with Tyre. A reference to "walled cities" in m. Arak. 9:6 is suggestive in this regard, including the fortress of Sepphoris and the citadel of Gush Halav (Gischala) and Jotapata among them. Thus it would appear that the Hasmoneans established fortresses and garrisons at least along the outer frontier of Galilee as well as in the principal administrative towns.[44]

To administer the area, moreover, to gather tax revenues as well as to maintain internal and external security, the Hasmonean regime would have placed officers in Galilee. As Hasmonean officers settled in the area, far from a "native aristocracy" emerging, a Judean aristocracy would have

---

44. Freyne, *Galilee*, 49-50.

consolidated its power in Galilee.⁴⁵ Since it is unlikely in the extreme that the traditional agrarian economy was suddenly monetarized, the finds of large numbers of Jannean coins at points in the area (such as Meiron in Upper Galilee) do not mean that the population was (suddenly) Jewish, but simply that the area had come under Hasmonean administration.

For the general situation on the level of the village communities one can only extrapolate from later rabbinic evidence as measured against comparative sociological and anthropological studies. In most traditional agrarian societies, villages were semi-autonomous communities. Josephus's frequent references to a city or town "and its villages" (or "Hebron and its daughters," 1 Macc 5:65) fits this model. Rabbinic texts repeatedly mention a village assembly (*knesset* = *synagōgē*) and its leaders, such as the *hazzan*, the *roshha-knesset* (= *archisynagōgos* in the New Testament), or the *gabbaim*. In most matters the village ran its own affairs according to time-honored customs and traditions (cf. the origins of English common law), the central government's agents intervening primarily for taxes and trans-local problems. Assuming that the Galileans were largely descendants of Israelites, then Galilean village communities would have run their community affairs according to the Mosaic covenantal principles and traditional covenantal laws and customs. In matters such as observance of the Sabbath or other common Israelite traditions (e.g. circumcision), the Galileans would have paralleled popular Judean and official Jerusalem customs that were also rooted in Israelite traditions. However, dues owed to the temple and high priesthood not in the ancient common Israelite tradition—but apparently included in "the laws of the Judeans," judging from the official Seleucid and Roman decrees cited above-would have been, to the Galileans, a new demand by a new ruler. Insofar as the temple-state itself had developed during the centuries that Galilee had been administered under a separate imperial province from Judea, all of the "laws of the Judeans" that pertained to the temple-state and its priesthood would have been new to Galileans. Indeed, assuming that "the laws of the Judeans" were basically the Torah (along with other, oral priestly and/or scribal laws), which was also the product of the early Second Temple priesthood under Persian sponsorship, the whole framing of the common covenantal traditions would have been new to Galileans.

I have discerned to this point how the Hasmoneans would have administered and maintained internal and external security in Galilee, on the one hand, and how the Galilean village communities would have continued to

---

45. Freyne, *Galilee*, 49–50.

The Expansion of Hasmonean Rule

run their own affairs in accordance with Israelite covenantal traditions, on the other. Structurally speaking, however, if the Galileans were to conduct their communal lives "according to the laws of the Judeans" in any more intensive a way, if they were to be integrated into the community of loyalty to the temple and Torah, then some agents of "secondary socialization" or "re-socialization" would have to intervene across the fundamental division between the two levels of community, rulers/temple and ruled/village. The only possibilities for such agency emerging would be for the rulers to delegate some of their officers or "retainers" to undertake such a program, or for some of those officers or retainers to take such a task upon themselves. Josephus happens to provide information on both of these two possibilities.

Judging from Josephus's accounts of the reign of Alexander Jannaeus (*Ant.* 13.324–394; *War.* 1.84–106), that is, for the first full generation of Hasmonean rule in Galilee, the ruler himself would have been completely preoccupied with wars of conquest and then, perhaps as an effect of those wars, virtual civil war with his own Judean people and/or retainers (scribal elements such as the Pharisees). It is difficult to imagine Jannaeus having directed much by way of a "Judaization" campaign in Galilee or Idumea. Moreover, it was Jannaeus who appointed as governor of Idumea not a Judean thoroughly acquainted with "the customs of the Judeans" but a prominent Idumean, Antipas. Only during the next decade, under his wife-successor Salome Alexandra Salome, were foreign conquests ended and the conflict with the Pharisees resolved such that attention could have been given to some possible program of pressing Judean laws and customs more actively on the Galilean (and Idumean) population. Thereafter, in rapid succession, the struggle between the rival Hasmonean factions for control of the state, the Roman conquest, and the overlapping Hasmonean and Roman civil wars would have preoccupied and exhausted the disintegrating Hasmonean regime. Thus if anything happened by way of Judaization in Galilee (or Idumea) it would have been under Salome Alexandra and/or by independent action by retainers of the government such as the Pharisees.

Josephus portrays the Pharisees as heavily involved in the politics and administration of the Hasmonean state. In fact, he provides a clear window onto their responsibilities and function in his accounts of how they were pushed out and then restored to their positions. In connection with interpreting "the laws of Moses" the Pharisees had been promulgating additional regulations (*nomima*) for the people which had become a certain body of "tradition" (*paradosis*) that had the status of state law. According to Josephus,

Hyrcanus at one point broke with the Pharisees and rescinded their regulations as state law (leaving only the laws of Moses as favored by the rival party, the Sadducees; *Ant.* 13.293–297). The Pharisees must have been among those who bitterly opposed Alexander Jannaeus, and suffered for it. But under Alexandra Salome, they were restored to their position of power in the administration of the state, and their regulations were restored as state law (*War* 1.110–112). That is, with regard to the question of who, if anyone, would have been the agents pressing "the laws of the Judeans" more aggressively upon the recently subjected Idumeans and Galileans, the Pharisees would have been the obvious ones. And since they had been in disfavor, perhaps even in overt conflict, with Alexander Jannaeus, the first time that they would have been able to devote time and energy to the "Judaization" of Idumea and Galilee would have been under Alexandra Salome. But this seems highly unlikely since they were absorbed in running domestic affairs under Alexandra and were focused on bringing the officers of Jannaeus to justice for having advised him to crucify eight hundred of his principal opponents.

The fact that one hundred years later the Pharisees are portrayed in the synoptic Gospel tradition as representing Jerusalem's interests in Galilee and advocating their special "tradition of the elders" is suggestive in this connection. Of course the portrayal of the Pharisees in the Gospels a hundred years later as representing the interests of the temple(-state) in Galilee which was no longer under Jerusalem jurisdiction is suggestive. Yet there is no indication in Josephus' accounts of Hasmonean rule or in the Gospels that the Pharisees were involved in teaching in Galilean villages. But that is just the point. It seems historically unlikely that much by way of "secondary socialization" or "re-socialization" of the peoples subjected to "laws of the Judeans" toward the end of the second century BCE was mounted by the Hasmonean regime or its retainers. Both Idumeans and Galileans would have continued to conduct their village life according to their own cultural traditions arid local customs. "The laws of the Judeans" would have governed their relations with the Hasmonean regime in Jerusalem, and in that connection perhaps also impinged upon certain facets of local self-government.

CONCLUSIONS AND IMPLICATIONS

From this investigation of the relations between the Hasmonean regime and subjected peoples, particularly the Idumeans and the Galileans, a thesis is emerging. Those relations, far from being susceptible of understanding in terms of religious conversion, must be dealt with in terms of the political-economic-religious structure of an ancient temple-state that expanded its territory and power during a period of imperial weakness. In the case of the Hasmoneans, the new incumbents of the high priesthood in Jerusalem were, to start with, illegitimate occupants of the office whose power depended on the military forces built up during the resistance against the declining Seleucid imperial regime. Beyond the confined ideology of 1 Maccabees there is no indication that Hasmonean expansion was a religious crusade. The Davidic-Solomonic imperial ideal may well have influenced Hasmonean ambitions, but from the regime of Hyrcanus onward the Hasmoneans employed non-Judean mercenaries in their professional army and established an increasingly Hellenized administration. They seized the opportunities of Seleucid decline to expand their own domains in Palestine. To understand this as the expansion of a religion does not fit the situation or the sources. It is clear from the Seleucid and Roman decrees that "the laws of the Judeans" were understood as pertaining to the polity or constitution of the state and its relations with its subjects. Thus when subject peoples were required to live according to those "laws of the Judeans," it pertained to the relations of the people in their village communities to the Hasmonean state. There is no direct evidence of any attempt to press the subject peoples to apply "the laws of the Judeans" in their conduct of local community and family affairs. Of course, insofar as observing the laws of the Judeans in relations with the central government impinged adversely on the conduct of local affairs, then structural conflict would have developed.

Two incidents in particular can be used to illustrate the resulting relations between the Jerusalem temple-state and the subordinate peoples as the Hasmoneans bequeathed the situation to subsequent generations. The first is the case of Costobar already examined above. The control of Idumea was managed partly by alliances the Hasmoneans and later Herod made with heads of powerful Idumean families, such as Antipas and Costobar. But whatever the official policy was with regard to Idumeans living according to "the laws of the Judeans," Costobar's family illustrates that it was not pressed upon local life in terms of suppressing indigenous Idumean religious practices and social customs. In the case of Costobar, the conflict came to a head for some reason, but even there the conflict that meets the eye is a rupture in the relationship of personal-political patronage and not one between Idumean traditions and Torah and temple.

Galileans under Jerusalem and Roman Rule

The second case can be taken from the Gospel of Mark's portrayal of the conflict between Jesus and the Pharisees and the scribes representing Jerusalem's interests in Galilee. The "controversy story" in Mark 7:1–13 starts out as a conflict between local Galilean custom and Pharisaic/Judean custom which the representatives of Jerusalem are portrayed as attempting to press upon the Galileans (Mark 7:1–5). But the story moves quickly to relocate the conflict between the basic (Mosaic/Israelite) covenantal commandment of God and "the traditions of the (Pharisaic) elders" which under Hyrcanus and then Alexandra Salome had been state law, and focuses upon how the temple-state's economic demands made upon local resources by "the traditions of the elders" impinged adversely upon local need as expected to be managed according to the basic covenantal "commandment of God" (Mark 7:9–13).

Whatever "Judaization" might mean when applied to the Hasmonean takeover of Idumea and Galilee, it was clearly not very thorough and effective in terms of "the laws of the Judeans" becoming the regulations of local community life. The relations between the Hasmoneans and these subject peoples must be understood in terms of the structural conflicts involved. Those structural conflicts were not resolved by the Hasmoneans and persisted into early Roman, Herodian times. To illustrate, I refer again to the cases of the Idumeans and Galileans involvement in events of 4 BCE and 66–70 CE. The fundamental conflict was not between the Romans on the one side and the Jews on the other, but between the Judean rulers, Herodian and high-priestly, and their Roman sponsors, on the one hand, and the peasant forces from the various districts ruled from Jerusalem, on the other. In 4 BCE, a popular Galilean insurrection paralleled other popular insurrections in Judea and Perea. In the course of events from the summer of 66 through 70, Galileans resisted Jerusalem control and direction, Idumeans came to the rescue of Judean peasant forces locked in conflict with the high-priestly rulers and their Herodian allies, and (small numbers of) both Galilean and Idumean insurrectionaries joined with two popular Judean insurrectionary movements in the final resistance against Roman reconquest, after the high-priestly and Pharisaic elements had joined the Romans. Some of these groups at points were fighting from or driven for refuge into the (fortress) temple. But it would be difficult to argue that they were fighting primarily for the Torah and the temple. Yet it is fairly clear that they were fighting against the rulers based in the temple and the leading Pharisees whose function may still have included interpretation of the Torah.

2

Conquest and Social Conflict in Galilee

INTRODUCTION

Both Judaism and Christianity have roots in Galilee. Historians of Christian and Jewish origins, however, are experiencing increasing doubts that the fundamental concepts on which most of the remainder of their conceptual apparatus rest are rooted in historical reality. According to the standard (Christian) scholarly scheme, Jesus was "Jewish" and called "Jewish" followers, who then founded "early Christianity" as a movement within "Judaism" alongside other "sects" such as the Pharisees, which constituted the principal competition. Once the mission spread to the Gentiles, early Christianity increasingly diverged and eventually broke away from its parent religion of Judaism. However one construes the particulars of the early formation of Christianity, this standard scholarly scheme places a great deal of weight on its knowledge of "Judaism."

In the last generation we have come to realize that what we have had in mind when referring to "Judaism" did not yet exist until well after the time of Jesus and the earliest "churches."[1] Rabbinic Judaism, whose literary expressions scholars had in mind when speaking of "Judaism," could

---

1. E.g., Neusner, "The Demise of Normative Judaism"; Cohen, *From the Maccabees to the Mishnah.*

not be said even to have begun taking form until at least two generations after Jesus. Moreover, it turns out that we have precious little evidence about the Pharisees, who we have been assuming were the predecessors of the rabbis.[2] Discovery of the Dead Sea Scrolls has revealed just how diverse movements among the Judean literate elite were during late Second Temple times. But all together the high priests/Sadducees, Pharisees, and Qumranites/Essenes comprised only a tiny fraction of the population of ancient Jewish Palestine. The limited information available on the occasional movements among the ordinary people indicates that they were very different in orientation and agenda from the literate Jewish groups such as Pharisees and Essenes.[3] We are only beginning to take a critical look at Galilee in particular, the locus of Jesus' ministry and of the formative rabbinic activity some generations later.

The recent retreat by many in the field to the concept of "formative Judaism" is both an admission that what we had been thinking of as "Judaism" was still in the process of formation and an assumption that there is some sort of continuity between what emerged as rabbinic Judaism and at least some of what went before. That assumption of continuity enables us to continue speaking of the central importance of the academy at Yavneh, of the rabbis having (supposedly) been placed in charge of Jewish society by the Romans after the destruction of the temple, and of the Pharisees as the predecessors of the rabbis. We write confidently of "sectarian Judaism" existing centuries before the appearance of any "parent body" of Judaism from which sects might have separated.[4] We assume that at the time of Jesus Galilee was inhabited by Jews who acknowledged both the temple and the Torah as the media of redemption.[5] And we assume the existence of Jewish synagogues in Galilee in which the Pharisees were the leaders.[6]

Most of these assumptions are simply unwarranted by any historical evidence. There is no evidence that the Romans ever placed the Pharisees and/or proto-rabbis in charge of Jewish Palestine.[7] The rabbinic stories on which we have been basing the foundation and authority of the rabbinic

---

2. Neusner, *From Politics to Piety*; Saldarini, *Pharisees, Scribes and Sadducees*.
3. Horsley, "Popular Messianic Movements"; Horsley, "Like One of the Prophets of Old"; *Jesus and the Spiral of Violence*.
4. Cohen, *From the Maccabees to the Mishnah*.
5. Freyne, *Galilee*.
6. Kee, "The Transformation of the Synagogue after 70 CE."
7. Levine, "The Jewish Patriarch (Nasi) in Third Century Palestine."

academy at Yavneh turn out to be variations on a foundational legend and not reports with any particular historical veracity, as two independent investigations have demonstrated.[8] By their own repeated admissions, the rabbis had very little influence let alone serious authority among the people in Galilee in the second century CE.[9] What influence they had gained by the third century was apparently based in the fact that some of their number became dominant socially and economically in Galilee.[10] The same Mishnaic literature that indicates that the rabbis had little influence among the people in the second century also indicates that there were numerous local variations in customs and observances. Further, the earliest consistent evidence for synagogues as religious buildings in Galilean towns and villages is dated to the second century CE or later.[11] It seems more likely that what the synoptic gospel traditions refer to as *synagōgē* was, just like what the Mishnah refers to as a *knesset*, a local (village or town) assembly concerned with community affairs of all sorts, not simply religious observances.[12]

THE CONQUEST AND "JUDAIZATION" OF GALILEE

It appears that we do not know that much about what became "Judaism" in Galilee until nearly the third century CE. This realization should lead us to examine with new eyes the (lack of) evidence for what Galileans were thinking and doing before, during, and after the time of Jesus as well as many of the standard generalizations we rely upon in our scholarly investigations, particularly the extent to which Galilee was "Judaized." It seems obvious that the history of Galilee should be reexamined. The explorations that follow will be rudimentary at best.

In order to sharpen the issues and invite serious re-thinking, let me state at the outset the conclusion to which the explorations below seem to

---

8. Saldarini, "Johanan ben Zakkai's Escape from Jerusalem"; Schaefer, "Die Flucht Johanan b. Zakkai aus Jerusalem."

9. Goodman, "The First Jewish Revolt."

10. Levine, *The Rabbinic Class of Roman Palestine*; Cohen, "The Place of the Rabbi."

11. Kee, "The Transformation of the Synagogue after 70 CE"; Flesher, "Palestinian Synagogues before 70 C.E."

12. The functions of the leaders of the *knesset* mentioned in the Mishnah are similar to those of local leaders in the Hauran just to the east of Galilee (Harper, "Village Administration in the Roman Province of Syria").

lead: *The Judaization of Galilee was the result of a series of conquests and involved long periods of social conflict.*

This thesis can be broken down somewhat in terms of historical phases. From ancient times the Galileans would have shared. a common ancient Israelite heritage with Judeans (and Samaritans). But after the heavy demands of Solomon the ten northern tribes of Israel rebelled against Jerusalem rule. Then the descendants of those northern tribes lived under different imperial provincial jurisdiction for over seven hundred years. Thus the crucial event that led to the later Judaization of Galilee must have been the Hasmonean conquest or forcible takeover of the area, apparently under Aristobulus in 104 BCE. The Roman conquest and reconquest of Palestine in the first century BCE and their reliance on Herodians as well as on the Jerusalem high priestly families as client rulers created further complications in Galilee's "Judaization." Beginning with the frequent changes of client rulers in mid-first century CE and continuing in the aftermath of the Roman reconquest in 67 CE, Galilee apparently experienced several decades of political vacuum. The Jerusalem authorities may well have attempted to expand their influence in the midst of this political vacuum. But it was apparently not until well after the Roman reconquest of Judea in 67–70 CE, indeed apparently not until after the Bar Kochba Revolt, that the (proto-)rabbis focused their attention on Galilee and eventually acquired some influence among the Galilean people for what became Rabbinic Judaism.

The obvious implications for "Christian origins" are that we can no longer use "Judaism" in Galilee as a foil for Jesus' ministry. Nor can we view the Pharisees (especially not as based in the synagogues) as another Jewish "sect" competing for influence with Jesus' followers in Galilee. It will facilitate reexamination to keep the old concept of "Judaism" out of our minds while surveying the history of Galilee.[13]

THE HASMONEAN CONQUEST OF GALILEE

Freyne simply assumes, and states repeatedly, that Jerusalem was the "cultural and cultic center" (or matrix) of Galilee, which was eagerly awaiting

---

13. In an attempt to maintain critical awareness of the ambiguity of the modern English word "Jews" when applied to people in antiquity, I will use the term "Judean(s)" when translating the Greek *Ioudais/oi* and when referring to people in Judea, and "Galileans" when referring to inhabitants of Galilee.

the opportune moment to be reunited politically in Hasmonean times.[14] Both during the centuries before the Hasmoneans and after their demise, he claims, Galileans were loyal both to the temple and to the Torah, even when they were no longer politically united with their supposed matrix: "What is particularly significant about this situation is the fact that religious and ethnic loyalties transcend administrative and political boundaries."[15]

To anyone familiar with the Hebrew Bible, however, it is puzzling to figure out just when and how such Galilean attachment to Jerusalem may have developed. David may well have been a "popular" king at the outset (2 Sam 2:4; 5:1–3).[16] But Jerusalem was a non-Israelite (Jebusite) stronghold that David captured with the help of his non-Israelite mercenaries as a capital for his rule over Israelites and the conquered Canaanites (2 Sam 5:6–10). Eventually two extensive popular revolts erupted against "Yahweh's anointed." The first, which apparently involved much of Israel, drove David and his court from Jerusalem and was put down only with difficulty by David's mercenary troops (2 Sam 15–19). The less ominous second revolt also involved much of Israel, although Judah remained loyal (2 Sam 20). Thus resubjugated to their messiah by David's professional army, Israel remained quiescent through the long reign of Solomon. Feeling overburdened by the "forced labor" instituted by Solomon to build the royal temple (and royal palaces and fortresses), however, the ten northern tribes rebelled against Solomon's ostensible successor Rehoboam, and remained independent of Jerusalem's rule for two hundred years before the Assyrians finally conquered the (Northern) Israelite regime in Samaria in 722/21. Beginning with Jeroboam, the frequently overthrown kings of Israel instituted their own cult centers at Bethel, Dan, Samaria itself, and elsewhere, and Jeroboam had his own legitimating history written, "the Elohist," a counterpart to "the Yahwist" history written to legitimate the Davidic dynasty.[17] Thus, while the same god Yahweh was ostensibly worshipped by Judahites and Israelites and while prophets in both Judah and Israel appealed to the same god Yahweh in their indictments of the exploitation, injustices, and (religious) disloyalties of kings, priests, and royal officials, somewhat different traditions were developing.

14. Freyne, *Galilee*, 38 etc.
15. Freyne, *Galilee*, 26.
16. See the distinction between the royal Jerusalem ideology of kingship and the popular "anointing of kings in Horsley, "Popular Messianic Movements."
17. See now Coote, *In Defense of Revolution*.

Galileans under Jerusalem and Roman Rule

During the political vacuum in the wake of Assyrian decline, of course; Josiah not only centralized political-economic-religious power in Judea, but reasserted Davidic rule in the north. At Bethel and elsewhere in "the cities of Samaria" he destroyed the "high places," defiled the altars, and slaughtered the priests (2 Kgs 23:15–20). The question is whether such carnage would have evoked the appreciation and loyalty of ordinary people in the north. Such cult centers were royal institutions economically burdensome to the peasant producers. Insofar as Josiah's policy in the north was the same as in the south, i.e., to destroy local centers of loyalty in order to centralize power in the monarchy and temple, however, such actions may only have evoked popular resentment of Jerusalem. Josiah's "reform" apparently did reach into Galilee ("as far as Naphtali," 2 Chr 34:6–7;" from Geba to Beersheba," 2 Kgs 23:8; and control of the district of Megiddo, 2 Kgs 23:29). But Jerusalem's period of influence over the north was brief and hardly seems to have been the basis for the persistent Galilean loyalty to Jerusalem as the cultural and cultic center that Freyne imagines.

As in the century before Josiah, so in the five centuries following his "reform," Samaria and Galilee were under separate political jurisdiction, usually a Persian, Ptolemaic, or Seleucid imperial province or sub-province. The second temple was a Judean (and, of course, Persian imperial) institution with no direct or official authority over other districts in Palestine, so far as we know. In fact, Galilee did not come under the direct control of the Jerusalem temple and high priesthood until just before 100 BCE, when the Hasmonean Aristobulus, son and successor of John Hyrcanus, gained control of it. Maccabean literature and Josephus's reports contain scattered references to Galilee during the rise of the Hasmonean dynasty. Nothing in those references indicates Galilean subjection or attachment to Jerusalem prior to Aristobulus.

Josephus (*Ant.* 12.138–144) cites a letter of Antiochus III to the governor of Coele-Syria and Phoenicia that included the provision: *politeuesthōsan de pantes oi ek tou ethnous kata tous patrious nomous.* Freyne argues that this means "the right to live according to the Jewish law was confirmed to all the Jews under Ptolemy the governor, and this must have included Galilean Jews also."[18] The focus throughout the letter, however, is on "the Judeans" in and around the city of Jerusalem and the temple, with particular attention to "the senate, the priests, the scribes of the temple, and the temple-singers." Moreover, if *tous patrious nomous* refers to the Torah

---

18. Freyne, *Galilee*, 36.

Conquest and Social Conflict in Galilee

(written and used in the temple-state of Judea), at what point and through what social-political process would it have become the traditional law among Galileans?

The pro-Hasmonean 1 Maccabees must be read critically. The archaizing author of 1 Maccabees represents the Hasmoneans and their allies as (the heirs of) "Israel," who, in chapter 5, rescue other "Israelites" or "their brethren/kindred" who are supposedly being attacked elsewhere in Palestine, such as "those in the territory" of Gilead and "those in Galilee" (1 Macc 5:9, 16-17, 23, 45; at 1 Macc 5:16-17, 23, the Jerusalem Bible has "countrymen" and "the Jews"; RSV has "the Jews," and NRSV still has "the Jews of Galilee!"). Thus even if we take the text at face value, it would be necessary to determine whether "Israel" and "kindred" referred only or primarily to Judeans who had come to be resident or captive outside of Judea or to other Israelites as well. Moreover, in Galilee both the persecution and Simon's rescue operation were confined to the immediate vicinity of Ptolemais (so 1 Macc 5:15; cf. 5:21-23), which hardly warrants a conclusion about the ethnic composition of all of Galilee.

The account of Gentile persecution and Hasmonean rescue of "Israelites" in 1 Macc 5, however, can hardly be taken at face value. The author does not even represent all the campaigns cited as rescue missions and others are not convincing as rescue missions. The account is heavily influenced from biblical passages such as Josh 9:12; Ezra 4:1; Neh 2:10, 19; 3:33; 4:1-2 ("the nations roundabout"); and Deut 20:13-15 (Judas' treatment of towns in Gilead, 1 Macc 5:28, 35, 44, 51).[19] From the sequence of places mentioned, it seems clear that 1 Macc 5 and 2 Macc 10-12 are following a common source. But what 1 Maccabees portrays as Gentile persecution, 2 Maccabees (12:2; 10:14) represents as Seleucid officials' repression. It does seem remarkable that "Israelites" in such diverse locations "roundabout" should suddenly and simultaneously have been attacked. Moreover, 2 Maccabees has no reference to an expedition to Galilee. Thus it is not surprising that the report of a rescue mission in western Galilee, with its lack of detail uncharacteristic of 1 Macc 5 and its general similarity to Judas's campaign in Gilead, has roused historians suspicion.[20] Judging from the phrase *pasan Galilaian allophulon* in 5:15, finally, it would appear that 1 Maccabees assumed that Galilee was comprised primarily of non-Judeans.

---

19. See further Schwartz, "Israel and the Nations Roundabout," 25-27.
20. Sievers, *Hasmoneans and Their Supporters*, 49-57.

The letter from Demetrius to the Jews cited in 1 Macc 10 mentions "three districts added (to Judah) from Samaria and Galilee" (10:30), subsequently referred to as "from the *chōra* of Samaria" and "three toparchies of/and Samaria" (10:38; 11:24). That these are then explicitly identified as the *nomoi* of Aphairema, Lydda, and Ramathaim, all added to Judea from southern Samaria, indicates that no Galilean territory was involved (the reference in 10:30 could be explained if, as is suspected, the Seleucids had linked Galilee with Samaria administratively; cf. Josephus, *Ant.* 12.154). The absence of any mention of Galilee in these arrangements between Demetrius and Jonathan throw into question the contention that Galilee was "essentially Jewish and that its inhabitants enjoyed the rights of Antiochus III's charter."[21]

The references in 1 Maccabees to Hasmonean and Seleucid military actions involving Galilee, along with the parallels in Josephus, indicate nothing about Galilean attitudes toward Jerusalem. The reference to the Seleucid general Bacchides taking the road to *galgala* and encamping at *maisalōth tēn en arbelois* and capturing it in 1 Macc 9:2 can hardly be read to suggest that "the Galilean peasants of the region had given some sign of their support for their Judaean brothers."[22] Indeed, this extremely difficult passage has been taken as a reference to Galilee only by reading it through Josephus's paraphrase in *Ant.* 12.421. It is not difficult to see what Josephus has done. Assuming that "Judea" was the greater territory claimed for Jerusalem rule in his own day,[23] he read *galgala* as Galilee (thus creating the awkward juxtaposition of "coming to Judea" and "encamping in Galilee" in his account) and the dative plural *arbolois* as a reference to Arbela, near the shore of the Lake. Moreover, he then embellished the brief story in 1 Macc 9:2 with a famous bit of "local color" influenced by the famous incident in which Herod ferreted out the brigands holed up in the cliff-caves near Arbela (perhaps reading *maisalōth* as a reference to "ascents").[24] If we focus on the text of 1 Macc 9:2, however, without Josephus's "clarification," there is no reason to find a reference to Galilee. Bacchides encamped *epi* = "at" *maisalōth*, a transliteration of the Hebrew *mesilot* = "routes," which

---

21. Freyne, *Galilee*, 40.

22. Contra Freyne, *Galilee*, 39.

23. A similar insertion of "Judea" for "his own country," *Ant.* 13.174 (cf. 1 Macc 12:35) can be read either as Judea proper or all Judean controlled territory in Palestine in the sense the historian himself was familiar with.

24. So *Ant.* 12.421, the legends of Herod's exploits near Arbela and Josephus's own experience in the area, *War* 1.304-313; *Ant.* 14.415-430; *Life* 188, 311.

must then be not "near" or "by" but "in" Arbelois, which must then be understood as a region, not a place name. After a convincing critique of alternative suggestions, Bar Kochva then offers a convincing explanation of how *arbelois* in the text could have resulted from the original Hebrew *har-bet-el*, "the hill-country of Beth-El" (see 1 Sam 13:2; Josh 16:1). Taken together with clear evidence of two place names just to the east, this locates Bacchides' encampment and military action just to the north of Jerusalem in Judea proper, the destination of his mission to confront Judas and army.[25]

Moreover that Jonathan left two-thirds of his troops in Galilee when he advanced on Ptolemais, troops who subsequently stood their ground against Seleucid troops (1 Macc 12:47–51), hardly indicates anything about Jonathan having "support" from Galileans.[26] Finally, we cannot take Josephus's report (*Ant.* 13.154) that Demetrius's generals believed that Jonathan was an "ally" of Galilee and that "the Galileans" were "his own" (people) as evidence for the Galileans' longstanding political-religious loyalties.[27] Josephus's account is suspect at just this point. He is paraphrasing 1 Macc 11:63, which reads, in the best LXX textual tradition, *boulomenoi metastēsai auton tēs chreias* (Demetrius's generals) "wishing to draw him (Jonathan) away from his purpose" (or perhaps "remove him from office"—NRSV). But Josephus apparently read *tēs chōras* as do some MSS of the LXX. Thus Josephus's insertion of the comment about Galilee and the Galileans into the 1 Maccabees account, prompted perhaps by the reading *chōras* before him, reflects his own view of the proper relations between Galilee and Jerusalem.

Schürer argued a century ago that Galilee must have come under Hasmonean rule when, according to Josephus's report, Aristobulus "made war on the Itureans and acquired a good deal of their territory for Judaea and compelled the inhabitants, if they wished to remain in their country, to be circumcised and to live in accordance with the laws of the Jews" (*polemēsas Itouraious kai pollēn autōn tēs chōras tē Ioudaiai prosktēsamenos, anagkasas te tous enoikountas, ei boulontai menein en tē chōrai, peritemnesthai kai kata tous Ioudaiōn nomous zēn*; *Ant.* 13.318). There is reason to believe that the Itureans (based in Lebanon around Panaeas) had by this time extended their power into Galilee as well as over Auranitis, Batanaea, and Trachonitis to the east.[28] Schürer's conjecture that the portion of Iturean-

---

25. Bar-Kochva, *Judas Maccabaeus*, 553–59.
26. Contra Freyne, *Galilee*, 40.
27. Contra Freyne, *Galilee*, 41.
28. Smallwood, *The Jews under Roman Rule*, 14.

controlled territory taken by Aristobulus was (part of) Galilee is based on several interrelated observations. The most telling are that Josephus does not say that Aristobulus subdued "the Itureans" themselves but only that he conquered a large portion of their territory; that Galilee had not hitherto belonged to the territory of the Jewish high priest, Hyrcanus' conquests having reached only as far as Samaria and Scythopolis; and that the districts north and east of Galilee were predominantly Gentile down to the time of the Herodians.

A comparison between Josephus's report of Aristobulus's actions in the north and that of Hyrcanus's conquest and Judaization of the Idumeans lends further support to Schürer's conjecture. In the case of Idumea Josephus writes that Hyrcanus "subdued the Idumeans" themselves, and "permitted them to remain in their country so long as they had themselves circumcised and were willing to observe the laws of the Jews" (*Ant.* 13.257). By contrast, in the case of Aristobulus, he distinguishes between "the Itureans" on whom the high priest made war and from whom he wrested territory for Judea, on the one hand, and "the inhabitants" of that territory (i.e., Galilee), whom he compelled "to be circumcised and to live in accordance with the laws of the Jews," on the other (*Ant.* 13.318). Moreover, all other territories except Gaulanitis, which was secured by Alexander Janneus, controlled by the Itureans were still intact well over a half-century later when the Romans finally assigned Batanaea, Auranitis, and Trachonitis, as well as Ulatha and Panaeas to Herod (*Ant.* 15.342-364).[29]

Recent archaeological work at Meiron in Upper Galilee provides numismatic evidence that further supports Schürer's conjecture. The numerous Hasmonean coins found in Stratum I (200-50 BCE, Hellenistic) are almost exclusively those of Alexander Jannaeus, while prior to those the coins are Hellenistic Tyrian mints. Some caution is in order since Jannean coins also predominate among Hasmonean coins found in Judean sites as well. But the sudden appearance of numerous coins of Alexander Jannaeus suggests that it was just before or at the beginning of his reign that Hasmonean rule became effective in upper Galilee (see, with a critical eye, Meyers, Strange, Meyers:xix, 155, Appendix C).

Still unclear, however, is just how "Jewish" this made the Galileans. That Ptolemy Lathyrus "was able to surprise the city of Asochis ... because it was the Sabbath" (Ant. 13.337) simply reflects that the defending troops

---

29. Ironically, Freyne's paragraph (1980:43) against Schürer on the "Judaization" of Galilee supports rather than weakens Schürer's conjecture.

were Judean and is not evidence that Lower Galilee was "Jewish."[30] Also, the establishment of Hasmonean rule in Galilee would have meant the imposition of a Judean administration (as Hasmonean officials settled into the administrative centers of the district), not the emergence of a "native aristocracy."[31] Moreover, the presence of Jannean coins does not necessarily mean that Meiron was a distinctively "Jewish" village, but only that Hasmonean coins circulated there.[32]

In order to understand the situation adequately we must refine our conceptual apparatus. Given the political power vacuum in the area in the wake of Seleucid decline toward the end of the second century BCE, it is historically unlikely that there was a circumscribed territory with clear boundaries known as "Galilee." The area could perhaps best be described as a frontier. When Hyrcanus took control of the Great Plain it is likely that Jerusalem's influence projected into lower Galilee. But it remained for Aristobulus to take control of Galilee from the Itureans.

Who the inhabitants of the area were ethnically and religiously is a separate question, once we note the difference between the Itureans, whose control of the area Aristobulus put to an end, and the inhabitants, whom Aristobulus subjected to the laws of the Judeans, according to Josephus. In the absence of any direct historical evidence or until archaeologists make some conclusive discovery that sheds light on the issue, we must rely on historical reasoning from some admittedly vague "knowns" to the "unknown." We know that ancient imperial rulers tended not to displace (and replace) the bulk of the populations they conquered or to interfere much in village community life of subject peoples, but simply to deport and replace the governing and administrative elite of the previous/conquered regime. The Babylonian practice is well represented as removing basically the ruling elite from the capital city (2 Kgs 24–25). Presumably this is how we should interpret the brief report of the Assyrian conquest of Galilee in 731 (2 Kgs 15:29) and of the capital city Samaria a decade later (2 Kgs 17). Unless we are to dismiss the account of the latter as merely Josianic/deuteronomistic propaganda, the displacement of people may have been more severe than usual when the Assyrians finally conquered Samaria itself. Still the figure of 27,290 people given in Assyrian imperial

---

30. Contra Freyne, *Galilee*, 44.

31. Contra Freyne, *Galilee*, 49–50.

32 Contra E. M. Meyeers, Strange, and C. L. Meyers, *Excavations at Ancient Meiron*, xix, 155.

sources would correspond roughly to the ruling elite and its political–economic–religious–military governing apparatus (which would have been approximately ten percent of the total population, judging from comparative sociological studies). In contrast with the settlement of foreigners in the capital city of Samaria itself after 721 (2 Kgs 17:24; *ANET* 284), however, there is no evidence of Assyrian settlement of people from elsewhere in the empire in Galilee, as Tadmor explains.[33]

The Persian regime even restored previously deported native elites to power, as in the case of Judea, hence is unlikely to have resettled Galilee with non-Israelites. Moreover, while the Hellenistic empires founded numerous cities in the ancient Near East, including in the areas surrounding Galilee, they did not interfere much with local village life. Thus, in the absence of any evidence for transplantation of peoples or for foundation or cities in Galilee itself, we may surmise that many if not most people in Galilee were the descendants of ancient Israelite tribes/clans, most likely what was left of the "tribes" of Naphtali and Zebulun (e.g., Naphtali's "high places of the field" from the Song of Deborah, Judg 5:18).[34] The (semi-)rugged terrain, including a series of mountains and valleys, reinforces such an assumption of traditional social life in Galilee.

There is nothing to warrant the reading of "religious conversion" into Josephus's report that "the inhabitants were compelled to be circumcised and to live according to the laws of the Jews" (*Ant.* 13.318). Thus most of the older as well as recent scholarly discussion of whether the "conversion to Judaism" was "forced" or "voluntary" is anachronistic and beside the point (recent treatment by Kasher). In accordance with the political history he is writing, Josephus's report means that the Hasmonean regime from this point governed Galileans and other recently subjected peoples such as the Idumeans just as they did the Judeans according to the Torah and its application by court scribes and regional officials.

Insofar as some of the inhabitants of Galilee may have been descendants of former Israelites, "the laws of the Judeans" would not have been totally strange. We know from numerous cross-cultural studies that even though they may not be literate, peoples most definitely have cultural traditions carried in oral forms, and that peasantries and other subjected peoples maintain their own "little" or popular traditions over against the

---

33. Tadmor, "Some Aspects of the History of Samaria during the Biblical Period"; Hayes and Kwan, "The Final Years of Samaria," 169, 178–79.

34. See Carol Meyers, "Of Seasons and Soldiers"; Stager, "The Song of Deborah."

"great" or official tradition maintained in literary form by a cultural elite (Scott). Assuming some continuity of Mosaic and other common 'Israelite traditions, descendants of the tribes of Naphtali and Zebulun would have had historical traditions (such as the exodus and "The Song of Deborah") and covenantal customs (such as the Sabbath and circumcision) akin to those subsumed in the Judean Torah and history-scrolls.

"Judaization" would have meant varying degrees of change depending on the ethnic and cultural background of the local villagers. Josephus provides a fascinating case of the prominent Idumean (family of) Costobar who, despite the ostensible subjection to "the laws of the Judeans" since the time of John Hyrcanus, persisted in indigenous Idumean cult and customs into the reign of Herod (*Ant.* 15.255). That seemingly special case, however, points to the general question that must be addressed when it comes to the extension of Hasmonean rule to subjected peoples such as the Idumeans and Galileans. The Idumeans apparently had different cult and customs from the Judeans. But even if (some of many) Galileans had traditions similar or parallel to those of the Judeans, those traditions and customs had undergone eight centuries of different development since the time of David and Solomon. How would the Galileans, whose customs would have differed in significant ways from "the laws of the Judeans," have become familiar with them? Assuming that it began with the Hasmonean takeover of the area under Aristobulus, how would the "Judaization" of Galilee have proceeded?

A CENTURY OF JERUSALEM RULE IN GALILEE

Even if we assume that subsequent Hasmonean High Priests continued Aristobulus's policy of requiring the Galileans "to live in accordance with the laws of the Judeans," we still have little or no direct evidence either of the extent to which the Galileans would have appropriated the Torah or of their attitudes toward the Hasmonean regime and the temple in which it was based during the forty years prior to the Roman takeover in 63 BCE. One would expect the principal agents of Judaization to have been what sociologists would call the "retainers" of a regime such as the Hasmonean high priesthood.[35] Such would have been professional guardians and interpreters of the Torah, scribes or sages such as the Pharisees who, as Josephus

---

35. Lenski, *Power and Privilege*; Saldarini, *Pharisees, Scribes and Sadducees in Palestinian Society*.

explains, had been "passing down to the people certain regulations handed down from former generations and not written in the laws of Moses" (*Ant.* 13:297).

John Hyrcanus had rescinded those rulings established for the people by the Pharisees sometime prior to the Hasmonean takeover of Galilee. It is doubtful, moreover, that much by way of systematic instruction in Jewish ways could have been accomplished under the reign of Alexander Janneus, immediately after imposition of the Jewish laws in Galilee, even though he continued the policy of forced Judaization of conquered peoples (Ant. 13.397). Whatever energies Alexander Janneus did not exhaust in new military conquests must have been devoted to the extensive resistance he evoked among his own people, particularly from the scribal or "retainer" elements through which his regime would supposedly have governed the populace. Josephus's reports of the virtual civil war raging in Jerusalem and Judea suggest that Pharisees and other retainers were likely among the thousands whom Janneus killed, among the 800 he brutally crucified, and among the supposedly 8000 who fled into exile for the remainder of his reign (*Ant.* 13.372–383).

On the other hand, when the Pharisees themselves gained control of the state under his wife and successor Alexandra Salome (76–67 BCE; *Ant.* 13.398–415), it is quite possible that the Hasmonean regime undertook more rigorous application of the laws of the Judeans and the rulings of the Pharisees in Galilee and other recently subjugated areas.

It is difficult to discern how the repeated Roman conquest of Palestine could have done anything but delay or even weaken the Judaization of Galilee. At one point Freyne takes some of the Roman decrees cited by Josephus to mean "that Galilee could claim to be Jewish, both in fact and tradition, and such claims were recognized and embodied in legal enactments by the Roman authorities."[36] Such would be a misunderstanding of political-economic relations under ancient empires, however. The decrees of Julius Caesar cited by Josephus pertain to the rulers Hyrcanus II and his successors, their jurisdiction over "the nation of the Jews . . . and the tribute and other taxes they must extract from their people to render" up to Rome (*Ant.* 14.193–210). The "rights and privileges" mentioned are either those specified by the traditional Jewish "laws" for the high priests or the fruits of certain lands previously and now again subject to the Hasmonean high priesthood (*Ant.* 14.195, 209), not rights and privileges of Judeans

36. Freyne, *Galilee*, 61–62.

generally, in which Galilee supposedly now shared.[37] The implications for Galileans are simply that they are to continue under Hasmonean rule, and presumably to be taxed by the regime in Jerusalem as well as by the Romans—through the regime in Jerusalem.

In fact direct Roman intervention touched off a generation of political and social turmoil in Galilee as in the rest of Palestine, including chronic "civil war" between rival Hasmoneans, compounded if not fueled by the empire-wide Roman "civil war" that encompassed much of the East. During that time, Galileans were the first among his future subjects to become acquainted with the repressive practices of the young Herod, whom his father Antipater had placed in charge of the district. Among his early exploits were the vigorous suppression of banditry along the Syrian frontier and the energetic collection of a special levy of taxes by Cassius (*Ant.* 14.159–160, 168–171, 274; *War* 1.204–206, 210–211, 220–221).

In the sustained resistance to Herod's conquest of his kingdom with the aid of Roman troops, the principal military forces were probably provided by the troops of the rival Hasmonean faction, including the garrisons that Aristobulus had stationed in fortresses throughout Palestine and which remained loyal to him and his sons Alexander and Antigonus (*Ant.* 13.417, 427; 14.83, 89, 413, etc.). But there was also popular resistance to Herod and the Romans, resistance that appears to have been unusually persistent in Galilee (*Ant.* 14.414–417, 421–430, 432–433; *War* 1.304–306, 309–313, 315–316; how do we read *Ant.* 14.450 vs. *War* 1.326?). Ordinary Galileans and Judeans alike had by this time sufficient experience of Herod's (and the Romans') ruthless treatment to resist the imposition of his rule.[38]

There is no more evidence for Galilee under Herod's rule than for the period of Hasmonean rule. We can only reason from what we know was happening generally under Herod to the two measures of Galilean "Judaism" suggested by Freyne: the people's likely relations respectively to the temple and to the Torah. Herod left the temple/high priesthood as institution intact, but for his own purposes. There were thus now three layers of government over the people, each of which laid claim to revenues

---

37. For fuller discussion of the Roman policy of alliance with and rule through native aristocracies with particular reference to the Jewish high priesthood, see Horsley "High Priests and the Politics of Roman Palestine."

38. For a criticism of Freyne's attempt to explain the resistance to Herod in Galilee as stemming almost exclusively from the remnants of Hasmonean aristocracy that had somehow become based there (e.g., Freyne, *Galilee*, 63–68) see see further below, pp 131–33.

in the form of tribute, tithes, or taxes, compared with the one level only a generation earlier under the last Hasmoneans. One of the principal reasons for the intensity of Herod's taxation of his subjects was his vast program of cultural buildings and military fortresses, and the centerpiece of his building projects, in grand Hellenistic style, was the rebuilding of the temple area in Jerusalem. After marrying into the Hasmonean family, Herod managed to do away with the last possible Hasmonean claimant to authority, and thereafter appointed his own men, from Babylonian or Egyptian Jewish families, to the position of high priest. The problems of legitimacy that we might surmise thereafter surrounded the incumbents of the high priestly office are confirmed by Josephus's narratives of the events following the death of Herod. Among the principal foci of popular outcry in Jerusalem was the illegitimacy and injustice of the high priest (*Ant.* 17.207–208; *War* 2.7). If there was such an outcry against the high priest in Jerusalem itself, it is difficult to imagine that the temple and high priesthood, increasingly under Herodian influence and patently tools of Herodian rule, would have gained respect in Galilee where resistance to Herod's conquest had been so intense.

The Pharisees and other "retainers" attached to the temple would have experienced a dramatic "demotion" and loss of status under Herod. There is no reason to believe that they completely withdrew into conventicles of piety,[39] for Josephus reports their continued involvement in political affairs and their attempts to influence policy, despite their refusal to sign loyalty oaths to Herod and Rome (Ant. 17:41–46). Moreover, several decades later they are still active in political affairs, indeed are at the center of political scheming in the aftermath of the initial revolt in the summer of 66 CE (*Life* 20–23). Their general status and political influence would have been greatly reduced, however, given the higher level of Herodian administration above them. In this situation the Pharisees evidently focused on maneuvering for influence at the Herodian court, judging from Josephus' account (*Ant.* 17:41-45). It is at least imaginable that they sought influence among the people of Jerusalem, where they were based. But there is no evidence that they would have sought to influence villagers in surrounding countryside, much less in Galilee.

There is thus little reason to believe that the Judaization of Galilee (insofar as that would have meant focus on temple and Torah) would have advanced much under Herod's heavy hand. The popular uprisings that

---

39. Contra Neusner, *From Politics to Piety*.

erupted in every major district of Herod's realm, in Galilee around Sepphoris as well as in Perea and Judea, did not take the form of movements to restore the temple and Torah, as had the Maccabean Revolt (according to 1 Maccabees), or a popular election, by lot, of high priestly officers, as did the Zealots (proper) in northwest Judea in the winter of 67–68 CE. Josephus reports, rather, that in each case the insurgents acclaimed one of their number as "king" (*Ant.* 17.271–285; *War* 2.56–65). In the present context it is inadequate merely to observe that these movements were informed by a tradition of popular kingship attested in Jewish biblical traditions (of Saul, David, Jehu, etc.). We must appreciate also what these traditions and movements stood over against. The tradition of popular kingship would have been opposed to traditions that served to legitimate either the temple or the Torah. There appears also to have been a revival of interest in kingship tradition among literate groups, perhaps also in reaction to illegitimate, Roman-sponsored Herodian kingship, and the literate form includes the "son of David" motif as well.[40] But popular kingship, even if it had included the Davidic motif, would not necessarily have been distinctively "Judean," since David had been an Israelite hero as well as a Judahite one, and since popular kingship had preceded David as well as continued on in northern Israel long after David's time (esp. Jeroboam and Jehu). Thus the revolt in Galilee, like those in Judea and Perea, seems to have been an assertion of independence of the principal institutions of Jerusalem rule as well as of Herodian tyranny.

GALILEE BETWEEN ROMAN RECONQUESTS (4 BCE—67 CE)

After the death of Herod, Galilee was placed under the political jurisdiction of his son Antipas (4 BCE—39 CE). This leaves us wondering just what influence the temple, high priests and their retainers such as scribes and Pharisees continued to wield in the territory they had supposedly ruled for the previous century. Again we have virtually no evidence. And again the decisive events would appear to be conquests, the Roman reconquests in 4 BCE and 67 CE. In this case, however, the conquests would, on the face of things, seem to limit the opportunities for further Judaization of Galilee rather than foster it.

Following the Roman devastation of Sepphoris and the surrounding area and enslavement of the people in retaliation for the uprising led by the

---

40. Pss Sol 17; Horsley, "High Priests and the Politics of Roman Palestine."

popular king Judas in 4 BCE, Antipas rebuilt and fortified the city to be "the ornament of all Galilee" and called it "Autocratoris," i.e., "imperial city" (*Ant.* 18.27). The rebuilt city was apparently Antipas's initial capital, and the city became a center of Roman political and Hellenistic cultural influence, remaining steadfastly loyal to the Romans and a focus for Galileans' resentment, as evident in Josephus's account of events in 66 (*Life* 38-39, 104, 346-348). Before long, however. Antipas was busy founding the completely new city of Tiberias, on the shore of the Lake, as his new capital. It is clear from the names of his officials and their descendants that Tiberias was also a center of Roman and Hellenistic influence (*Life* 32-35). Cultivation of the Torah and tithes and offerings to priests and temple (an economic drain on the Galilean peasant producers that would have stood in rivalry with Antipas's taxation for building projects. etc.) were clearly not high on Antipas's agenda in Galilee.

Theissen has recently claimed that Antipas depicted himself on his coinage "as a pious Jew."[41] His assumption, of course, is that Galilee was basically "Jewish." We have no evidence, however, regarding how Antipas's subjects may have viewed images on coins. Moreover, the non-Judean as well as Judean descendants of former Israelites shared the tradition of Mosaic Covenantal prohibition of images. Thus the coinage of Antipas apparently cannot tell us much about the Judaization of Galileans.

A more appropriate question to ask would be whether Antipas did anything to foster the Judaization of Galilee. On this question, the indications from literary evidence are negative. Two of Josephus's reports suggest fairly clearly that, if anything, Antipas was oblivious to the religious-cultural sensitivities of his subjects, regardless of their provenance, and that the Jerusalem authorities and their representatives had (or chose to have) little or no authority over Antipas and his officials. First, Antipas apparently built his new "royal" administrative city on the site of a graveyard, which "was contrary to Judean tradition" (*Ant.* 18.38). Second, the royal palace there was lavishly decorated with representations of animals in a style contrary to the laws (*Life* 65). The Herodian capital was hardly advancing the cause of Judaization.

After the demise of Antipas a relative power vacuum ensued in Galilee, with frequently changing political jurisdictions, from Agrippa I (39-44) to Roman governors (44-54) to continued Roman governors in western Galilee around Sepphoris but assignment of eastern Galilee around

---

41. Theissen, *Gospels in Context*, 29.

Conquest and Social Conflict in Galilee

Tiberias and Tarichaeae to Agrippa II from 54 on. We can imagine that the Jerusalem authorities and/or their representatives such as scribes and Pharisees may have attempted to exert more influence in Galilee, but we have no evidence—unless we give credence to Mark's Gospel.

Mark represents the Pharisees, and to a more limited extent, the scribes, as present in Galilee during the ministry of Jesus. Clearly the picture in Mark 2:1—3:6 of the Pharisees watching Jesus' every move cannot be taken at face value. Ancient governments, unlike some modern regimes, did not keep their subjects under regular surveillance.[42] But that Pharisees, as representatives of the Jerusalem temple and high priesthood, were present in Galilee during the reign of Antipas and/or after Antipas was deposed seems highly unlikely, given their focus on influencing affairs in the Jerusalem temple state.

Upon the withdrawal of effective Roman power in the summer of 66, the Jerusalem authorities immediately exerted their claim to Galilee (*War* 2.562–568). That is, in their minds, Galilee, like Idumea, belonged under the rule of Jerusalem. Making their authority effective, on the other hand, was quite another matter. The utter failure of Josephus's mission to maintain control in Galilee, as documented even through his self-serving accounts, indicates just how fragmented and parochial the various areas of Galilee were and how little authority was commanded in Galilee by either the temple or the Torah.

Following the Roman reconquest of Galilee in 67, our sources dry up. There is little that can be said with certainty. But rather than assume a state of affairs on the basis of modern scholarly assumptions, we should acknowledge that there is simply no evidence that the Pharisees or proto-rabbis exerted influence, let alone dominance, in Galilee following the Roman reconquest and the destruction of the temple and high priestly government in Jerusalem. Apparently Agrippa II was restored as ruler in eastern Galilee, and presumably Roman officials administered western and upper Galilee in some manner, In contrast with the situation under Herodian rule, there was a power vacuum in Galilee from the middle of the first century and well into the second. The Yavnean rabbis, fleeing the Roman devastation of Judea in the aftermath of the Bar Kochba Revolt, reestablished themselves in Galilee toward the middle of the second century. Even then only gradually did they come to have much influence among the Galileans, who appear to

---

42. See Giddens, *Nation-State and Violence*.

have been resistant to their rulings.⁴³ The rabbis' efforts over a longer period of time eventually effected a deeper and longer lasting Judaization of Galilee. That finally successful Judaization of Galilee, however, at least in the nascent overlay of rabbinic culture, was ironically the indirect result of the final Roman reconquest of Judea in reaction to the Bar Kochba Revolt.

THE EARLY JUDAIZATION OF GALILEE AND SOCIAL CONFLICT

This brief survey, on fragmentary evidence, of the erratic historical process in which Jerusalem conquered and ruled or influenced Galilee should raise a number of important questions in our minds regarding out previous working assumptions about Galilee. Just how "Jewish" could Galilee have become in a few generations of Jerusalem rule? Would Galileans have been positively or negatively or rather ambivalently disposed toward the temple and the high priestly government in Jerusalem? Would the Torah have been operative in Galilee in some way? And what influence would the Pharisees have had and in what social role(s)?

In order even to approach such questions we must, first, recognize the basic social structure in ancient Palestine.⁴⁴ The fundamental social division or opposition in Palestine was not Judaism versus Hellenism or observance versus non-observance of the Law or, eventually, Jewish versus Christian. The fundamental social division indicated in our sources was between what appears in various aspects as rulers versus ruled, taxers versus taxed, city/court/temple versus village/town, and official/learned tradition versus popular/local tradition. Yet this fundamental division is not between separable entities that can be understood in isolation. It involves rather relationships of exploitation and domination as well as shared cultural heritage and mutual influence. Perhaps most important to recognize is that we cannot speak simply of one "Jewish" "society" or "community" with its traditions and rules, but must come to grips with different communities on at least two (overlapping) levels: local village or town communities that had their own semi-independent social forms, on the one hand, and the community(ies) centered around the urban-based governing apparatus, on the other. The vast majority of ancient people's lives were largely defined and determined by their membership in families and village or town

---

43. Goodman, *State and Society in Roman Galilee*.
44. See Horsley, *Sociology and the Jesus Movement*, chaps. 4–5.

communities. Villages and towns were semi-independent, self-governing, and relatively self-sufficient communities. But villages and towns were subject to higher level communities/authorities with political, military, or religious power, such as cities, temples, and high priests, and other rulers regional and/or imperial, often in multiple layers. That basic division between rulers and ruled in Palestine was complicated in the case of Galilee by the regional differences rooted in the history sketched above.

In order even to approach such questions we must, second, make one or another procedural assumption about the cultural background of social life in Galilee: that is, whether or not there was continuity with ancient Israelite traditions. If we assume the population was non-Israelite at the time of its takeover by the Hasmonean regime in 104 BCE, then the situation in Galilee would have been somewhat like that in Idumea, with little common cultural tradition shared with the Judeans. If we assume the population was Israelite, then Galileans were likely to have held certain important cultural-religious traditions in common with Judeans and the "official" traditions of the Torah. The fact that we find materials of Galilean provenance in the Gospels which allude to Israelite traditions in apparent independence of Judean texts such as the Torah reinforces the second alternative.

Thus, although biblical history and the subsequent political history of rule over Galilee give no support to the assumption that Galileans looked to Jerusalem as their cultic and cultural center, it seems highly likely that the cultural traditions of many Galileans were Israelite in provenance, and therefore may have had certain similarities to what had become officially sanctioned or sponsored traditions in Jerusalem. That would appear to be the appropriate basis on which to reassess the fragmentary evidence available on whether and/or in what ways Galileans may have developed loyalty or attachment to the temple and Torah.

GALILEANS AND THE TEMPLE[45]

As the now familiar generalization has it, temples were built by kings, at least in the ancient Near East. The books of Ezra and Nehemiah make it

---

45. In this section I am working with very different presuppositions than those of Freyne, *Galilee*, chap. 7. Assuming that Galilee was somehow primordially Jewish and oriented toward the temple as its cultic and cultural center, Freyne: (a) anachronistically separates the religious from the social and cultural dimensions; (b) works on functionalist assumptions about the integrative effect of a temple; and (c) on the assumption of the necessity of some "cult center," finds no alternative, pagan or syncretistic cult center

abundantly clear that the second temple in Jerusalem was sponsored by the Persian imperial regime, whose general policy was to sponsor the restoration of local temples and laws such as those of Judea in what became the Torah. It was not a new practice that sacrifice was offered for both Rome and the Roman emperor. The temple with its high priesthood was the governing political–economic–religious institution in Judea in a double sense: It was the means through which the empire controlled Judea, and it was the institution through which the Judean rulers controlled and drew revenues from the people. We need only recall the decree of Caesar cited above: All those peoples of Palestine subject to Jerusalem "shall also pay tithes to Hyrcanus and his sons just as they paid to their forefathers" (*Ant.* 14.203).

In Judea, which had been ruled by a temple-state since the late sixth century BCE (and before that a small "kingdom" under the Davidic monarchy for four hundred years), there was probably a relatively high degree of interaction between the high priestly regime and the local village communities. That does not mean, however, that Judean people were unambiguously "attached" to the high priesthood and temple. Even in Judea, with centuries of temple heritage, it is clear from "intertestamental" literature such as 1 Enoch, Psalms of Solomon, the Dead Sea Scrolls, and so on, that prominent scribal groups sharply condemned the high priestly rulers. Moreover, in their scenarios for a reformed and renewed "Jerusalem" or "Zion" they wasted little imagination on a restored or rebuilt "temple."[46] In the early first century BCE there had been virtual civil war against the high priest Alexander Janneus; Herod installed "foreign" Jewish families into the priestly aristocracy; widespread popular outcries broke out against the high priest at the death of Herod; and the high priests were the first to be attacked by the popular insurrection in the summer of 66 CE. Thus, even in Judea, where there was a long-standing historical basis for loyalty to the temple, popular crowds as well as literate scribal groups had for centuries sharply criticized or condemned the priestly aristocracy and/or temple-establishment.

By comparison with Judeans, Galileans had none of the historical basis for attachment to the temple while having a recent basis for resentment of Jerusalem rule. Galilee not only stood at a distance from Jerusalem, but it

---

constructed in Galilee under Hellenistic rule; hence he concludes (d) that Galilean "attachment to the temple" was "very strong." Every one of those key assumptions can now be seen as unwarranted, and the conclusion is at odds with the evidence he himself presented that Galileans ignored regulations regarding tithes and offerings.

46. That is exactly the opposite of the claim in Sanders, *Jesus and Judaism*, chap. 2; cf. Horsley, *Jesus and the Spiral of Violence*, 286–92.

had only recently come under Jerusalem's rule through conquest. Both the structure and the history of the situation suggest that there is little reason to look for much Galilean loyalty to the temple.

At the level of the rulers and their officials in the principal cities, Sepphoris was clearly the principal military and administrative center in Galilee under the Hasmoneans and may well have continued with close relations to the temple and high priestly families under Herod. The Roman installation of Antipas altered the governing structure, however, and set up overlapping and rival layers of rule. Antipas and his officials, first in the rebuilt Sepphoris and then in the new city of Tiberias, were in a position of competition for the tax or tithe revenues produced by the Galilean populace. It is difficult to imagine any special attachment to the temple or reason to advocate its support by Herodian officials in Sepphoris and Tiberias.

At the level of villages and towns, we can simply revert to the fundamental and apparently decisive evidence laid out but not followed by Freyne.[47] As Rabbi Judah said, "the people of Galilee know naught of the terumah of the temple chamber . . . and know naught of things devoted to the priests" (m. Ned. 2:4); they were reluctant to pay the tithes; and there is little or no evidence of compliance with the "half-shekel" tax, which had only recently been imposed in any case. The apparent situation behind Josephus's report that (he and) his two colleagues quickly "amassed a large sum of money from the tithes which they accepted as their priestly due" is as telling as his report that they wanted to return to Jerusalem with their "take." Josephus and his colleagues were sent by the high priestly regime in Jerusalem to try to take control of Galilee in the breakdown of imperial order after the summer of 66. They would have arrived well after harvest time, it would seem. That is, tithes had not already been collected at the threshing floors or otherwise paid to priests in these Galilean communities. Suddenly, to officials from the Jerusalem high priestly government, people "anted up." Does this story testify to "attachment by the Galileans to priests from Jerusalem"[48] or to a hiatus in or lack of any regularized pattern of obligations supposedly due to temple and priests? After all, Galilee had not been under direct temple and high priestly political (and economic?) jurisdiction for the previous seventy years (unless for three years under Agrippa I, 41–44). It would appear that we have no reason to believe "that the picture of m. Bik. 3:2; m. Ta'an. 4:2, portraying devout countrypeople

---

47. Freyne, *Galilee*, 277–87.
48. Freyne, *Galilee*.

gathering to bring their offerings, also applied to Galilean Jews once the *maamadoth* system had been set up there."[49]

Comments about pilgrimage to the temple, particularly at the great so-called "pilgrimage festivals," tend toward extreme hyperbole.[50] Considering the physical limitations of Jerusalem and the temple courtyards, it is clear that only a small fraction even of the Judean population could have made a pilgrimage at any given festival. One must therefore be highly skeptical about just how important pilgrimage would have been for any significant portion of the Galilean populace. And one must be critical about what constitutes evidence for Galileans making pilgrimage. It seems inappropriate to take the story about the youthful Jesus and his family in Luke 2 as a historical account, given Luke's theological agenda. Yet the passing reference to Pilate having mingled some Galileans' blood with their sacrifices and the eighteen killed by the collapse of the tower of Siloam in Luke 13:1–5 may provide evidence of some pilgrimage activity by Galileans.

In particular two incidents mentioned by Josephus must be examined. At Pentecost in 4 BCE, after Archelaus had already bloodied the people protesting his father's tyranny at Passover, "a countless multitude flocked in from Galilee, from Idumea, from Jericho, and from Perea, although it was the native population of Judea which was preeminent" (*War* 2.43). But Josephus also indicates that this gathering was utterly atypical because of recent events. The people came "not only for the religious observances but because they resented the reckless insolence of (the Roman officer) Sabinus" as well (*Ant.* 17.254); "it was not the customary ritual so much as indignation that drew the people in crowds to the capital" (*War* 2.43). A widespread uprising was in its nascent phases, so this is hardly good evidence for pilgrimage. It is interesting that Josephus makes no reference to any significant number of Galileans or Pereans at the preceding Passover festival.

Josephus's variant accounts of the second incident, under Cumanus (49–52), leave us pondering what to make of his inconsistent use of terms of reference, among other things. In the *War* (2.232–235) he has the Samaritan villagers killing one "Galilean" among "many *Ioudaioi* going up to the festival," while in the *Antiquities* (20.118–120) he has numerous "Galileans" killed while on their way through Samaria to Jerusalem, and then "Galileans" urging a mass of *Ioudaioi* to take arms in assertion of their liberty. The second account also makes it seem that such pilgrimages were

49. Contra Freyne, *Galilee*, 294.
50. Freyne, *Galilee*, 287–93, following Safrai, "Synagogues."

a regular occurrence. We must conclude that pilgrimage was not unusual for Galileans, but there is no reason to think that it was a regular pattern for very many Galileans.

Thus the Galilean relationship to the temple and high priesthood would appear to involve a fundamental structural social conflict compounded by regional and historical differences. It is difficult to imagine how the temple and high priesthood could have had much of an integrative effect for Galileans. If some sort of identification with Jerusalem as a symbolic center did develop for some Galileans, then we would expect that to have been an ambivalent relationship, since they were at times governed and taxed from that symbolic center.

GALILEANS AND THE TORAH[51]

Some critical rethinking may be necessary before we can even pose the historical inquiry appropriately in regard to the presence and function of the Torah in Galilee under Jerusalem rule or influence. As for evidence, we have references that may be relevant to the question in both Josephus and the Synoptic Gospels. But those references rarely refer to "the Law," as in the phrase, "the Law and the Prophets." Rather Josephus refers in various terms, almost always in the plural, to *oi nomoi, ta nomima, oi patrioi nomoi*, and so forth—"the laws," "the customs/rulings," "the ancestral customs." And the Gospels refer to a particular custom or to "the traditions of the elders" versus "the commandment of God" (see esp. Mark 7:1–13). The idea that "the Law" was at issue between Jesus and the Pharisees or that "the Law/Torah" was operative in Galilee is likely an influence from modern scholarship's own roots in Pauline-Lutheran influenced discussions of "The Law"

---

51. Procedurally there is no point in framing this discussion as an argument with Freyne's presentation. In both his grand historical survey (*Galilee*) and his more popularized version (*Galilee, Jesus, and the Gospels*), the research and conceptualization pre-date recent recognition of key issues that call our older assumptions into question. Neusner has made clear how inappropriate is Freyne's use of rabbinic sources (Neusner, Review of Freyne). And the main argument driving Freyne's whole construction of Galilean history—that Galilee, in contrast to Judea, was not dominated by "the Zealots"—turns out to be beside the point, since there has turned out to be no evidence of "the Zealots" as dominant anywhere in first-century Palestine (Smith, "Zealots and Sicarii"; and Horsley, "The Sicarii"). Thus there is no point in arguing against a treatment that finds in several incidents recounted by Josephus "extreme (or rigorist) Jewish sectarian views" of "the halakhah" or a "Zealot ideology" that somehow jumped from the temple captain Eleazar in Jerusalem in the early summer of 66 to the riff-raff of Tiberias in a few weeks' time.

and from recent modern discussions of "Judaism" as basically a "religion" in which there were particular "redemptive media" such as Torah and temple. We should rather attend to the terms used in our sources themselves. We should be open to the possible differences between (a) a Torah scroll proper, (b) "laws" or "customs" generally that may include or refer in some way to what is also in the Torah scroll, (c) rulings advocated by Pharisees, scribes. or sages but not actually in a scroll of Torah (i.e., unwritten "Torah" or "traditions of the elders"), and (d) local-regional customs which may well have had roots in the same original covenantal tradition out of which the Torah proper had grown (the last is an example of what anthropologists refer to as the "little" or popular tradition, while the first three all belong to the "great" tradition, some of which is written and some oral). With such possible differences in mind, we can examine several incidents in Galilee recounted by Josephus for what they indicate about whether common Israelite covenantal traditions/customs and/or more particularly Judean ethnic or ancestral traditions and/or scribal "traditions of the elders" and/or a scroll of Torah itself were involved in a given case.

Motive of the Peasant Strike over Gaius's Statue

The widespread protest over the attempt to place Gaius's statue in the Jerusalem temple apparently involved a peasant strike—refusal to plant crops—and this took place at least partly in some areas of Lower Galilee (*Ant.* 18.261–288; *War* 2.184–203; Philo, *Gaium* 230–232). Both Josephus's and Philo's accounts emphasize that what inspired the protest was the violation of the Judean law. All three accounts, however, are heavily charged with apologetic rhetoric. We simply have no way of knowing the degree to which the Galilean peasants who became caught up in the protest were motivated in the way portrayed by the Flavian Jewish historian and the Alexandrian Judean theologian. It may be more plausible historically to surmise that such people were more motivated by the (reports of) mass movement of Roman and auxiliary troops through their land. In such colonial or imperial situations as the Palestinian people under Roman rule, however, "religious" symbols take on a heightened importance as people's political autonomy is removed and their economic circumstances disintegrate.[52] So it is conceivable that protest rooted more in long-standing grievances crystallized around a symbol such as the bust of the emperor. On the

---

52. More extensive discussion in Horsley, *Jesus and the Spiral of Violence*, chap. 3.

basis of Josephus's and Philo's reports it is difficult to determine whether the motives of the Galilean participants focused specifically on the violation of the Torah itself and/or the prospect of the bust being placed in the temple (as a symbolic center). The Galileans in this case could have been motivated simply by the violation of one of the basic "commandments of God" (in the common Israelite covenantal tradition) or simply by the statue itself as objectionable. That is, while the accounts of this incident tell us much about the Judean apologetic rhetoric of Philo and Josephus, they do not tell us much at all about the Torah proper (as distinct from the common covenantal tradition) in Galilee.

Motives in the Burning of Antipas's Palace in 66

Josephus writes that he had instructions from the Jerusalem koinon "to press for the demolition of the palace . . . which contained representations of animals . . . forbidden by the laws" (*Life* 65–66). Capellus and the other *protoi* of Tiberias, however, were no more concerned about the violation of the laws in 66 than Antipas and their fathers' generation had been when Tiberias was built over graves and the animal decorations set in place forty or fifty years earlier. "Jesus son of Sapphias," leader of the party of sailors and destitute, along with "some Galileans," set the whole palace on fire. Nothing in this account even suggests that Jesus and the Galileans were motivated by the violations of the laws, or at least the prohibition of images in particular. That is rather the reported concern of the Jerusalem council. Nor can we trust Josephus's attribution of motives to his opponents in the situation, i.e., that Jesus and the Galileans were after spoil (gold leaf on the roof), since it was Josephus himself who ended up with spoil confiscated from the conflagration (*Life* 295). One could imagine that destitute Tiberians and the Galileans were more motivated by resentment at the luxury of the "king's palace" built and maintained by their own labor and produce (cf. Luke/Q 7:25: "What then did you go out to see? Someone dressed in soft robes? Look, those who put on fine clothing and live in luxury are in royal palaces"). This incident thus does not provide evidence of Galilean interest in the Torah. Instead it is evidence for the conscious flouting of the laws and/or the official rulings on the part of Herodian rulers and their officials, who must have set a certain tone or cultural style in this Galilean capital city.

The Demand that Two Renegade Royal Officials Be Circumcised

When two officials of Agrippa II from Trachonitis joined Josephus in Galilee in the fall of 66, reports Josephus, *oi Ioudaioi* demanded that they be circumcised as a condition of remaining (in Tarichaeae/E. Galilee), a demand Josephus himself resisted (*Life* 112–113). Sometime later "the crowd" clamored against Josephus that these refugee royal officers should conform to "the customs" (*ethē*) of those among whom they were living, and claimed that they were "sorcerers" making it impossible to defeat the Romans (*Life* 149). This apparent doublet of a report is puzzling. It is highly unusual for Josephus to use the term "the Judeans" in his accounts of affairs in Galilee in the Life. Are "the Judeans" here different people from those to whom he refers repeatedly as "the Galileans" or "those around John of Gischala/Jesus son of Sapphias/etc.?" Does "the crowd" in Tarichaeae in the resumption of the story, *Life* 149–154, refer to different people from "the Judeans" in the initial report? (The *palin/*"again" in *Life* 149 relates to the immediately preceding conflict between the crowd and Josephus, *Life* 132–144, not to the initial report of the demand to circumcise the foreign nobles in *Life* 112–113). If *oi Ioudaioi* in the initial report is not a broad term inclusive of Galileans and refers rather to some Judeans present in Tarichaeae, then this report tells us little about Galileans' views.

In any case, whether either "the Judeans'" demand for circumcision in the initial report or the crowd's concern about "customs" in the sequel refers specifically to the Torah is highly doubtful. In numerous other places Josephus uses phrases such as *oi nomoi patrioi ton Ioudaion* when he wants the reference to be explicitly to "the ancestral Judean laws." The term "customs" suggests that the reference is more likely to the general Israelite (and not distinctively Judean) custom of circumcision, which would have had deep historical roots in Galilee prior to the arrival of the Torah from Jerusalem. Josephus says explicitly in the second report that the crowd was also concerned about the nobles somehow being "sorcerers" in a special political-religious sense, that is, they were officers of the Roman client ruler against whom the people are in rebellion.

Supplying Oil to "the Judeans" in Caesarea Philippi/Syria

Josephus charges in two accounts that John of Gischala had profiteered in supplying olive oil to "the Judeans" in Caesarea Philippi or Syria generally

(*Life* 74; *War* 2.591–593). The incident does indicate that those Caesarean or Syrian Jews, like Josephus, recognized oil grown and pressed in Upper Galilee as satisfying purity requirements (*ta nomima*, *Life* 74). Does this imply a ruling based on some concept of an approved *eretz Israel* delineated already, in mid-first century CE by some authorities, perhaps in Jerusalem (cf. *Ant.* 12.120)? Josephus's report of the incident, however, says nothing about either the use and/or acceptance of the Torah or Pharisaic rulings in Galilee itself.[53]

Jesus Son of Sapphias Holding in His Hands "the Laws of Moses"

To incite the Tarichaean mob against him, says Josephus, Jesus son of Sapphias, the *archon* of Tiberias, held up in his hands "the laws of Moses," claiming that Josephus was about to betray "the ancestral laws" (*Life* 132–135). It is more difficult than usual to know how to sift through the rhetoric in this account. Josephus has one of his two arch-enemies in Galilee refer to him here as "your commander in chief." It is clear from Josephus's overall narratives of affairs in Galilee that most of the different feuding groups in Galilee did not recognize Josephus as such a "commander in chief." This leads to doubts about the intended tone of the adjoining phrase "the patriarchal laws." Is Josephus portraying Jesus as mocking him and his supposed agenda which, as Josephus himself unabashedly indicates, most groups in Galilee saw through? Assuming that Jesus did waive "the Mosaic laws" in his hand, the incident suggests that there was a scroll of Torah around, at least in a town the size of Tarichaeae. We can imagine that, whether it was read regularly or not, it could have served well as a symbol for the people's independence of Roman rule. What is striking about Josephus's account (besides his virtual admission of the double game he was playing) is that he couches his own defense not in terms of loyalty to the laws of Moses, but in terms of his intent to use the spoil taken from the baggage train of the wife of the king's overseer (*epitropos*) to build fortifications for Tarichaeae (*Life* 141–142). That is, concern for defense of the Torah/the laws of Moses was apparently not a burning issue for the Tarichaeans or his readers or both.

---

53. It is hardly acceptable critical historical procedure to take at face value Josephus's attributions of motives to actors in his accounts, particularly in the case of his own rivals—in this case that John of Gischala was motivated by profiteering rather than piety. And one must be suspicious of Josephus's defensive comments about his own authorization of John's action, *Life* 16.

Josephus's Sensitivity to Observance of the Sabbath in Tarichaeae and Tiberias

Josephus says at one point he dismissed his soldiers for the sabbath (*Life* 159). Assuming that the account indicates observance of the sabbath in Tarichaeae, is observance of the sabbath an indication of observance of the Torah or of Pharisaic/scribal sabbath regulations? The sabbath was one of those basic covenantal "commandments of God," deeply rooted in the Israelite roots of Galileans well prior to their subordination to Jerusalem. Its observance in Galilee does not imply use of the Torah.

Josephus's accounts of these incidents in Galilee give very little by way of indication that the Torah was important in Galilean life of the first century. One story may indicate that a copy of the Torah scroll was available in a large town. But another story suggests that defense of the Torah was not a major issue, even in the excitement of the revolt in 66. A few of the incidents give information only about the basic Israelite covenantal stipulations about images or sabbath or the traditional custom of circumcision. One may imply that at some level there already existed some authoritative ruling regarding purity of oil, but it provides no information on observance in Galilee itself. We thus have evidence of observance of and concern about the basic commandments of the Mosaic covenant among Galileans, but little evidence one way or the other regarding either the functioning of the Torah or the presence of "the traditions of the elders" in Galilee.

In Conclusion

What may be most remarkable about this survey of evidence on the temple and Torah in Galilee is that there is little to suggest that either one was of central, defining importance for life in Galilee. However much temple and Torah may have been the principal "redemptive media" for priests or Pharisees based in Jerusalem (or for Jews in the diaspora), no currently available evidence indicates that they had central significance in Galilee such that it would emerge in a situation of crisis. Some of the incidents Josephus reports, however, do indicate that fundamental principles of the Israelite covenantal heritage did have such defining significance that came to the fore in historical crises. But it is also evident that in those crises where the basic covenantal commandments of God had defining significance for Galileans, they stood in conflict with representatives of the Jerusalem temple authorities, or rather they were involved in fundamental social conflicts in which the Jerusalem authorities or their representatives were "caught in the middle," given the structure of the imperial situation. Ironically, in such overt social conflicts, the Galileans who take their stand on covenantal principle stand opposed by or to those whom we have been accustomed to labelling the leaders of Judaism. What this suggests is that we need a different set of terms and concepts with which to analyze and reconstruct Palestinian history in the early Roman period.

THE ROLE OF THE PHARISEES IN GALILEE

Our best, and almost our only, sources for the Pharisees in Galilee, as for Galilean life in general, are the Synoptic Gospels. As with the temple and Torah, we must free our thinking of the old synthetic conceptualization that linked the Pharisees closely with both the Law and the synagogue. Synagogues have been understood as religious buildings and the Pharisees as the leaders of the synagogues, and these as standard features of life in Galilee as well as the diaspora, where, for example, the Matthean church stands over against "the synagogue down the street" led by the Pharisees who constitute the principal religious competition.[54]

In first century Galilee, however, the *synagōgai* mentioned in the Gospels were not (yet) buildings in the villages of Galilee, nor were they distinctively religious, and the Pharisees were not their leaders. There is virtually no archaeological or textual evidence for the existence of synagogue buildings until the second century CE and most evidence is much later.[55] It has been standard procedure to take NT references to *synagōgai* as evidence for a widespread presence of "the synagogue" (i.e., a building) in Palestine, above all in Galilee.[56] In the Synoptic Gospels and Acts, however, only two uses of *synagōgē*, Luke 7:5 and Acts 18:7, clearly and unambiguously refer to a building. In all of the Markan occurrences (e.g., 1:21, 23, 29; 3:1; 6:2; and the Matthean and Lucan parallels) the assumption is that the *synagogai* are local assemblies, with nothing in the texts to suggest that buildings might be involved. Texts such as Mark 13:9 and Luke 12:11 indicate that "synagogues" means local assemblies with political jurisdiction

---

54. Kee, "The Transformation of the Synagogue after 70 CE," 15-22.

55. Gutmann, *The Synagogue*, 72-76; Kee, "The Transformation of the Synagogue after 70 CE," 1-14.

56. See, e.g., Hengel, "Proseuche und Synagoge."

and authority to keep the peace and to discipline troublemakers. Thus not only were the synagogues not buildings but they were not simply religious. Hoenig has gathered evidence that *knesset* in early rabbinic literature "applied to 'assembly' and designated all communal activities." He then lays out numerous tannaitic sources indicating that the "town-square" (*r'hova shel 'ir*, the *agora*, which is misleadingly translated "marketplace") was the location of the *ma'amadoth* prayers for fasting, trials, general assemblies, the bringing of first fruits, and prayers for rain.[57] As Safrai sees, but buries in his treatment, the synagogue was thus the people, the community, the congregation assembled to conduct community affairs such as fundraising, public projects, or prayers.

There is no evidence, moreover, to suggest that the leaders of the local assemblies were the Pharisees. Recent claims that the Pharisees were local religious leaders and brokers in Galilean villages are based on Lukan editorial phrases which are not good evidence for affairs in Galilee.[58] There were apparently often more than one *archisynagōgos* or *rosh ha-knesset* (mistranslated as "ruler of the synagogue"). In tannaitic times, judging from repeated references in the Mishnah, neither the head(s) of the assembly nor the *hazzan* nor the *parnasim* nor the *gabaim* were sages, scribes, or Pharisees. These officers of local assemblies were rather indigenous leadership from among the members of the local community. For their part, the rabbis viewed association with the *amme ha-aretz* as highly problematic— "morning sleep and midday wine and children's talk and sitting in the assemblies of the peasants put a man out of the world" (m. Abot 3:11). It seems highly unlikely that the Pharisees were leaders of local assemblies if the later rabbis, by their own clear indication, played no such role.

Who then were the scribes and Pharisees? What was their social position and role? Of the three sets of evidence, the least reliable and helpful is from Rabbinic sources.[59] Read critically, however, both Josephus's reports about the Pharisees and the Gospel harangues provide evidence about their social-political role. And in using the extremely limited evidence on Pharisees, we should keep in mind that besides speaking from different interests and points of view, our sources provide information on different aspects of the Pharisees' concerns and roles. As noted above, several of

---

57. Hoenig, "The Ancient City-Square."

58. Moxnes, *Economics of the Kingdom*; Saldarini, *Pharisees, Scribes and Sadducees*, 175–76.

59. Saldarini, *Pharisees, Scribes and Sadducees*.

Josephus's reports about the Pharisees' activities or actions under different rulers indicate that they were what comparative sociologists such as Lenski would call "retainers," that is, representatives of the rulers who help govern or, at times, govern themselves.[60] As we noted briefly above, under John Hyrcanus, the Pharisees were the guardians and interpreters of the laws and promulgators of additional rulings. Under Alexandra Salome they virtually administered the temple-state, and under Herod they simply lost status but did not abandon their political function. Finally, Josephus's reports of events in 66–67 in Jerusalem and Galilee indicate that leading Pharisees quickly stepped into prominent roles in the attempt to control the volatile situation until the high priestly government that remained in Jerusalem could negotiate with the Romans (*Life* 21, 191, 197).

If we take Josephus's portrayal of the Pharisees' role under the Hasmoneans seriously, recognizing that they did not back away from politics under Herod and after, is it then historically credible that they would have been active in Galilee at the time of Jesus as the representatives through whom the Jerusalem rulers attempted to exert influence even after they no longer enjoyed direct political jurisdiction over Galilee? The impression given toward the beginning of the Gospel of Mark that scribes or Pharisees were hanging around every village assembly where Jesus preached and healed is not credible. On the other hand, the Markan portrayal of the Pharisees as authority figures in the Jerusalem temple-state with expertise in the Law is highly credible historically, in agreement with the accounts of Josephus. Not surprisingly, they are mentioned less frequently in Mark once Jesus arrives in Jerusalem, where the high priests are directly in charge.

In recent years scholars both of Mark and of the Synoptic Sayings Source Q are increasingly inclined to place the origin of both in or close to Galilee. Thus it does not matter whether we penetrate to a pre-Q or pre-Markan level in order to discern how their representation of the Pharisees may be pertinent to the concerns of Jesus and other people in Galilee. Not surprisingly, given the new sense we have of the Pharisees as having been "retainers" of the high priestly government in Jerusalem and particularly the guardians and interpreters of the Torah, their portrayal in Q and Mark involves both the temple and their traditions of interpretation. Our sense that both the woes against the scribes and Pharisees in Q and Jesus' disputes with the Pharisees and scribes in Mark involve primarily the (ritual) Law and/or purity regulations is the product of an older synthetic conceptual

---

60. Lenski, *Power and Privilege*; and Saldarini, *Pharisees, Scribes and Sadducees*.

apparatus heavily influenced from Protestant theological debates.[61] And indeed the concern with purity is a motif in the anti-Pharisaic Gospel material. The main issue, however, is not purity, not legalism, not ritual law.

In Mark 7:1–23 we miss the issue either if we read the story in terms of oral versus written Law or if we read it as concerned primarily with purity codes.[62] The story may begin with a question about cleanliness. But it becomes quickly apparent that the purity issue is only a foil for, and is placed in stark contrast with, a religious-economic issue and the religious-political role of the Pharisees. Moreover, in the overall literary context of Mark, the story in 7:1–23 is part of a broader conflict between Jesus and the authorities, beginning with the Pharisees' attacks and escalating into the high priestly plot to capture and execute him. We miss the point if we focus only or primarily on the Pharisees concern for purity and do not locate it in the broader conflict between Jesus and the Jerusalem rulers and their agents—both literarily, in the Markan overall narrative, and historically assessing the Markan narrative against the background of what we know of the structural social conflict in first century Palestine.

Reading Mark 7 in the context of the particular social conflict at play in Galilee, however, requires greater precision with regard to particular items in the story:

(a) The scribes who join the Pharisees in 7:1 are said explicitly to have "come from Jerusalem." Instead of taking the Markan placement of the scribes (and Pharisees) in Galilee at face value, it should be read as "stage setting" to bring them into direct conversation with Jesus. But that does not make the Pharisees local leaders. While ostensibly operating in an outlying district they are, like the scribes, advisers and representatives of the temple-state in Jerusalem, just as the Herodians are the retainers of the regime of Antipas.

b) Mark makes the parenthetical comment in 7:3 that the Pharisees and *pantes oi Ioudaioi* do not eat unless they wash their hands. There is no reason to read "Jews" here, as if a universal Jewish practice were in focus, rather than simply "Judeans."[63]

---

61. J. Z. Smith, *Drudgery Divine*.

62. For readings of Mark 7:1–23 on standard concepts of purity, ritual law, etc., see Banks, *Jesus and the Law*, 132–46; Westerholm, *Jesus and Scribal Authority*, 62–85; and Booth, *Jesus and the Laws of Purity*.

63. The only other occurrences of the term *Iodaioi* Mark are in ch 15, where it appears on the lips of Pilate in the trial and on the lips of soldiers and the chief priests in mockery, as well as in the inscription on the cross. Reading these phrases also as "(king of) the Judeans" makes sense given the dramatic reinterpretation Mark is giving to "the messiah"

(c) Then in 7:5 the Pharisees and scribes accuse the disciples not of violating the Law, but of not living according to "the traditions of the elders." In the ensuing counterattack Jesus charges that the Pharisees abandon, indeed make void, the commandment of God in order to cling to their tradition (7:6–13). Now assuming the consensus that "traditions of the elders" refers to the "oral Torah" propounded by Pharisees and others, it is evident from the specific example Jesus uses in his indictment that the issue is not simply oral versus written Torah. Jesus does not refer to the Torah explicitly, and there is no indication that he has some written word or "scripture" in mind. That is true even if the text of Mark 7:10 "quoting" Moses has been conformed to the LXX text of Exod 20:12; 21:17 or Deut 5:16.

(d) Ironically, modern scholars and translators have "cleaned up" the language of a passage in which Jesus is blatantly scatological in slamming the Pharisees' obsession with cleanliness. An ancient copyist apparently anticipated the problem by changing an omicron to an omega in 7:19, leading many modern theologians to conclude that Mark's Jesus, in good Pauline and Lukan fashion, was "declaring all foods clean." But that is not the *lectio difficilior*, in which Jesus says in effect that it is the process of what was ingested being evacuated into the outhouse that purifies all foods. Since many scholars dismiss Mark 7:19c as a gloss anyhow, it hardly seems credible to focus a reading of Mark 7:1–23 on the traditional English version phrase "Thus he declared all foods clean."

The difficulty with grasping the real concern in Mark 7:1–23 using the old conceptual apparatus is indicated by many interpreters' sense that Jesus' first response is almost unrelated to the Pharisees' question. But of course Jesus—in no uncertain terms—is dramatically changing the focus. Jesus charges the Pharisees with making void the actual commandment of God precisely through "the traditions of the elders." In the illustration Jesus offers, the Pharisees and scribes encourage people to devote their property to the temple, which means that that property cannot thereafter be used for other purposes, such as the support of elderly parents, thus blocking the fulfillment of the commandment to "honor your father and your mother." The meaning of the commandment of God is concrete, not just spiritual, inseparably social-economic as well as religious, just as the Pharisaic "traditions of the elders" are economic as well as religious regulations. What is more, the traditions of the elders express the economic interest of the temple in Jerusalem, at least in the illustration given. But, charges Mark's

---

and related terms/concepts and the irony with which he writes repeatedly in chap. 15.

Jesus, that is counter to the commandment of God, which is concerned rather for the welfare of impoverished non-productive elderly people.

In Mark 7:1–23, Jesus is attacking the scribes and Pharisees not primarily on the matter of purity codes, but for the effects they have on the people in exercising their religiously-legitimated role as supervisory retainers of the sacerdotal government in Jerusalem. The same indictment is expanded in the last part of the harangue (7:15–23), where Jesus indicts the Pharisees as violators of the decalogue, the traditional principles of social justice. This reading is confirmed later in the Markan narrative, 12:38 through 13:2: "Beware of the scribes who, among other things, devour widows' houses" is illustrated by the widow giving all she has. That is, her whole "house," or basis of livelihood, has just been "devoured" as the effect of the scribes exercising their religio-political-economic role.

The woes against the Pharisees and scribes in Q (Luke 11:39–52) are a similar indictment of effects of their social role, not a dispute primarily about purity codes. Although Q is now being placed solidly in Galilee, it is still being (mis)read through the remaining vestiges of anti-Judaism in Christian exegesis and through an apolitical understanding of Jesus. There is simply no indication in Q of a Gentile mission, and it is Christian eisegesis to find in Q a condemnation of "all Israel."[64] If anything, one of the principal concerns of Q is a prophetic mission of the renewal of Israel, as articulated in the last saying, Luke 22:28–30/Matt 19:28: the Twelve are to be on twelve thrones not "judging" but "doing justice for" the twelve tribes of Israel.[65] Most of the prophetic threats of judgment in Q are directed at the Q people themselves. Otherwise there is the prophetic lament over the Jerusalem ruling house in 13:34–35, and the prophetic woes against the Pharisees which we should examine here.

Because the issue of the Law, particularly when associated with the Pharisees, has loomed so large in Christian exegesis, scholars have tended to read the Q woes against the Pharisees as focused on interpretation or understanding of the Law. On the basis of Luke 11:42 (these you ought to have done, without neglecting the others) and on the assumption that cleansing the cup and tithing were at the heart of Pharisaic interpretation, some have argued that the Q-people are not even rejecting the cultic laws here but radicalizing the Torah, thus being in effect another Jewish sect

---

64. On this point and generally on "Q" see Horsley, "Q and Jesus," 183; and Horsley, "Questions about Redactional Strata and the Social Relations Reflected in Q."

65. First explained in Horsley, *Jesus and the Spiral of Violence*, 201–6.

in competition with the Pharisees.[66] At the opposite pole, others view the Q people as redefining purity in ethical terms, reading the woes more as general ethical exhortations.[67]

But what if we read these woes more concretely in the context of the structural social conflict in Galilee between Jerusalem rulers and their retainers, on the one hand, and the Galilean villagers in their semiautonomous communities on the other? In focus is not the Torah and not even purity rules or cultic laws, but the social functions or role of the Pharisees. In fact only three of the seven indictments even mention or allude to what might be termed laws and/or Pharisaic concerns about purity (11:39–40, 42, 44). But virtually all of them focus on the social role of the scribes and Pharisees as "retainers" and indict them for one after another of their practices or effects on the people.

The first woe, in Luke 11:39–41, does indeed refer to their concerns about ritual purity. As Neusner has documented, it even appears to be in touch with what would have been particular Pharisaic twists of the time.[68] But both Luke's version (Q?), explicitly, and Matthew's version, implicitly, quickly shift the vessels into metaphors: "inside you/they are full of extortion and rapacity." Nothing subtle about that woe. Rhetorically the Pharisees are mocked for their purity concerns, but the primary concern of the Q woe is the rapacious effects of their governing or supervisory effects on the people.

Tithes, the subject of the woe in 11:42, were hardly a matter of ceremonial law, but of taxes. The reference to "mint, dill, and cumin" is hyperbole and caricature, probably full of sarcasm and ridicule. It is not even clear that such minor items were supposed to be tithed, at least in later rabbinic literature. The charge that the Pharisees were obsessed with even the minor items, not even cultivated, such as mint and herbs, serves to indicate how rigorous they were about the principal cultivated products subject to tithes/taxes such as grain, on which the very survival of subsistence producers themselves depended. And if the Pharisees or scribes, as representatives of Jerusalem, were still insisting on payment of tithes in addition to the taxes that Galilean peasants were paying to Antipas (including for the major building projects, first in Sepphoris and then Tiberias) and the tribute they were rendering to Caesar, they were indeed neglecting justice and

66. Wild, "Encounter between Pharisaic and Christian Judaism"; and Schultz, Q.
67. E.g., Kloppenborg, *The Formation of Q*.
68. Neusner, "First Cleanse the Inside."

compassion. (Note the clear allusion to the prophetic covenantal exhortation demanding *mišpaṭ, ḥesed, ṣedeq*, and *emet* in such passages as Hos 4:1; 12:7; Mic 6:8; Zech 7:9: "Thus says Yahweh Sebaoth, 'Render true judgment, show kindness and mercy each to his brother, do not oppress the widow, the fatherless, the sojourner, or the poor'"). It is at least conceivable that the "heavy burdens" in 11:46 included the multiplication of rules by scribal interpretation. More likely, however, the burdens refer to the tithing and other dues which the people owed. One of the functions of the scribes and Pharisees would have been policy for and instruction about tithing. The reference to the Pharisees not touching those burdens with one of their fingers is probably an allusion to how such interpreters-overseers responsible for application of the laws and regulations could help alleviate the burdens through their scribal role, if only they would.

The accusation that the Pharisees are like "unmarked graves" which the people walk over unsuspectingly may be the most clever indictment of all. Like the accusation that began with cleansing the outside of the cup, this charge surely picks up on one of the Pharisees' concerns, that about contamination of ritual purity. But by charging that they themselves are like unmarked graves from which people are exposed to danger unawares, Q's Jesus shifts the focus to political-economic relations: the danger to which the people are subjected unawares comes from the Pharisees themselves.

As for building the tombs of the prophets in 11:47–48, the custodians of such memorials to the dissident figures of earlier times would have been precisely retainers such as the Pharisees. But it is more than irony or hypocrisy or mystification for the representatives of the rulers to be cultivating the sacred memory of those who had protested against earlier rulers, and perhaps paid with their lives.

The final indictment is the most comprehensive and the one that comes closest to dealing with the Torah. Even without a definitive reconstruction of the original Q text, we can discern that Matthew's accusation of shutting the kingdom of heaven (23:13) and Luke's accusation of "taking away the keys of knowledge" (11:52) are parallel and even synonymous or equivalent expressions. As in prophetic passages (e.g., Isa 1:2–3), "knowledge" here is covenant keeping, which would be synonymous with living under or according to the rule or kingship of God, the possibility of which has been blocked by the Pharisees, but opened now with the ministry of Jesus.

Throughout these woes in Q/Luke 11:39–52, the focus is not on the Torah, but on the political-economic-religious role of the scribes and

Pharisees. Jesus indicts them for the ways in which they, partly in their role as official interpreters of the laws, were having detrimental effects on the lives of the people. The indictments include mocking or sarcastic references to the Pharisees' special concerns about purity codes, but the focus is clearly on the effects of their role as official interpreters and intermediaries for the Jerusalem government. Thus we find in both Mark and Q condemnations of the scribes and Pharisees for the detrimental social-economic effects they have on the people, apparently just by virtue of their social-political role as retainers.

SUMMARY IMPLICATIONS

In both Mark 7 and again in the Q woes against the Pharisees, Jesus is apparently appealing to the basic Israelite covenantal tradition, "the commandment of God" or fundamental covenant-keeping. Perhaps this indicates how we should reconceptualize what may have been happening in Galilee following the take-over by the Hasmoneans and under continuing rule or influence by the Jerusalem authorities. If our assumption of continuing Israelite tradition in Galilee under foreign imperial rule is correct, then Jesus and other Galileans were rooted in Israelite tradition that had much in common with the official traditions followed in Jerusalem and advocated by scribes and Pharisees. But the official Jerusalem-based tradition and the popular Galilean tradition were not the same, despite sharing the basic covenantal heritage, and they functioned to legitimate and advance different interests.

The high priestly families whose base was the temple and the intellectual legal retainers representing the temple-state apparatus understandably worked to advance their own interests, although after the Roman take-over that was entangled with, dependent on, and to a degree in competition with, Roman imperial interests. Galilean villagers and townspeople, on the other hand, as illustrated perhaps in Mark 7:6–13 and Luke/Q 11:52, would have appealed to the Israelite covenantal tradition against the practices and effects of those who ostensibly shared that covenantal tradition. It was, among other things, a struggle over who could claim Israelite covenantal tradition and in what way.

Insofar as the rabbis who later established domination in Galilee were the direct or indirect successors of the Pharisees and scribes based in Jerusalem, then scribal-rabbinic groups were the historical winners of that struggle in Galilee. As of the middle of the first century CE, however, neither

"Judaism" nor Christianity" existed in Galilee. That is, neither what we know later emerged as rabbinic Judaism, which was more than a "religion," and what we know emerged as proto-orthodox Christianity, which was at least a "religion," existed yet in general, hence could not have been forces in Galilee.

Some of the historical phenomena which may be relevant to the later emergence of rabbinic Judaism and proto-orthodox Christianity can be approached in the broader context of the Judean and Roman conquests of Galilee and the continuing efforts by Jerusalem institutions and groups to influence or control Galilean affairs. Such efforts at control were occasionally resisted by certain Galileans on whom we every so often have windows, such as in the resistance to Herod of 40–37 BCE, the insurrection led by the popular king Judas in 4 BCE, the Jesus movement(s) which began in the 30s, and the highly fragmented assertion of regional independence in 66–67 CE. Yet there is no evidence of any unifying institution, religious or political, anywhere on the Galilean scene until rabbinic Judaism began to consolidate its influence in late antiquity, and even then there remained both Christian and pagan communities particularly in the cities.

Shifting Rulers / Jurisdictions in Galilee
late second century BCE: Seleucid decline and Iturean control

104–63	Hasmoneans
63–47	shifting Roman and (rival) Hasmoneans
47–40	(Hyrcanus II—Antipater) Herod
40–37	struggle between Herod/Romans & Antigonus/Parthians
37–4	Herod (with high priesthood weakened but still intact)
4BCE—39 CE	Antipas (with high priesthood still intact)
39–44	Agrippa I (with high priesthood still intact)
44–54	Roman governors (high priesthood still intact)
54–66	Sepphoris/West, Roman gov.; Tiberias/East, Agrippa II
66–67	independent, with high priesthood asserting authority
67–	Roman authorities
ca. 200	Rabbinic Patriarchate (recognized by Rome?)

3

Power Vacuum and Power Struggle in 66–67 CE

THE GREAT REVOLT, WHETHER in Judea or Galilee, was a complex series of events. It requires a multifaceted critical approach, a consideration of many factors and their interrelation. I will focus on three principal aspects: (1) our main sources, Josephus's histories, which must be read suspiciously and critically; (2) the political and economic structure of the Roman imperial order, particularly the fact that Rome worked initially through indirect rule in Judea and Galilee; (3) the developments and differences within the districts of Judea and Galilee. In sum, we must consider the interactions and effects between the distinct and various political and economic structures and particular histories of Roman Judea and Galilee as part of the contingent dynamics of key actors and unfolding events.

FIRST PRINCIPLES: KEY STRUCTURAL AND HISTORICAL FACTORS

The structure of ancient societies was such that religion was embedded in all aspects of daily life, including political and economic activities. Since the fundamental social forms were the household and village communities, it is difficult to identify structures that provided inter-village or regional coherence. While some peoples may have had a certain common awareness as *ethnoi*, "nationalism" is a modern concept that is anachronistic when applied to ancient societies. I understand the specific case of the Great Revolt, therefore, as a conflict rooted in a society with an interlocking religious–political–economic structure, which was under stress because Judeans and Galileans had experienced Roman conquest and reconquest three times in the sixty years from 63 to 4 BCE. In response to the severe Roman practices of scorched-earth slaughter and devastation, people fled to any place that seemed more secure (Yodefat, Yaffo, Gamla, Jerusalem); and rather than simply be slaughtered, some attempted to resist.

Some factors are pertinent particularly to the Great Revolt in Galilee. First, Galilee had been independent of Jerusalem and/or under a separate division of imperial administration for over eight hundred years prior to its takeover by the Hasmoneans and its rule by Herod. Significant aspects of Judean society and history, such as the centuries of interaction with the temple and high priesthood and the Maccabean Revolt, were not part of Galilean collective memory. We must take seriously what anthropologists call the differences between the "great tradition" and the "little tradition," in this case the differences between elite and partially written traditions developed in the Jerusalem temple-state and the Israelite popular tradition that was presumably cultivated in Galilean village communities.[1]

Judeans in Galilee during the first century BCE and the first half of the first century CE were probably Hasmonean and then Herodian administrative officials and their service personnel. There is no evidence for institutionalized mechanisms by which Galileans would have been socialized into greater conformity with Jerusalem-based traditions. Galileans may well have had an ambivalent relation to the temple and high priesthood. Further, there is clear evidence that Galileans, like their Judean cousins, were hostile to Herod and Herodian rulers generally.

This antipathy notwithstanding, after the death of Herod, for seventy years leading up to the Great Revolt, Galilee was controlled mostly by Herodian client kings. In establishing his rule directly in Galilee and building two major cities within twenty years, Antipas must have made a great impact on Galilean village society. Suddenly the rulers of the Galileans lived right in their midst, and a new or rebuilt capital city was accessible

---

1. I have discussed the division between and the relationship between the Israelite popular tradition and the Judean scribal tradition in many publications. See the recent discussion in "Contesting Authority," in *Text and Tradition*, chap. 5.

from nearly every village. Such major building projects required resources from the only available source, the productive peasantry.

After the removal of Antipas, the Romans imposed frequent changes of rulers in Galilee—not exactly stable and consistent rule in a time first of drought and then social unrest. In their policy of indirect rule through client kings and .temple-states, the Romans expected indigenous aristocracies such as the Jerusalem high priests to maintain order in the society under their charge. Once the Great Revolt erupted in the summer of 66 CE, the only chance for the Jerusalem aristocracy to retain its position of power and privilege was to attempt to regain control of the society (Judea and Idumea). Presumably Agrippa II and his officials in Tiberias and Tarichaeae were faced with the same problem.

JOSEPHUS AND HIS AGENDA AS AGENT AND HISTORIAN

In approaching the Great Revolt[2] in Galilee we face a dilemma that inevitably involves circular reasoning. In order to use our principal source, Josephus, a highly interested central participant in the events he portrays and so, with good reason, highly suspect in his portrayal of these events, we need to understand the role he was playing in Galilee. In order to understand that role, we must understand the character and strategy of the provisional government in Jerusalem that sent him to Galilee. Yet our only source for the latter is Josephus's own characterization of that provisional government, its circumstances, and its strategy. Nevertheless our situation is not utterly impossible. Considerable debate about how Josephus's histories should be read and critically assessed has led to fairly persuasive hypotheses about the merits of his different portrayals of events and about the character and agenda of the provisional government in Jerusalem.[3]

Josephus's *War* and his later *Life* are often seen to stand in conflict with regard to the formation of a provisional government in Jerusalem and,

2. As explained in the Introduction (see 16–18 above), I am using "the Great Revolt" instead of "the Jewish Revolt" or "the Jewish War," which were influenced by the Flavian imperial propaganda about the Romans great victory over the Jewish people.

3. It is interesting that several independent recent analyses of Josephus's histories, each working with a different reconstruction of the Great Revolt itself, have come to roughly the same conclusion about the relative reliability of Josephus's *War* and his *Life*: Horsley, *Galilee*, 72–76; Jossa, "Josephus' Actions in the Galilee"; Rappaport, "Where Was Josephus Lying."

more importantly, that Jerusalem provisional governments' strategy with regard to the popular insurgency already underway against the Romans. In the *War* Josephus claims that "those who defeated Cestius, after going back to Jerusalem, attracted those who still supported the Romans to their side, some by force and others by persuasion and, gathered in the temple, appointed several commanders for the war," among whom was Josephus, sent to Galilee (*War* 2.562). In the *Life*, on the other hand, "the principal men of Jerusalem" only pretend to go along with the Great Revolt in order to regain control of the country and stall for time until they can negotiate with the Romans. In that connection "they dispatched me [Josephus], with two other priests, to induce the disaffected [in Galilee] to lay down their arms and ... to wait and see what action the Romans would take" (*Life* 28–29).[4]

If we read the War more completely and critically, however, its conflict with the Life is more apparent than real. Josephus indicates clearly in later passages in the War that the actual strategy of the aristocratic Jerusalem provisional government was exactly as claimed in the Life. In the assembly supposedly held in the temple after the Roman military forces were expelled (*War* 2.562–568) the principal leaders of "those who defeated Cestius," in particular Simon bar Giora and Eleazar ben Simon, were—evidently on purpose—not appointed among the "generals to conduct the war." Further, the renegade high priestly temple captain Eleazar ben Ananias was sent to Idumea where he would have difficulty taking any further dramatic revolutionary initiatives. Those appointed to key positions, especially in Jerusalem itself, were stabilizing priestly aristocrats. Subsequently in the *War* Josephus indicates that the high priest Hanan, one of the two heads of the Jerusalem junta, took action to suppress the more insurrectionary forces in the countryside, in hopes of moderating the conflict, apparently to buy time for an accommodation with the Romans (2.651–654). Later, in Josephus's account of the aristocratic junta's struggles against the Zealots, a coalition of brigand bands from the Judean countryside who invaded Jerusalem in the winter of 67–68 CE, and particularly in Josephus's encomium on Hanan (4.319–322), Josephus indicates that the real strategy of the high priests and leading Pharisees was to regain control of the society and negotiate a

---

4. Cohen (*Josephus in Galilee and Rome*) provides an extended argument from comparison of key texts for the difference between the *War* and the later *Life* on this issue. Rajak (*Josephus*, chaps. 4 and 6) and Bilde (*Flavius Josephus*, chaps. 2 and 5) critique Cohen's identification of a conflict between the two histories and provide a critically established alternative reading that moves in the same direction as the argument here.

settlement with Rome.[5] Thus this cannot be dismissed either because it appears only in the later *Life* or because it is simply an "apology" by Josephus. As he indicates clearly in both versions of the Great Revolt and his role in it, the aristocratic junta was attempting to carry out what was in effect a "counter-revolution" in Jerusalem, and Josephus himself was sent to Galilee basically to assert control of the situation there.

Others have independently recognized similarly that the provisional government in Jerusalem was not all that revolutionary, indeed, was attempting to regain control of the volatile situation and reach accommodation with the Romans. Although he still characterizes it as "popular," Jossa notices that the provisional government in Jerusalem does not give positions of command to the very leaders of the defeat of Cestius[6] and that Josephus's behavior in Galilee can hardly be characterized as anti-Roman.[7] Instead, he adopted "the tactics of waiting and trying to keep open the possibility of a mutual understanding with the Romans."[8] Still working on the sense that the accounts in the *War* and the *Life* conflict, Rappaport recognizes that however "apologetic" the latter may be, it is by far the more credible account historically: in the *Life* Josephus is admitting that he and the aristocratic junta in Jerusalem were pursuing a two-faced policy, pretending to go along with the Great Revolt while hoping for negotiation with the Romans. Josephus had been forced into this admission by Justus of Tiberias' accusation, based partly on his self-portrayal as a revolutionary general in the *War*, that Josephus was responsible for drawing Tiberias into the appearance of revolt.[9] Jossa concludes that "it is impossible to share those scholars' opinions who want the Jewish aristocracy involved against the Romans together with the Zealots and victim only of their own weakness."[10]

We can thus secure an hypothesis to build upon in reading Josephus's histories, our principal sources, that the provisional high priestly government in Jerusalem sent Josephus to Galilee as part of their general strategy of attempting to control the volatile situation at the end of the summer of 66 CE in order to regain the favor of the Romans and negotiate a settlement that would preserve their own positions as client rulers. That conclusion

5. Hosley, *Galilee*, 72–75.
6. Jossa, *Josephus' Actions in the Galilee*, 269–72.
7. Jossa, *Josephus' Actions in the Galilee*, 273–77.
8. Jossa, *Josephus' Actions in the Galilee*, 277.
9. Rappaport, "Where Was Josephus Lying," 282–85.
10. Jossa, *Josephus' Actions in the Galilee*, 272.

is confirmed by what Josephus did and did not do in Galilee, according to both of his accounts of his activities there. Although he portrays himself in the *War* as the great Jewish general, a worthy foe for the future emperors, Vespasian and Titus, and much beloved by his own people, Josephus fails to portray himself engaging the Roman forces in battle in any significant way—with the notable exception of the siege of Jotapata. Interpreters have long since become suspicious of his claim to have fortified all those cities and villages (*War* 2.573). His grossly exaggerated claims about the size of his army have never been credible (*War* 2.576, 583). Except for Jotapata, Josephus and his military forces engaged the Roman's forces or Agrippa's royal forces rarely and then in relatively insignificant connections, as in checking each other's maneuvers. In what is virtually the only case (*Life* 115-118), Josephus and 2,000 infantry (he claims) skirmished briefly and tentatively with a small Roman force under the decurion Aebutius on the frontier between Galilee and the Great Plain near Besara and Herod's old military colony of Gaba.

Josephus did have military forces under his command in Galilee. But instead of using them against the Romans, he used them to control affairs in Galilee, in various connections. Whatever control Josephus was able to exercise in Galilee was based on his own, apparently private, army, which he claims consisted of 4,500 mercenaries and a "body-guard" of 600 (*War* 2.583). Those figures are likely inflated, and even if these mercenaries were the same as the "brigands" he paid in Galilee (which I doubt), the effect was the same. While he did not use them against the Romans in any significant encounters, he did use them to control certain areas and general affairs in Galilee. Whatever his credibility, he claims to have "taken by storm" the cities of Gabara, Sepphoris (twice), and Tiberias (four times) as well as to have deployed his own hoplites (obviously 10,000 is a gross exaggeration) against Tiberias at one point (*Life* 82, 321-331). He indicates at several points that he deployed a commander with troops to control Tiberias (*War* 2.616; *Life* 89, 272). He kept most of his troops and bodyguard always with him, dismissing them only for the special occasion of the Sabbath (*Life* 159), relying on them for his own security and "forceful suasion" (e.g., the distinction in Life 240-242, 243). He effectively neutralized potential rival fighting forces, such as the brigand bands that formed in various regions of Galilee. Indeed he simultaneously co-opted both these brigands and the Galilean peasants by conning the latter into paying the former to serve as mercenaries—who of course were to take orders from him. He even adapted a standard use of military forces in ancient politics: as he candidly admits in the *Life* (79, 228; cf. *War* 2.570) the Galileans who dined with him as his "friends" and served as envoys to Jerusalem (while under guard!) were really local Galilean magistrates ("those in office") whom he had taken as hostages for the acquiescence of the Galilean villagers and whose consent he could use to legitimate his actions.

Insofar as the provisional government in Jerusalem was attempting to control the active conflict that had erupted in 66 CE and insofar as the "general" they sent to Galilee was using his own military forces not to fight against the Romans but to control the Galileans and Galilean cities, events in (Judea and) Galilee cannot be understood in terms of a simple binary opposition of pro and anti-Roman forces or of "the peace party" and "the war party."[11] The Jerusalem provisional government delegated Josephus to take control of Galilee and he proceeded to do so with the help of the military forces at his disposal. But the Galilee already had Roman-installed rulers. Galilee had not been under the jurisdiction of Jerusalem authorities since the death of Herod the Great, at which point the Romans had placed Galilee under the rule of Antipas. Thereafter Galilee was ruled by Agrippa I and later partitioned, the western part of lower Galilee apparently under the control of the city of Sepphoris, itself accountable to the Roman governor in Caesarea, while eastern lower Galilee was under the client king Agrippa II from 54 CE on. Thus, after a century under Hasmonean and Herodian rule from 104 to 4 BCE, Galilee had not been under Jerusalem's jurisdiction for the following seventy years prior to the Great Revolt. In sending Josephus and his aristocratic priestly colleagues to attempt to take control of affairs in Galilee during the summer of 66 CE, therefore, the high priestly provisional government in Jerusalem was reasserting Jerusalem rule over Galilee (*War* 2.562–568). Josephus's elaborate accounts of the attempts by the Jerusalem junta to replace him is further indication that the leading high priests and Pharisees believed that they should control affairs in Galilee (*War* 2.626–631; *Life* 189–335). As noted above, the high-priestly led provisional government in Jerusalem could have entertained no illusions that, in the long run, they were independent of Roman rule. Rather they were attempting to assert control over Galilee as part of their overall strategy to regain control of the Judean and Galilean people in order to regain the confidence of the Romans in their ability to maintain order. But they were clearly taking the opportunity of the vacuum of effective Roman

---

11. Cf. Cohen, *Josephus in Galilee and Rome*, 183–85.

control of Galilee through Sepphoris and Agrippa II's governing apparatus in Tiberias and Tarichaeae to intervene in an area not designated by Rome as under their jurisdiction. What Josephus encountered and contributed to in Galilee and then subsequently portrayed in his histories was thus far more complex than a simple anti-Roman revolt. It was instead a variety of interrelated and overlapping conflicts including urban-rural hostilities, class conflict within the cities, hostility toward and acquiescence in Roman and/or Herodian rule, and response to and rejection of Jerusalem authority—including plenty of mutual manipulation and negotiation and shifting alliances. Far from examining the Great Revolt in Galilee in general, it is necessary to focus on particular cities, areas, or groups in order to begin to comprehend the shifting dynamics of the power struggles from the initial outbreak of the Great Revolt in the summer of 66 CE to the Roman reconquest in the summer of 67 CE.

GALILEE IN 66–67 CE

Of the two rival capital cities, Sepphoris, Antipas' "ornament of all Galilee" and still "the greatest city of Galilee," remained unswervingly loyal to (and dependent on) Roman rule.[12] Through Josephus or otherwise, the high-priestly provisional government in Jerusalem attempted to assert its authority in Sepphoris. The capital city of western lower Galilee, however, for its part consistently resisted its advances, for example refusing to talk with either Josephus or with the priestly Pharisaic delegation Jerusalem sent to replace him in Galilee (*Life* 123–124). While waiting for the inevitable Roman reconquest of the area, Sepphoris therefore resourcefully engaged the brigand-chieftain Jesus and his horde of several hundred as mercenaries to protect it from the hostile Galileans (*Life* 104–111). Josephus would appear to have been engaged in some sort of mutually manipulative game with Sepphoris. It is not at all clear how to understand Josephus's accounts of his interaction with the city. He claims to have taken it by storm twice (*War* 2.646; *Life* 82, 374, 395–396). Yet he also claims to have served at one point as a mediator making it easier for Sepphoris, as the only unit consistently loyal to Rome, to maintain its position and he came to a "mutual understanding" with Jesus the brigand-chief and his horde serving as the city's protectors (*Life* 30–31, 107–111). He also says that he was "inveigled into

---

12. See further E. M. Meyers, "Sepphoris."

Power Vacuum and Power Struggle in 66–67 CE

[further] fortifying the city"—which was already an exceptionally strong fortress (*Life* 347; *War* 3.61; cf. 3.34).

Tiberias, the other principal city in Galilee, was sharply divided along class lines between the "ten principal men" headed by Julius Capellus and the "party of sailors and the poor" led by Jesus son of Sapphias (*Life* 32–35, 64–67, 69, 296). The third party mentioned by Josephus, headed by his rival historian Justus son of Pistus (*Life* 36), does not appear to play much of a role in his subsequent accounts. Josephus himself repeatedly consulted and collaborated with Capellus and the "leading men," who were consistently pro-Roman and pro-Agrippa, repeatedly attempting to have royal troops take over the city. As the Roman reconquest worked its way toward Tiberias, these Herodian elite of Tiberias fled to Agrippa in the Roman camp and pleaded for Vespasian's mercy (*Life* 34, 155; *War* 2.632; 3.453–454). Jesus and the Tiberian "riff-raff," on the other hand, killed "all the Greeks" and burned and looted the royal palace at the beginning of the Great Revolt and at the end actively resisted the Roman army both at Tiberias and then at Taricheae (*Life* 66–67; *War* 3.450, 457–459). Josephus suggests that these two classes fought for control over Tiberias throughout the brief "revolt" in Galilee and, led a pitched intra-city battle or a "purge" by one side or another as the Roman army marched closer (*Life* 353).

Josephus's main concern was his own control of Tiberias, the machinations of which complicate his narratives. After taking control he placed one of his own officers, Silas, in charge of the city (*Life* 89; *War* 2.616). Then for one reason or another, he repeatedly had to reassert his control, claiming to have taken the city by assault four times (*Life* 82, 155–174, 317–35; *War* 2.632–646). Josephus provides clear indications that his assertion of control over Tiberias was part of the general agenda of the provisional government in Jerusalem) headed by high priests and influenced increasingly by leading Pharisees such as Simon son of Gamaliel. When he first arrived, Josephus pressed upon the "council and principal men of the city" the orders of the Jerusalem koinon that the royal palace be demolished because it contained "representations of animals . . . forbidden by the [Judean] laws" (*Life* 64–65). Similarly Josephus's lengthy account of the Jerusalem priestly Pharisaic envoys' negotiations to replace him reveals the Jerusalem council's continuing agenda of control in Tiberias. However it may have accorded with that of the Jerusalem council, moreover, Josephus had his own agenda which he repeatedly had to disguise because it ran counter to the popular interests in Tiberias. He repeatedly collaborated with the Herodian upper class of Tiberias who were loyal to Agrippa, for example, handing over the spoil taken from the royal palace to Capellus and the leading men to hold in trust for the king, while effectively delaying the time when Agrippa would reestablish control.

Just as Sepphoris' loyalty to the Romans can be explained from its history, so the position of the "principal men" of Tiberias can be explained from the history of that royal city. Tiberias had been founded by Antipas only a half-century before the Great Revolt as a royal city of a Roman client king. At least among its Herodian elite, it seems to have retained its identity as a small royal administrative city, never having been under Jerusalem's jurisdiction and having experienced only about a decade of direct Roman rule. The Herodian elite, however, had reason for some resentment over the city's loss of status, since under Agrippa I it had become reduced to a toparchy capital, like Tarichaeae, and had lost the royal bank and archives (*Life* 37–39). That, along with the formidable opposition of the party of the poor and sailors led by the city magistrate Jesus, may explain why Tiberias was more vulnerable to Josephus's manipulations than was Sepphoris.

Tarichaeae (Magdala) just northwest of Tiberias along the shore of the Sea of Galilee, also the center of a toparchy under Agrippa II, appears to have been more solidly in the control of the leading residents who remained loyal to Agrippa. Two of the "leading men," Dassion and Jannaeus son of Levi ("the most powerful man of the Tarichaeans") were "very special friends of the king" and still secure in their positions (*Life* 131; *War* 2.597). Josephus entrusted them with goods taken from one of the king's officers in an ambush for safe return at the appropriate time. The interests of the dominant Tarichaeans were apparently similar to those of Josephus and those of the Jerusalem koinon. Tarichaeae proved his most dependable ally in Galilee, and his most comfortable "headquarters" (*Life* 97, 159–160, 276, 304). He benefited from their support particularly in difficult dealings with Tiberias (*War* 2.635–641; *Life* 97–98). Josephus distinguishes carefully between the dominant Tarichaeans and the refugees from other towns and peasants from the surrounding area who came together in and around Tarichaeae at times and were eager to resist royal or Roman rule, as well as Josephus's leadership (*War* 2.598–602). "The indigenous residents, intent on their property and city," had from the beginning opposed the war and were simply caught in the middle between the Roman attack and the resistance of the rebellious nearby peasants and Tiberian lower class (*War* 3.492, 500–501). Although they were taken captive, Vespasian restored these leading Tarichaeans to their town (*War* 3.532–535). Again as with Sepphoris and the Tiberian elite, their history helps explain the stance of the dominant Tarichaeans: their interests and orientation lay with the established imperial order.

For Josephus to have presented Gabara (about ten miles north of Sepphoris) as the third of the "chief cities of Galilee," it also must have been an administrative town (*Life* 82, 123, 203; identical with the village of Gabaroth? (*Life* 229, 235, 240, 242–243). In the escalation of social conflict during the summer of 66 CE, some people from Gabara joined with some from Sogane, Tyre, and Gadara (?) in attacking Gischala (Gush Halav) to the northeast, which proceeded to counterattack (*Life* 44). Once Simon, the leading resident of Gabara, became fast friends with John son of Levi, however, the two towns formed a lasting alliance (*Life* 123–124). Assuming that the "house of Jesus" was anything like the "great castle as imposing as a citadel" described by Josephus, there were some extremes of wealth and power in the area. Gabara stoutly resisted Josephus's attempt at taking control. Although Josephus claims to have taken Gabara by assault, he makes no mention of fortifying it (mentioning rather the village of Sogane, nearby). Vespasian's "first objective" as he launched his reconquest of Galilee was Gabara. Finding no combatants in the town, "he slew all the males who were of age . . . and also burned all the surrounding villages and towns," enslaving the remaining inhabitants (*War* 3.132–134).

What happened in Gischala (Gush Halav) and Upper Galilee during the Great Revolt cannot be separated from the rise to prominence of John son of Levi. It is difficult in the extreme, however, to reconstruct the rise of John from Josephus's polemics against his principal rival for control in Galilee. Gischala was a key regional town in the rugged hill country of Upper Galilee along the frontier with territory controlled by Tyre. As is usually the case during times of social conflict in a frontier region, fugitives gathered along the frontier near Gischala in 66 CE (*War* 2.588, 625; *Life* 372). Toward the outset of the widening disorder, as mentioned above, the towns of Gabara and Sogane to the southwest and some elements from Tyre had attacked Gischala, which then counterattacked and fortified itself (*Life* 43–45). Such are the circumstances from which John rose to become Josephus's principal rival in Galilee. Josephus's charge that John got his start as a brigand has at least some credibility, since it is in just such circumstances that communities (such as the city of Sepphoris) rely on strongmen for protection and leadership. Whatever his origins, John built a following from the fugitives along the Tyrian frontier (*War* 2.587–588). His first conflict with Josephus revolved around local autonomy and local leadership versus control from above (i.e., by Josephus as a representative of the Jerusalem junta). Josephus's complaints about both John's seizure of the imperial stores of grain in the villages of Upper Galilee and about John's scheme to supply pure olive oil to the Jewish inhabitants of Caesarea Philippi simply suggest that John had outmaneuvered him in bolstering his own local power as opposed to Josephus's design to enhance his regional power. John and Gischala, however, next moved to challenge Josephus for influence in the rest of Galilee. John sought alliances in Tiberias, in active conflict with Josephus's attempt to control the city (*War* 2.614–625; *Life* 84–96; cf. 368–372). Gischala reversed the earlier conflict with Gabara, John cementing a friendship with the town's strongman, Simon (*Life* 123–124, 235). John also started cultivating central figures in the Jerusalem provisional government, supposedly establishing the second co-commander there, Jesus son of Gamala, as "an intimate friend" (*Life* 204) and forming links with leading Pharisees who played an increasingly influential role in the provisional government. The struggle in Galilee created unlikely bedfellows: peasants and refugees in Upper Galilee forged alliances not only with their former enemies, the elite of Gabara, but with scribal officials as well as the lower class of Tiberias and, finally, the Pharisaic delegation from Jerusalem. Josephus almost met his match in maneuvering for control of Galilee.

Throughout both of Josephus's accounts of affairs in Galilee, "the Galileans" are consistently hostile to the cities and/or the urban elite of Sepphoris and Tiberias and to those who dominate Gabara and Tarichaeae as well, in both accounts "the Galileans" usually refers to the people from the countryside (*chōra*), i.e., the peasantry, in a given area or in Galilee as a whole (e.g., *War* 2.602, 621–622; 3.199; *Life* 102, 243), often in distinction from the people of Tiberias and/or Sepphoris. Josephus uses *hoi galilaioi* to refer to the Galilean peasantry regardless of whether they are loyal to himself in the *Life* (30, 39, 66, 143, 177, 351) just as he had in the *War* (2.621–622; 3.110, 199, etc.). The only variation is that from a perspective beyond Galilee, "the Galileans" can refer to all residents of Galilee, including people in Sepphoris and Tiberias. Josephus thoroughly distorts his relationship with the Galilean peasants insofar as "the Galileans" figure as the key to his self-defense in the *Life*. He even has them acclaim him as "the benefactor and savior of their country" (*Life* 244, 259) when the delegation arrives from the Jerusalem provisional government to displace him from his command. In moments of greater realism and candor, however, he admits several examples of how he co-opted the Galilean peasants in his attempts to control one or another of the cities or to counter John of Gischala and how be kept their leaders as hostages under guard because he did not trust them (e.g., *Life* 79, 228). Obviously we should be extremely suspicious of Josephus's apologetic narcissism and of his claims about the peasants' devotion to himself. Indeed, Josephus himself indicates at several points that, far from being deceived by and loyal to him, the Galileans distrusted, challenged, and opposed him. While he presented the Jerusalem provisional government's concerns to the Herodian elite in Tiberias, the Galilean peasants in the area were helping to loot the royal palace (*Life* 66). They were not fooled by his secret plan to return goods they had plundered from the king Agrippa's finance officer and they were suspicious of his protection of the foreign officers of the king (*War* 595–597; *Life* 126–131, 149–152). Not surprisingly, they suspected that his real intention was "to betray the country to the Romans," distrusted his protestations to the contrary, and even (he says, credibly enough) attempted to kill him (*Life* 132–148; *War* 2.598–610). While peasants often appear overly trusting of those seeking alliances with them in times of social disruption and revolt, the Galilean peasants appear to have been healthily skeptical of the "general" from Jerusalem, and appear to have cooperated mainly when it suited their own concerns.

The Galilean peasants' hostility to the cities and/or city elite in Sepphoris and Tiberias is indisputable. It must have been present and at times intense, or Josephus could not have exploited it for his own purposes, as he repeatedly claims to have done. "The Galileans ... had the same detestation for the Tiberians that they had for the Sepphorites" (*Life* 384). This hostility had built up for decades out of the people's resentment at the way they had been treated by their rulers in the cities (e.g., *Life* 30, 39, 177). Josephus's tirades against his rival historian Justus, who held some official administrative position in Tiberias, provides a specific example of the intensity of the peasant resentment as well as of the reason for it in their rulers' exploitative machinations: "The Galileans, resenting the miseries which he had inflicted on them before the war, were embittered .against the Tiberians" (*Life* 392). Indeed, "the Galileans had cut off bis brothers' hands on a charge of forging letters prior to the outbreak of the hostilities" (*Life* 177). Not surprisingly, the Galilean peasantry seized the opportunity of the collapse of effective Roman or Herodian royal rule to exercise their intense hostility against those whom they viewed as their exploiters in Sepphoris and Tiberias (e.g., *Life* 66–67, 374–378, 381–384). While claiming to have mitigated its most extreme potential manifestations, Josephus unabashedly admits that he used the Galileans' hostility to Sepphoris in his attempts to control that city (*Life* 30, 107, 374–377). As in the case of the burning and looting the royal palace in Tiberias, the peasants in the area made common cause with the party of poor and sailors led by Jesus son of Sapphias inside the city against the Herodian elite who controlled the area on behalf of the king, just as their predecessors had for Antipas and Agrippa I. Given the political-economic structure of the Roman imperial order, Josephus's report that the peasantry's hostility to the Sepphoris and Tiberias elite was closely related to the latter's loyalty to Rome and/or king Agrippa II is highly credible. One incident concerning Tiberias should be sufficient to illustrate the conflicting power relations, in which their opposition to their ultimate rulers, the Romans, was connected with their hostility to their immediate rulers in the capital cities, in the very structure of the situation:

> The principal men from the council [of Tiberias] had written to the king inviting him to come and take over their city. The king promised to come, writing a letter in reply, which he handed Crispus, a groom of the bed-chamber, Judean by race, to convey to the Tiberians. On his arrival with the letter he was recognized by the Galileans who seized him and brought him to me. The news created general indignation and all were up in arms. On the following day large numbers flocked together from all quarters to the town of Asochis . . . loudly denouncing the Tiberians as traitors and friendly to the king, and asking permission to go down and exterminate their city. For they had the same detestation for the Tiberians as for the Sepphorites. (*Life* 381–384)

The historical role of the cities in Galilee as elsewhere in the Roman imperial order can be seen in the eventual Roman reconquest, in which troops from bases in the city resubjected the countryside, re-establishing the traditional power-relations in no uncertain terms. Both infantry and cavalry "made constant sallies and overran the surrounding country devastating the plains and pillaging the property of the countryfolk, invariably killing all capable of bearing arms and enslaving the weak" (*War* 3.59–63, 110).

For all the intense Galilean peasant hostility to the cities of Tiberias and Sepphoris, however, there is little in Josephus's accounts to indicate that they were actively engaged in a revolution against the Rome-imposed political-economic order. To the extent that they were armed, they had done it on their own (Josephus's claims to have organized and armed an army being utterly incredible). Yet there is no evidence that they mounted major or frequent attacks against the cities, hence difficult to imagine that they would have except for Josephus's restraining influence. The only remotely "insurrectionary" activity Josephus describes was clearly an ad hoc local occurrence.

> Some adventurous young men of Dabaritta [a village on the western slope of Mount Tabor] lay in wait for the wife of Ptolemy, the king's overseer, She was travelling in great state, protected by an escort of cavalry, from territory subject to the royal administration, into the region of Roman dominion, when, as she was crossing the Great Plain, they suddenly fell upon the cavalcade, compelled the lady to fly, and plundered all her baggage. They then came to me at Tarichaeae with four mules laden with apparel and other articles, besides a large pile of silver and five hundred pieces of gold. (*Life* 126–127)

Indeed it would be difficult to argue that the Galilean peasants were actively engaged in a revolt or insurrection in any sustained and organized way, unless defending yourself against the intentionally punitive and retaliatory Roman reconquest can be construed as somehow revolutionary. Once the Roman military briefly "pacified" Galilee and then withdrew in the summer of 66 CE, the Galilean villagers simply enjoyed the temporary realization of a typical peasant fantasy: living independent of taxation and other exploitation by landlords and rulers. Apparently the power-relations were such that the Roman agents in Sepphoris and the royal officers in Tiberias temporarily felt unable to carry out their usual duties of tax-collection and social control. Even villages in immediate proximity to the ruling cities were able, temporarily, to take a position remarkably independent of their once and future rulers. The village of Shikhin, for example, was resistant to direction from Jerusalem as well as temporarily independent of Sepphoris' and Roman rule (*Life* 230–233). Sepphorites, for their part, felt sufficiently vulnerable to potential attacks from the surrounding villagers that they hired the brigand Jesus and his horde of 800 to defend them. And the Herodian elite of Tiberias repeatedly attempted to arrange for Agrippa to reassert control there. But aside from the raid on the royal palace early on, we know of no organized popular assault on either city or on the urban elite (the attack on the Greeks in Tiberias was by the urban lower class there).[13]

---

13. A critical, skeptical reading of *Life* 373–380 suggests that if Josephus did take

Galileans under Jerusalem and Roman Rule

Some villagers did resist the Roman reconquest, in which the Roman troops systematically slaughtered and enslaved the people and destroyed their villages without consideration of whether combatants were present. Many peasants simply fled to mountain strongholds such as Tabor or fortress towns like Jotapata or Gischala. Whatever Josephus's role there may have been historically, the Romans conducted a major siege and assault at Jotapata, so those gathered there did "go down fighting."[14] Josephus's recitation of the heroics of a few Galileans from nearby villages such as Saba and Rumah has a ring of credibility (*War* 3.229–233). Josephus claims that at Japha, "the largest village in Galilee," near Nazareth and Sepphoris, the villagers offered heroic resistance to the Romans attack (*War* 3.289–306). Similarly at Tarichaeae, although the residents of the town were quiescent, Galileans from the nearby countryside offered resistance (*War* 3.492–502). And "a vast multitude" who had fled to Mount Tabor held out as long as possible against the relentless Roman attack (*War* 4.45–61).

Throughout Josephus's accounts of affairs in Galilee, it is clear that the Galilean peasants' activity was distinct from, if at points similar to, the actions of the large troops of brigands that formed out of the social dislocation leading up to the Great Revolt.[15] Josephus's accounts, moreover, must be read critically in any attempt to discern banditry and to distinguish it from ad hoc insurrectionary activities by rebellious bands of peasants still based in villages.[16] The behavior of brigand bands in 66–67 CE in Galilee appears to have been every bit as diverse as the other local and regional conflicts examined above, with the situation in and around Gischala being unique insofar as banditry can, but rarely does, flow directly into peasant revolt. Factors such as taxation, indebtedness, drought and famine, repressive political administration, and in Galilee in particular shifting political jurisdictions and frequent change of rulers during the 40s and 50s contributed to the social and economic difficulties of the peasantry and the rising incidence of banditry. In the years just prior to the outbreak of the Great Revolt banditry escalated to epidemic proportions in Galilee as well

---

Sepphoris by assault, he used his own trained mercenaries. Yet it would be credible that the Galilean peasants would only have needed a little encouragement and the occasion of such an assault to take out their resentment on the ruling elite of Sepphoris.

14. See Aviam, "Yodefat/Jotapata."
15. Horsley, *Galilee*, 85–86, 264–68.
16. Contra Schwartz, "Josephus in Galilee, 296–300."

as in Judea.[17] In Galilee banditry was of relatively greater importance in the developing social turmoil, in contrast to Judea, with its diverse types of popular resistance, such as prophetic movements and "dagger men." Josephus's accounts indicate that the large brigand groups already in existence constituted one of two principal kinds of resistance to the initial Roman attempt to regain control of Galilee in the summer of 66 CE. While Sepphoris was welcoming the Roman forces, "all the rebels and brigands fled to the mountains in the heart of Galilee" where they were able temporarily to hold off a Roman legion (*War* 2.511). As happened repeatedly later in Judea, the Roman practice or systematic devastation ironically generated the very insurrection they were supposedly suppressing by generating thousands of fugitives (e.g., *War* 2.504–505; cf. 3.60–63). Other fugitives from the Greek and Syrian cities' attacks on their Jewish inhabitants or dependent villages may also have swelled the ranks of the brigands (*War* 2.457–480; *Life* 77–78, 105).

Epidemic banditry, however, while perhaps an indication of social breakdown, is not necessarily revolutionary. Once Galilee slipped into political anarchy, it would be difficult to view the large brigand horde that formed as fitting Hobsbawm's model of "social banditry," flexible as his discussion is.[18] The large brigand bands appear rather to have become pawns in the struggles between the principal leaders and cities during the year leading up to the Roman reconquest. As already noted, Sepphoris, which remained loyal to its Roman patrons, hired Jesus and his band of 800 as mercenaries to defend them against the potential attacks of the Galilean peasants-and Josephus. (Presumably the Jesus hired by Sepphoris is different from "the Galilean named Jesus" mentioned later as "staying in Jerusalem with a company of 600 men under arms" whom the Jerusalem junta engaged to protect the Pharisaic delegation sent to displace Josephus in Galilee, *Life* 200.) The greatest manipulator of bandit groups in Galilee was probably Josephus himself. The source of the power he wielded in Galilee

---

17. See further, Horsley, "Josephus and the Bandits"; Horsley, "Ancient Jewish Banditry"; Isaac, "Bandits in Judaea and Arabia," 176–83; Shaw, "Bandits in the Roman Empire."

18. In a rather quantitative analysis of brigands supposedly involved in revolt in Galilee, Schwartz ("Josephus in Galilee," 297–300), while apparently following my earlier work on banditry in many key respects, states that it is "marred by the author's naïve (or ideologically motivated) over-use of the 'social bandit' model, derived from E. Hobsbawm (1959, 1969)," apparently preferring the analysis of Blok ("The Peasant and the Brigand"). The analysis of the English social historian, however, is far more sophisticated and flexible in raising questions about and accommodating differences in political-economic circumstances and power relations than that of Blok.

during 66–67 was surely his own mercenary force and bodyguards. But he also manipulated the peasants into a "protection racket," paying for their freedom from harassment from bands of brigands who then were to report to and take orders from Josephus:

> I also summoned the most stalwart of the brigands and, seeing that it would be impossible to disarm them, persuaded the people [*to plēthos*] to pay them as mercenaries, remarking that it was better to give them a small sum voluntarily than to submit to raids upon their property. I then bound them by oath not to enter the district [*chōra*] unless they were sent for or their pay was in arrears, and dismissed them with injunctions to refrain from attacking the Romans or their neighbors. (*Life* 77–78)

Throughout his manipulation of both peasants and brigand groups Josephus's "chief concern" was in effect counter-revolutionary: "the preservation of the peace in Galilee" (*Life* 78). Even if there was any revolutionary potential among the bandit groups of Lower Galilee, it was cut off by the city of Sepphoris, Josephus, and perhaps other local power-holders, who used them as mercenaries in the service of other interests.

Only in Upper Galilee around Gischala, so far as we know, did the escalating banditry flow into rebellion and perhaps even stimulate wider peasant revolt, rather than be manipulated by those attempting to restore the established order.[19] Through Josephus's sharp hostility to his principal rival for influence in Galilee we can still discern two significant aspects of the relationship between John, the bandits in this frontier area, and the people of Gischala. Bandits, many of whom were fugitives from across the frontier in the villages of Tyre, constituted a significant part of the fighting force that provided the basis of John's expanding influence in Galilee (e.g., *War* 2.588, 625; *Life* 94, 101, 233, 292, 301, 304, 371–372). However partially or completely John dictated their actions, his agenda appears to have been relatively revolutionary, especially when compared with that of Josephus. John's attempt to "seize the imperial grain stores in the villages of upper Galilee" was a clear act of revolt against Roman rule (*Life* 71–73). Moreover, in contrast to the capitulation of Tiberias and Josephus's self-serving surrender at Jotapata, John and his forces at Gischala resisted as long as they could and then headed for what must have appeared as the center of revolt and a more defensible fortress in Jerusalem (*War* 4.98–120). In the introduction to his account of the Gischalans' final struggle to maintain

---

19. See further Horsley, "Ancient Jewish Banditry."

their independence, Josephus himself explains how perhaps the escalation of banditry in the area stimulated the Gischalan peasants to revolt.

> In Gischala, a small town in Galilee, . . . the inhabitants were inclined to peace, being mainly farmers [*geōrgoi*] whose whole attention was devoted to the prospects of-the harvest. But they had been afflicted by the invasion of numerous gangs of brigands, from whom some members of the community had caught the contagion. (*War* 4.84)

As Hobsbawm points out, although rare, this is exactly what can happen in certain circumstances. The earlier attacks on Gischala by Tyre, Gabara, and Sogane undoubtedly contributed both to the escalating banditry in the area and to the politicization of the peasants of Gischala. Thus from these and related factors, in contrast to what happened in Lower Galilee, the peasants and brigand groups in and around Gischala joined in common insurrection against Roman rule, as well as resisted Josephus's machinations as a representative of Jerusalem rule.

To summarize this survey of events in Galilee in 66–67 CE: there was no unifying ideology and no coherent anti-Roman revolt in Galilee.[20] There were, instead, a number of interrelated local or regionally based conflicts. Sepphoris remained consistently loyal to Rome. Tiberias split between its Herodian elite and a more revolutionary popular faction. "The Galileans," by which Josephus refers to the villagers of Lower Galilee, directed their hostilities against Sepphoris and the ruling elite of Tiberias, often making common cause with the popular party in the latter city. Although the elite of the toparchy capital Tarichaeae remained loyal to Agrippa II, there was less conflict with the surrounding villagers who were ready to resist Roman reconquest. Any "revolutionary" potential of the burgeoning brigand bands was vitiated by their hiring as mercenaries by Sepphoris and Josephus and perhaps others. Distinctively in Upper Galilee in and around Gischala, Josephus's principal rival for influence in Galilee, John, led a coalition of peasants and brigand bands partly composed of refugees from the Tyrian frontier, and both challenged Josephus for domination of Galilee and resisted the Roman reconquest, finally fleeing to join the resistance in Jerusalem. With the exception of the Herodian "leading men" of Tiberias and the elite who dominated Tarichaeae, all of the various towns and groups

---

20. Contra the archaeological evidence and suggestions of Berlin, "Romanization and Anti-Romanization in Pre-Revolt Galilee"; and Avshalom-Gorni and Getzov, "Phoenicians and Jews."

successfully resisted Josephus's attempts to assert Jerusalem's or his own control in Galilee. In sum, I conclude that there was no coherent, unified, anti-Roman "revolt" in Galilee in 66–7 CE, but rather a number of overlapping but independent conflicts, rooted in local and regional history within the broader structure of the Roman imperial order in Judea and Galilee. While local or regional in their particular manifestations, these conflicts' principal common division was between the rulers, who were based in cities, and the ruled, whether in cities or villages.

JUDEA AND JERUSALEM

It is pertinent to compare the conclusions of this analysis of multiple conflicts raging in Galilee in 66–67 CE with the patterns discernible in the Great Revolt in Judea and Jerusalem. There also, although there was more of a coherent and sometimes coordinated revolt, local factors rooted in local history were of crucial importance. The principal division, again, was between urban-based rulers and village- or city-based ruled. The Great Revolt in Judea and Jerusalem, however, differs from that in Galilee, insofar as the former gained momentum and intensity long after the latter was fully suppressed by the Roman reconquest. Events in Galilee, moreover, were relatively remote and detached from events in Judea and Jerusalem. Ancestral Judean-Jerusalem institutions of the temple and its high priesthood played little or no role in Galilee, while these were central to the Great Revolt in the south.

It is important to distinguish the structural roots of the Great Revolt from its sequence and patterns.[21] Judea was ruled by a temple-state headed by an ancestral high-priestly aristocracy. As is increasingly evident from recent analysis of post-exilic prophetic literature, apocalyptic literature, and Qumran literature, however, the imperially sponsored temple-state and high-priestly incumbents had never been completely accepted by all elements in Judean society, nor even by the scribal retainers of the temple-state. Periodic conflicts had emerged among rival priestly groups, whether between rival high-priestly factions or between the ordinary priests and

---

21. I have researched and discussed the structural political-economic-religious divisions and conflicts in Judean history in several books and articles, particularly in *Jesus and the Spiral of Violence*; *Sociology and the Jesus Movement*; *Galilee*; *Jesus and Empire*; and *Scribes, Visionaries and the Politics of Second Temple Judea*. See also Chaps. 1 and 2 above.

Power Vacuum and Power Struggle in 66–67 CE

the incumbent high priests. Such recent recognitions must make us all the more uncertain about the basic loyalty of the Judean peasants to the temple and supposedly hereditary high priesthood. The Hasmonean dynasty, itself an "illegitimate" upstart family of rebels who consolidated their position by arrangement with imperial regimes and wars of expansion, evoked substantial opposition and internal division, particularly in its last generations. After systematically eliminating the Hasmoneans, the Roman-installed client king Herod reconstituted the priestly aristocracy from Judean priestly families from Egypt and Babylon. These families had no previous relations either with the Judean priestly clans or with the region's ordinary people. Thus the priestly aristocracy that the Romans entrusted with control of Judea after Herod's death and the deposition of his son Archelaus had little legitimacy, their power depending on Roman patronage that worked primarily through Roman governors. The priestly aristocracy, moreover, became increasingly predatory on the people they ruled. They built themselves lavish mansions in the New City in Jerusalem while gradually manipulating Judean peasants into indebtedness, through which they could exploit their labor and extract their produce. This pattern of exploitation was further compounded by the remaining Herodian families who had established estates at various points, including the Judean hill country northwest of Jerusalem.

Social conflicts escalated steadily during the decades preceding the outbreak of revolt in the summer of 66 CE. In Jerusalem itself, where the populace was economically dependent on the temple apparatus, these included protests over the oppressive or insensitive actions of Roman governors.[22] The priestly aristocracy did little to mediate.[23] In the countryside popular prophets led movements of liberation inspired by fantastic visions of a new exodus or new conquest (Theudas and the "Egyptian" Judean prophet respectively). Particularly after the drought and famine of the late 40s deepened the crisis for many Judean peasants, the always endemic social banditry became epidemic at times, a telling sign of the breakdown of social order.[24] Far from attempting to mitigate such circumstances and attend to the disintegrating social order, the four principal high priestly families exacerbated it, competing for influence with and appointment by

---

22. Among many treatments, Horsley, "High Priests and the Politics of Roman Palestine."

23. Horsley, "Menahem in Jerusalem."

24. Horsley, "Josephus and the Bandits"; Horsley, *Jesus and the Spiral of Violence*.

the Roman governors and even gathering gangs of thugs which they used both to seize tithes from the threshing floors, depriving the ordinary priests of their living, and to attack each other.[25] In this respect I appreciate and affirm the important, careful analysis of Martin Goodman in delineating the high-priestly factions and their struggle for power, particularly in the last decades prior to the Great Revolt, as one of the principal factors leading to its outbreak. The fundamental division was between the increasingly exploited peasantry and frustrated Jerusalem populace, on the one hand, and the high-priestly and Herodian aristocracy and Roman rulers, on the other. In order for a revolt to happen, however, as has been pointed out for modern times, the ruling class must come to a point where it can no longer effectively rule. And the struggle between various high-priestly factions compounded the illegitimacy of the priestly aristocracy and their alienation from the people and the ordinary priests sufficiently that by the mid-60s they could no longer control Judean society, to the specific extent that they were no longer able to collect the tribute for Rome, which was in arrears (*War* 2.405).

In Jerusalem and Judea the sequence of the Great Revolt unfolded in three phases: the initial eruption in the summer of 66 CE; the temporarily successful attempt by the high priestly aristocracy and leading Pharisees to control it from late 66 CE through early 68 CE; and the coalescence of popular forces from the Judean countryside and their entry into Jerusalem during 68 and 69 CE, where they held our against the Roman reconquest until Jerusalem was destroyed in 70 CE.

The first phase not only was concentrated in Jerusalem, but involved Jerusalemites, including ordinary priests and renegade high priests as leading participants. In the deteriorating series of events leading up to more revolutionary actions, the Jerusalem "crowd" engaged in protests over what they considered outrages and provocations by Florus, the Roman governor and his troops (*War* 293-332). Eventually the Jerusalemites began fighting back against the Roman troops unleashed to "pacify" the city (*War* 2.325-329), and Florus simply withdrew, leaving the ruling aristocracy to bail themselves out of the now uncontrollable situation (*War* 331-332). A more serious act was the symbolic one of the cessation of sacrifices for the emperor by the priests, led by the renegade high priest, the temple-captain Eleazar son of Ananias (*War* 409). Despite abuse by Florus, the high priests,

---

25. Horsley, *Jesus and the Spiral of Violence*, 46-47; Goodman, *Ruling Class of Judaea*, 20 passim.

other "notables" and leading Pharisees desperately attempted to calm the crowd and keep minimal control on the deteriorating situation while attempting to obtain help from the Roman officials and Herodian client king Agrippa II (*War* 2.318, 320, 333–342, 410–421).

The situation had degenerated into class warfare within the city, with the renegade Eleazar son of Ananias leading the rebellious ordinary priests and populace against his own father as well as other aristocrats in attacks on their mansions, the royal palaces and their garrisons, and the public archives where debt-records were kept all significant targets of popular resentment against the ruling class (*War* 422–441). They were joined by the *sicarioi*, the terrorist group now led by Menahem (a descendant of the teacher Judas, who had organized the Fourth Philosophy and resistance to the Roman tribute in 6 CE) who were apparently intent on taking the leadership of the Great Revolt now underway in Jerusalem. The Jerusalemites and priests led by Eleazar, however, suspicious of Menahem's "messianic" pretentions, rejected their leadership (*War* 433–438). After the urban insurrectionaries massacred the Roman garrison, Cestius Gallus, the Legate of Syria, launched an expedition to put down the rebellion (*War* 499–500), At this point the rebellion spilled beyond the bounds of the city, as Judean rebel forces effectively opposed the Roman troops' march on the city, their attempt to take control of it, and their retreat, which turned into a rout. High-priestly elements attempted to turn the city over to the Romans, but fighting forces apparently from the countryside now joined with urban elements to drive the Romans effectively out of the country (*War* 517–555).

Although it eventually involved surrounding villagers, the first phase of the Great Revolt in Judea was both based largely in Jerusalem and took place mainly in the city, The first phase was, moreover, as much a class war of the ordinary priests and populace of Jerusalem against their high priestly rulers as it was a rebellion against Roman overlords. In addition to battling Roman troops, the insurrectionaries attacked the public archives housing the records of debts and the mansions and even the persons of the high-priestly rulers and drove out King Agrippa II. The claim that the "ruling class" of Judea was actively involved in the revolt at this stage cannot be supported from a critical reading of Josephus's accounts. Eleazar son of Simon, who emerged from these battles in control of Roman spoil, may have been an ordinary priestly leader, but nothing indicates that he was from a high-priestly family. And Simon bar Giora, who captured much of the Romans' baggage in the rout of Cestius Gallus at Beth Horan, was not a priest, let alone a high priest, but a leader of popular forces generated from the province of Akrabatene. While a few renegade military officers of Roman client kings participated in these battles, there is no mention of any members of the Judean "ruling class" as involved in action against the Romans other than the temple-captain Eleazar son of Ananias, who led cessation of sacrifices for the emperor and the attack on the public archives.[26]

In the second phase of the Great Revolt some of the high-priestly figures who had not already fled Jerusalem apparently managed to put together a provisional government in a desperate attempt to reassert control over their society (and then to reach some accommodation with the Romans). Given the Roman system of indirect rule through native elites, this was their only chance of retaining their position of power and privilege. As discussed above, Josephus's portrayal of the transition in *War* 2.562–568 is simply incredible, because it contradicts itself. It cannot have been "those who had pursued Cestius" who engineered the appointment of generals because those who pursued Cestius were either sent out to remote posts, as in the case of the high priest Eleazar son of Ananias, or excluded from any role in the provisional government and conduct of affairs, as in the case of both Eleazar son of Simon and Simon bar Giora. The provisional government was clearly dominated by high-priestly figures, headed by Ananus son of Ananus and Jesus son of Gamalas, and eventually included leading Pharisees such as Simon son of Gamaliel. Whether or not the high-priestly provisional government had to "pretend" to be organizing resistance to the inevitable Roman reconquest, they were clearly attempting to control the society. Not only did they push the earlier revolutionary leaders out of the way, but Ananus even sent an "army" into the district of Acrabatene to push Simon bar Giora out of the area where he was still "ransacking the houses of the wealthy" (*War* 2.652–653). The principal division remained that

---

26. Goodman's basic argument that "the power struggle within the Jewish ruling class" was a "crucial link in the chain of causation" (*Ruling Class of Judaea*, 19) of the Great Revolt is a crucial supplement to discussion of the "causes" of the Revolt. His careful and detailed analysis agrees with my own limited analysis (Horsley, "High Priests and Politics of Roman Palestine"), as he comments in several notes. The contention that members of the Judean ruling class were involved in the Great Revolt, however, is based on only these three figures. His discussion seems inconsistently critical in rejecting or accepting particular accounts in Josephus's histories and involves inconsistently applied criteria for speculating about the class-standing of leaders such as Eleazar ben Simon and Simon bar Giora. Eleazar son of Ananias would rather appear to be the proverbial "exception that proves the rule"—in this case the sole renegade member of the high priestly aristocracy, and not a typical case from which a broader generalization can be made.

between the high priestly "coup" or "counter-revolution" and the popular urban and countryside rebels whom they were attempting to suppress or manipulate.

In the third phase of the Great Revolt in Judea and Jerusalem, popular forces emerged from various districts of the countryside and moved into Jerusalem both to take control of the city and to prepare for the Roman reconquest. The emergence of these popular movements was either directly provoked by the Roman advance in 67–68 CE or made possible by their delay in advancing toward Jerusalem until 70 CE, after Vespasian had secured his position as emperor. First, bands of what Josephus calls "brigands" forming in flight from the Roman "scorched-earth" practices in their advance toward Jerusalem through northwestern Judea coalesced in Jerusalem, forming a coalition calling itself the "Zealots."[27] They attacked wealthy Herodians still in the city, probably because of their previous exploitation of the peasants in northwest Judea, where many Herodian estates were apparently located (*War* 4.138–142). When the leaders of the high-priestly provisional government became alarmed and attempted to check the Zealots, the latter invited forces from the Idumean countryside to enter the city. The latter eliminated the high-priestly leaders of the provisional government, Ananus and Jesus (*War* 4.228–235, 316), after which most of them withdrew again to Idumea. John of Gischala and his followers from Upper Galilee meanwhile moved into alliance with the Zealots, then split with them, in the principal factional strife among the popular forces now controlling Jerusalem from the summer of 68 CE to the summer of, 69 CE. Simon bar Giora, who had meanwhile been building his popular movement in southeastern Judea and Idumea, finally entered Jerusalem with the most numerous fighting force of all, and thereafter controlled most of the city outside of the temple, still in the control of John and the Zealots (Horsley 1984).[28] Each of these peasant forces from the countryside, moreover, attacked the Herodians and/or the priestly aristocrats who still remained in the city) thus continuing the class warfare from the first two phases of the Great Revolt.[29]

27. Horsley, "The Zealots."
28. Horsley, "Popular Messianic Movements."
29. Goodman's historical construction of leading figures and their followers engaged in the Great Revolt (*Ruling Class of Judaea*) seems to work on limiting assumptions about (insurrectionary) movements. He appears to assume that only figures from the ruling class are capable of leadership and, therefore, that any leader in the Great Revolt must have been from the ruling class. And he appears to assume that the principle or even only

Galileans under Jerusalem and Roman Rule

By the time the Romans finally mobilized their forces for the reconquest, there were thus four popular groups from different districts of the countryside in Jerusalem awaiting their assault: the Zealots from northwest Judea, the Idumeans from the south, John's smaller contingent from Upper Galilee, and finally the largest force, under Simon bar Giora, from southeastern Judea and Idumea. Their parallel but uncoordinated emergence may seem somewhat similar to popular insurrections in the twentieth century. In Mexico in 1910-14, in Algeria and Viet Nam in the 1950s and 1960s, and in El Salvador in the 1970s and 1980s, rebel movements emerged in several different areas of the countryside, at first separate if not competing and only gradually forming "national liberation fronts." In ancient Judea, similarly, even once they had all entered Jerusalem, as long as the Romans delayed their attack, these popular forces feuded with and fought each other. Not until the Romans advanced did they combine forces to resist the siege and eventual Roman attack. The third phase of the Revolt was thus carried out by several peasant movements, only they fought from the fortified city of Jerusalem, not by guerrilla warfare in the remote countryside, as had the Maccabees and their twentieth century counterparts.

---

motive for leadership in revolt is the drive for power and the only motive for ordinary people to fight is monetary reward (and that men can be mobilized into fighting forces only after they have been transformed from peasants into bandits ready to respond to such monetary inducement). Comparative material from biblical history as well as modern "peasant revolts," however, indicate concrete revolts are formed in far more complex combinations. Most popular movements produce popular leaders from among their own ranks, usually marginal figures previously involved in some contact with affairs outside the usual village relations who then make alliances with other leaders, including higher status figures. Often local "big-men," prominent local figures, take leading roles in a crisis situation, e.g., as leader of "peasant revolts" (e.g., Sheba, who led the second massive revolt against King David [2 Samuel 20]). Simon bar Giora and John of Gischala may well have been local "big-men" at the beginning of the Great Revolt. Sometimes, but rarely, an alienated ruling class figure becomes leader of a popular movement or revolt (e.g., David's son Absalom became leader of the first massive popular revolt against David [2 Samuel 15-19]; Jeroboam, Solomon's officer over forced labor for the tribe of Joseph, became leader of the ten northern tribes' rebellion from the Davidic monarchy [1 Kings 12]). The renegade Eleazar son of Ananias appears to have retained a following as long as he was operating within the city of Jerusalem, but disappeared from a serious leadership role once sent out to the remote district of Idumea. As I have attempted to demonstrate in several different cases (Horsley, "Josephus and the Bandits"; "Popular Messianic Movements"; "Menahem in Jerusalem"; and "The Zealots"), these are the sorts of social relations and social circumstances that should be taken into account in analysis of the various groups and leaders involved in the Great Revolt if we are to attain any precision in our historical construction.

4

Bandits, Messiahs, and Longshoremen
Popular Unrest in Galilee around the Time of Jesus

THAT OUR TEXTBOOKS USE Pharisees, Sadducees, and Essenes/Qumran as the principal comparative material for Jesus and the synoptic gospel tradition is a mark of how removed we have been from the social world of Jesus and his followers. These groups represented a tiny minority at the upper echelons of ancient Judean society. As the rulers or representatives of the rulers of the society, they were Jesus' opponents. But they surely do not provide appropriate parallels to Jesus and his movement. To reach a more concrete and precise understanding of Jesus we would need to know about life among the common people of ancient Palestine. Until archaeologists make some unexpected discoveries, however, we are dependent on literary sources, and that means, except for the gospel tradition itself, information provided by, and usually about, the elite who could write. About the only time that ordinary people made the pages of literary historical sources was when they caused trouble for the elite. Thus for information on the common people we must focus on figures and movements or incidents that disturbed the tranquility so valued by the rulers.

We have known of movements among the common people through the histories of Josephus. But in our defensive posture vis-à-vis modern scientific criticism—and choosing to view Jesus in our own image—we have tended in recent generations to ignore embarrassing features of Jesus' ministry such as healing miracles and opposition to the established order and concentrate on Jesus' teachings abstracted from concrete historical context.

Galileans under Jerusalem and Roman Rule

As we now begin to take more seriously the concrete circumstances of Jesus and his movement, we are left ill-prepared to evaluate our fragmentary data and to formulate the appropriate historical questions. It seems clear that comparisons with figures and movements among the peasantry bring us closer to the concrete social context of Jesus and his movement. Because our information is so limited and fragmentary, it seems appropriate as well as attractive to utilize figures and movements from anywhere in Palestine and movements over several generations around the time of Jesus. How might things appear differently, however, were we to focus only on popular movements in Galilee?

Although we have some other data for the social-historical context, we are dependent basically on Josephus for fragments of information on popular phenomena in Galilee. That he was there himself gives us at least a minimal reason for taking his accounts seriously. But he is a hostile witness who despises the popular leaders and movements which he was attempting to control as a representative of the government in Jerusalem. And the principal agenda in his reports is either a glorification of his own role as a great general in a war of monumental import (*The Jewish War*) or a self-serving defense of his own actions (*Life*). One recent analysis of Josephus' accounts of events in Galilee has concluded that they are utterly unreliable, but then constructs a highly simplified alternative history based selectively on some of Josephus' statements with no apparently consistent criteria of selection.[1] A more recent study of Josephus provides a more sophisticated grasp of the historical context in which Josephus must be read and suggests that, with a continually critical and somewhat skeptical eye, we can utilize Josephus' accounts for cautious historical reconstruction of circumstances and events ancient Galilee.[2]

Further investigations of affairs in Galilee must take into account the work of Freyne. It is just one more indication of the stimulation he has provided that some of his generalizations may require qualification. Of some importance for the discussion below, for example, he assumes and asserts but has not demonstrated "Galilean attachment to the temple generally" or "the basic loyalty of Galilean Jews for Jerusalem and its temple: But there would appear to be more reason to conclude that ordinary Galileans would have viewed Jerusalem and the temple somewhat critically as the center from which they were ruled and taxed.

---

1. Cohen, *Josephus in Galilee and Rome*; cf. the review by H. R. Moehring.
2. Rajak, *Josephus*.

BANDITRY: ENDEMIC AND EPIDEMIC

Much of the discussion of Jesus and his historical context in the last generation worked on the assumption that Judea was a hotbed of violent rebellion against Roman rule. The modern scholarly construct of "The Zealots" crystalized the issue for most of that discussion. Closer analysis of our sources for the period, particularly the histories of Josephus, have indicated that although there was indeed widespread revolt in 4 BCE as well as in 66–70 and 132–135 CE, there was very little violent insurrectionary activity anywhere in Jewish Palestine in the interim. There was a good deal of social unrest, including periodic protests over particular abuses and some distinctive types of popular movements. But there is no evidence for any organized or longstanding "nationalist" or "resistance" movements such as that imagined in the Zealot movement. The group actually called the Zealots did not even emerge until the middle of the Great Revolt of 66–70. An important part of this new view of the diversity among popular movements at the time is the recognition that *lēstai* is not just another term that Josephus used for "the Zealots," but in fact, in most cases, a term for what appears to be "social banditry." If that is the case, then far from being "revolutionary," the *lēstai* were simply what Hobsbawm calls a "pre-political" form of social protest against particularly local conditions and injustices, and lacked a larger view of the whole society or a critique of the dominant social order.[3] Only when conditions seriously disintegrated in the 60s did this banditry typical of most peasant societies escalate into epidemic proportions and merge with a wider peasant revolt against the high priestly rulers as well as Roman rule.

Freyne has been at pains to argue that Galilee was not full of revolutionary activity against Roman rule.[4] Still working on the assumption that Judea itself was filled with revolutionary ideology, he insists that Galilee, by contrast, was strikingly calm and peaceful. Recognition of the actual pre-political (and non-revolutionary) character of ancient Judean and Galilean *lēstai* would provide strong support of his contention regarding Galilee which is further reinforced by the realization that the whole picture of a nationalist revolutionary movement in Jewish society lacks historical evidence. Freyne, however, appears to have understood the concept of "social banditry" in terms of the old concept of "the Zealots," as if it were a political

---

3. Hobsbawm, *Primitive Rebels*, chap. 2; Hobsbawm, *Bandits* (rev. ed.).
4. The dominant theme that recurs throughout Freyne, *Galilee*.

or even revolutionary phenomenon with a "religious component."[5] Ironically, then, the phenomenon of banditry in Galilee becomes subsumed into his earlier concern to deny that there was revolutionary ideology and activity in Galilee. Freyne's development of a concept of banditry far broader than that in the literature of banditry and his application on it like a social scientific model to Galilean material, however, serves as a stimulus to review critically both concept and procedure.

Studies of banditry such as Hobsbawm's, upon which I depended heavily in previous analyses of ancient Judean and Galilean banditry, attempt to make generalizations about typical characteristics of social phenomena that recur across several societies, hence should not be used in a wooden, "cookie cutter" manner. Hobsbawm tends not to make generalizations with "never" or "always" in them. In characterizing social banditry and other forms of "primitive rebellion" he was writing comparative social history, not constructing law-like models of social science. We would be moving far beyond Hobsbawm's stimulating characterizations to think that we can "apply the criteria for social banditry" to a given situation (my emphasis). Rather, we can only attempt to reconstruct some aspects of ancient social history where our limited sources allow, utilizing Hobsbawm's comparative material and analysis to formulate appropriate questions.

This means that we must attend to what sort of characteristics the comparative material indicates often pertain to "social banditry" and take note of the significant variations and contingencies. For example, although bandits usually share the religion or values of the people from whom they come, they are not especially religious, and social banditry could hardly be called a "religious phenomenon." Although brigands often enjoy the support of the peasants in their area, nothing in the literature on banditry would suggest that there would ever be a "widescale popular uprising' in reaction to suppression of brigands. Hobsbawm suggested that often (but by no means always) social bandits do get involved in "righting wrongs," as in the case of Eleazar ben Dinai; but it would surely be rare to find bandits "conducting an independent judicial system on behalf of the peasants." (The latter sounds more like a revolutionary regime, and probably occurs only in modern times, although Gottwald and others might see the "judges" of early Israel as an ancient example.) One of Hobsbawm's principal points was that banditry is a prepolitical and "primitive form of social protest." One of the things that ordinary social banditry lacks is a sense of "the new order"

---

5. Freyne, "Bandits in Galilee."

that one might hope for. Another principal point is that social banditry sometimes but rarely precedes or escalates into wider peasant rebellion. If there is a situation of wider insurrection, then not only has the situation changed dramatically from that in which social banditry usually arises, but the character and role (and size) of brigand groups has changed. Thus if we want to appreciate the possible impact or role of social banditry in the origins of wider revolts, we cannot juxtapose incidences of ordinary social banditry in a non-insurrectionary situation and those of banditry in the midst of a wider rebellion (and we must be sensitive further to situations of transition and aftermath).

In order to achieve some degree of precision with regard to social phenomena it would be prudent to use the concept of "social banditry" somewhat as Hobsbawm does in regard to European phenomena. That limited and relatively precise usage seems to fit most of the cases for which Josephus uses *lēstai* with the exclusion of the cases in which he qualifies the term ("another species of banditry") or utilizes it as a political epithet (e.g., for the Zealots proper in Jerusalem when they are no longer operating as brigands). Freyne uses the concept more broadly to include not only rural phenomena but urban as well, e.g., those whom Josephus clearly indicates were "another species" of bandit's (i.e., the terrorist group called the Sicarii). He even includes groups for which Josephus never uses the term *lēstai*, such as Jesus son of Sapphias and the "faction of "the sailors and the destitute" in Tiberias (who, along with some Galileans, attacked the royal palace there in 66),[6] and the "young men" (*neaniskoi*) of the village of Dabaritta (who Josephus claims as some of the "guards" posted in the great plain in his more boastful account in the *War*, *Life* 126–129; cf. *War* 2.595–598). It is unclear, however, what the Sicarii in Jerusalem, the *neaniskoi* of Dabaritta or the *aporoi* of Tiberias have in common with those Josephus calls *lēstai* in an unqualified sense, other than the carrying out an attack on the rulers' persons or property.

In his lengthy argument that Galilee was not a hotbed of revolutionary activity, Freyne was still operating with the scholarly construct of "the Zealots" as a longstanding and widespread movement. One of the principal supports of that construct was the assumption that Josephus ordinarily used *lēstai* in reference to "the Zealots." Freyne is thus understandably at pains to explain away Josephus' reports about the *archilēstēs* Ezechias murdered

---

6. Josephus does label them "the brigand-band" a year later as they resisted the Roman take-over of Tiberias (*War* 3.450).

by the young Herod in 47 BCE and the *lēstai* dwelling in the caves near Arbela nearly a decade later. His claim that Ezechias and his band were Hasmonean nobles enables him to conclude that there "was no widespread involvement of the whole population."[7] This suggestion, however, lacks evidence and historical credibility.

First, his conception of a "native" "land-owning" nobility does not fit the historical situation of Galilee under the last of the Hasmoneans as the Romans were taking control in the eastern Mediterranean. That the mothers of the murdered brigands were appealing to Hyrcanus would appear to be decisive against the hypothesis that the brigands were Hasmonean nobles, for they could hardly have appealed to the rival (enemy) Hasmonean ruler. Like other principalities in the ancient Near East, the Hasmonean regime in Palestine had high ranking and intermediate officers who commanded the military and/or collected the taxes and/or otherwise administered political-economic affairs. The highest ranking officers in particular enjoyed substantial income from prebendal estates, and they and other officers in charge of tax-collection in regional centers surely came into control of additional agricultural and other revenues, perhaps through the credit-debt mechanism. But that does not constitute being a "large landowner." The basis of their power and wealth was their office in the regime. It seems difficult to imagine what sort of basis they could have had in the countryside to be able to sustain a struggle against Herod for years and decades, as imagined by Freyne.

Second, Josephus, who provides our only sources for these and related events, writes nothing that would suggest that Ezechias and company were Hasmonean nobles. It would appear, rather, that Freyne's claim is dependent on and an important component of a much oversimplified reconstruction of events in Palestine in the 50s and 40s BCE. Freyne believes that Herod's murder of Ezechias (in 47?) "caused the Hasmonean aristocracy that was prepared to go along with Roman rule to join Antigonus rather than Hyrcanus," and uses as an illustration "the second in command (*hypostratēgos*) in Jerusalem," Peitholaus, who "fought against Alexander, *Ant.* 14.84, but for Antigonus, *Ant.* 14.120!"[8] The situation and unfolding events in Palestine (focused on the conflict between the Hasmonean rivals Hyrcanus and Aristobulus), however, compounded by the shifting sides of

---

7. Freyne, *Galilee*, 68, with the claim simply reasserted without further argument or documentation in "Bandits in Galilee."

8. Freyne, *Galilee*, 63, 93n20.

the Roman civil war, were far more complex than a simple opposition of Hyrcanus, Antipater, and his son Herod siding with Rome vs. the Hasmonean nobles siding with Antigonus and the Parthians. In fact, according to Josephus, Hasmonean officials had begun to defect nearly a decade before Herod's appointment as governor of Galilee. Peitholaus had deserted not to Antigonus but to his father Aristobulus with 1000 men in 56 BCE, and was killed by Cassius (in 52?) when he was attempting to rally Aristobulus' partisans (*War* 1.172, 180). Moreover, to complicate matters, Caesar himself had sent Aristobulus back to Syria. Evidently the political sides were constantly shifting and, for Hasmonean officers, the outcome was utterly unclear, with much maneuvering for position. In 43 BCE, several years after the elimination of Ezechias, Malichus, a Hasmonean officer loyal to Hyrcanus, had Antipater poisoned, whereupon Herod avenged his father's death by having Malichus assassinated (*War* 1.223–230; *Ant.* 14.280–293). And the next year, also in and around Jerusalem, Malichus' brother Helix attacked Herod's brother Phasael (*War* 1.294–296). Thus there had been power-struggles going on within the Hasmonean regime for some time, apparently unrelated to Herod's elimination of Ezechias and his brigands in Galilee. Moreover, the return of Antigonus from exile seems unconnected with these struggles within the Hasmonean regime in and around Jerusalem, and connected with the political schemes of petty rulers in Tyre and Chalcis (*War* 1.297).

The prolonged struggle for control of Palestine between Antigonus and Herod, in connection with which the former obtained the backing of the Parthians and the latter was named "king" of the Jews by the Romans, did not emerge until 40 BCE, long after the elimination of Ezechias, and even longer after Cassius' defeat of Peitholaus. Josephus says nothing that would suggest that the Galileans who resisted Herod's conquest between 39 and 37 BCE were in some way continuing Peitholaus' struggle. Moreover, he gives no indication that the different points at which Herod fights against resistance to his rule in Galilee involve the same people, let alone that their "leaders, Ezechias and the others, were aristocrats."[9] Indeed, far from suggesting the "cave-dwelling brigands were the same as "the garrisons of Antigonus" who had fled Sepphoris, Josephus indicates that these are two different groups by his presentation of these two actions by Herod in immediate sequence in both accounts (*War* 1.304; *Ant.* 14:413–415), and even gives the impression that the brigands had been active in the area of

---

9. Freyne, *Galilee*, 67.

Arbela for some rime. Moreover, "the usual promoters of disturbance in Galilee" mentioned a few paragraphs later appear to be yet a third group and one connected in some way with "the cities" which Herod fined a hundred talents in punishment (*War* 1.315–316; *Ant.* 14.432–433). There is no reason to locate resistance to Herod among Hasmonean officers and government functionaries.

There was apparently resistance to Herod's conquest of his kingdom at all levels of society, including the peasantry. And the Galileans had had direct experience of his brutal efficiency as their *strategos* since 47, symbolized best perhaps in his rigorous collection of the special levy of taxes by Cassius in 44 (*War* 1.219–221). After reading about continuing and apparently diverse resistance to Herod one begins to wonder what Josephus had meant earlier by "all Galilee" having gone over to Herod (*War* 1.291; *Ant.* 14.395). Perhaps he meant those in charge in the district. His reports of a later incident, however, indicate that at least some of the officers or "nobles" (*dynatoi*) in Galilee had become supporters of Herod. Following a victory by Antigonus in Judea, "the Galileans, rebelling against their officers/nobles (*tōn para sfisi dynatōn*), drowned those who were partisans of Herod in the Lake" (*Ant.* 14.450; *War* 1.126). So at least some of the former Hasmonean *dynatoi* had prudently cast their lot with Herod—and underestimated the intensity of the people's continuing resistance. There is thus simply no basis in Josephus' accounts of the prolonged struggle for control of Palestine for suggesting that, in the incidents involving Ezechias and the cave-dwelling brigands, it was some Hasmonean nobles who were spearheading the resistance to Antipas and Herod over several decades. Ironically, to reconstruct Ezechias and the cave-dwelling brigands as the remnants of Hasmonean nobility injects a special religious-political dimension back into resistance groups in Galilee, whereas to allow the brigands to be brigands would support Freyne's own principal contention about Galilee, that it was not full of religiously motivated revolutionary activity.

Josephus' accounts of Ezechias appear indeed to be straightforward reports of brigand activity and its suppression:

> Herod, . . . discovering that Ezechias, a brigand-chief at the head of a large horde, was ravaging the district on the Syrian frontier, he caught him and put him and many of the brigands to death. This welcome achievement was immensely admired by the Syrians. (*War* 1.204)

As I explained previously, the activities of Ezechias and his brigands can be easily understood as the product of fifteen years of social disruption and dislocation caused by the Roman conquest and reorganization of Palestine, and the ensuing civil war in Palestine as well as in the Roman empire (including the struggles among Hasmonean factions).[10] As Hobsbawm and others have pointed out, such conditions can produce widespread banditry as peasants are driven off their land or their livelihood simply destroyed in the course of the wars. More particularly in this case, Josephus reports that, after taking control of the country, the Romans confined the Hasmonean regime to the territory it had previously controlled (before Jannaeus' conquests of Hellenistic cities), and restored the Palestinian/Syrian cities to independence (Scythopolis and Gamala are in the list, *War* 1.166; *Ant.* 14.88). This would almost certainly have meant also that the villages in the surrounding areas would have come under the control of those cities or their rulers, meaning either alien domination or displacement for peasants in such border area villages. This picture is confirmed by the decrees of Julius Caesar (with the Senate) restoring some of this border area to Hyrcanus' (and Antipater's) rule, dated between 48 and 44 BCE, i.e., around the time Ezechias and his band would have been active. That is, "the kings of Syria and Phoenicia, as allies of the Romans, had been permitted to enjoy the fruits of the places, lands and farms formerly under Hasmonean control" (*Ant.* 14.190–212, esp. 209). Bandits often operate in frontier areas. But in this case the frontier areas were the location of the most sustained turmoil and dislocation. Hence it is highly credible that displaced people would have formed brigand groups and would be raiding the "Syrian" cities or territories to which they had been subjected.[11] It is then similarly credible that, after Caesar had imposed a new arrangement for the control of Palestine, Antipater and his son as the energetic governor of Galilee, were attempting to assert their control in an area long under uncertain or inefficient control. The Syrians may have been delighted at Herod's killing of the brigands,

---

10. Horsley, "Josephus and the Bandits," 53.

11. Freyne, "Bandits in Galilee," argues that Ezechias and company must be displaced Hasmonean nobility rather than brigands because the raids were against the Syrians, and bandits attempting to "right wrongs" would have attacked the social oppressors within Galilee. But "pre-political" bandits do not yet enjoy a critical assessment of the overall social system and circumstances to which they are subjected and focus on the immediate local circumstances. In this case, the immediate source of their displacement and malaise was subjection to or encroachments by the Syrian cities, midst the general turmoil of the time.

Galileans under Jerusalem and Roman Rule

But not so at least some people in Galilee. And some of the ruling elite in Jerusalem, increasingly anxious about the concentration of power in the hands of Antipater and his sons, used Herod's murder of Ezechias' brigands and the resulting popular outcry as an occasion to attempt to clip Herod's wings. "The principal men of the Judeans" complained to Hyrcanus that

> Herod had killed Ezechias and many of this men in violation of our Law, which forbids us to slay a man, even an evildoer, unless he has first been condemned by the Synhedrion ... And everyday in the temple the mothers of the men who had been murdered by Herod kept begging the king and the people to have Herod brought to judgment ... (*Ant.* 14.167–168)

That ordinary people would appeal to the king for redress of injustices, even against the abuses of his officers, is a typical occurrence according to Hobsbawm.[12] Moreover, that Herod not only took a substantial body-guard with him to Jerusalem, but "first posted garrisons throughout Galilee" (*War* 1.210) suggests that Herod had already encountered some sort of serious outcry there. "The leading Judeans" in Jerusalem would not have been worried about brigandage on the Syrian frontier and probably not even about the lives of several bandits in the remote border area. But they were anxious to check Herod's rise, and the popular protest in/from Galilee over Herod's murder of the brigands provided the opportunity.

As noted already, the struggles between rival Roman rulers and the turmoil within Palestine continued for the next decade following the suppression of Ezechias and his band. Given the continuing displacement of people that such turmoil inevitably entailed, it would not be surprising if banditry had been a continuing phenomenon, Thus there is no need in historical reconstruction, as well as no indication in Josephus' reports, to resort to the Hasmonean nobility to explain the substantial numbers of brigands centered around the rough terrain and caves near Arbela. Although Josephus takes great relish in recounting the prolonged campaign and particularly the unusual means necessary for Herod finally to ferret out the "cave-dwelling" brigands, he provides little direct information from which we can speculate any further about their origins or role in Galilee during Herod's conquest of his kingdom. Under the tight control and sharp repression of Herod's regime it would have been difficult for banditry or any other form of protest to emerge. For the reign of Antipas in Galilee we simply have no information.

12. See Horsley, "Josephus and the Bandits," 46, 54.

Just before the outbreak of the revolt in 66, however, banditry was escalating to epidemic proportions in Galilee as well as in Judea. Relatively speaking, the now sizeable and multiplying brigand groups were far more important in Galilee than in Judea (with its diverse types of resistance) as forces in the Jewish revolt. Escalating banditry flowed imperceptibly into, or became the form assumed by, the gradually expanding insurrection in the district. Josephus' reports suggest that the sizeable bands of brigands already in existence constituted one of the two types of resistance to the Romans' initial attempt to "pacify" Galilee. As Sepphoris, the strongest city of Galilee, welcomed the Roman forces, "all the rebels and brigands fled to the mountain in the heart of Galilee" where they temporarily held off a whole Roman legion (*War* 2.511). Clearly, as Josephus recounts "the whole of Galilee had not yet revolted from Rome" (*Life* 28). Ironically, the Romans' "scorched earth" practices expanded the very rebellion they were attempting to suppress by creating thousands of fugitives (e.g., *War* 2.504–505; 3.60–63), and compounding the numbers of fugitives from Greek and Syrian cities' attacks against their Jewish inhabitants and their tributary Jewish villages (*War* 2.457–480). Many such fugitives would have joined or formed bands of brigands, particularly in northern Galilee and along the border with Ptolemais (*Life* 77–78, 105). Whether or not we believe Josephus that John of Gischala was himself a brigand, (and recognizing his tendency to exaggerate numbers) it is highly credible that "he mustered a band of four hundred men, for the most part fugitives from the region (*chōra*) of Tyre and the villages in that neighborhood" (*War* 2.587–588; cf. *Life* 372).

To understand adequately the central importance of the brigands in the "revolt" (or is it simply "anarchy"?) in Galilee, we must take into account the complexity of the situation, between cities (even opposing factions within cities), countryside, brigand groups, etc., and the struggle for dominance between Josephus, John of Gischala, and others. Moreover, it seems more and more likely (to me at least) that Josephus really was playing a moderating role, a double game, of pretending to organize defensively while attempting to control the situation, as he insists in his *Life*. Thus Josephus can argue both that he must pretend to organize resistance "on account of the brigands" and that he was the only one who could protect (the more respectable leaders of) "the Galileans" from the brigands (*Life* 175, 206). In the anarchic conditions it was perhaps an obvious solution, given that it would have been impossible to disarm and disband the brigands, to "persuade the people to hire them as mercenaries" and then to "bind them by oath not to enter the district (*chōra*) unless they were sent for or their pay was in arrear," and to order them not to attack either the Romans or their neighbors (*Life* 77–78). Some of the grossly exaggerated army that Josephus himself commanded may well have been such "mercenaries" (cf. *War* 2.583–584). Others such as John of Gischala, of course, could play the same game. Not surprisingly in the conditions of an anarchic "revolt" it is not always possible to distinguish between the activities of brigands and the raids and guerrilla actions that would be taken by popular rebel forces, such as the plunder of Ptolemy's (wife's) baggage by the *neaniskoi* of Dabarirta (*Life* 126–127; *War* 2.595).

Epidemic banditry that flows into rebellion, however, is not necessarily revolutionary. That the sizeable force led by Jesus could sell their services to the pro-Roman city of Sepphoris probably illustrates the "pre-political" perspective that Hobsbawm suggests is typical—i.e., they were almost certainly not "revolutionary" against either the Romans or the dominant city in the area. Of course, Jesus and his band may rather have been making common cause with Sepphoris against Josephus whom *they* saw as pro-Roman and/or a representative of Jerusalem's unwelcome attempt at domination (and it may be Josephus who invented the "large sum" in payment in a report that lacks credibility in other regards, *Life* 104–111).

In at least one instance in Upper Galilee the escalating banditry appears not simply to have constituted or flowed into rebellion but to have stimulated wider peasant revolt. Through Josephus' extremely hostile account of John and the rebellion in Gischala we can discern how the influence of a sizeable band of brigands in the area led peasants of Gischala, previously quiescent, into active rebellion (*War* 4.84–85). Overall in Galilee one has the impression that the revolt did not become all that widespread among the peasantry. Clearly, however, large numbers of people in the border areas or in the villages devastated by the Romans swelled the ranks of the brigands who provided the principal rebel forces that Josephus was eager to hold in check in the anarchic conditions of 66–67 in Galilee.

Although the brigands constituted substantial elements of the armed forces among the shifting factions in Galilee, those Josephus refers to as "the Galileans" were apparently the potential "revolutionary" elements. "The Galileans" are clearly country people, peasants. They are sharply hostile to the cities, particularly Sepphoris and Tiberias (*Life* 97–100, 374–385). To believe that this is because of their loyalty to Josephus is to accept that latter's self-serving apology. To assert that they are "militantly nationalist, but not essentially revolutionary"[13] "involves either an extremely narrow or a confused picture of what would have constituted revolution in antiquity. Josephus' statements about how he checked the potential attacks by the Galileans also indicate that these peasants in arms were hostile to the cities from which they had been ruled and ready to attack them, particularly when they were loyal to the Romans or Agrippa.

THE POPULAR KINGSHIP OF JUDAS SON OF EZECHIAS

I have argued that the movement led by Judas son of Ezechias in 4 BCE was one among several similar movements that assumed a distinctively Israelite form, that of popular kingship. In previous presentations of the results of analysis of Josephus' hostile reports, I have treated Judas' movement together with the two other principal movements in 4 BCE that he views as similar, that led by Athronges in Judea and that led by Simon in Perea. With our focus now more narrowly on Galilee, it may be useful to isolate the reports on Judas and to compare the reports on the other movements in order to "double check" Josephus' treatment of these movements as similar in form.

The descriptions are brief and parallel:[14]

> At Sepphoris in Galilee, Judas, son of Ezechias (the brigand-chief who once overran the country and was suppressed by king Herod), having organized a sizeable force, broke into the royal armories, armed his followers, and attacked the others who vied for power. (*War* 2.56)

> There was Judas, son of the brigand-chief Ezechias (who had been a man of great power and who had been captured by Herod only with great difficulty). This Judas, when he had organized at Sepphoris in Galilee a large number of desperate men, raided the palace. Taking all the weapons that were stored there, he armed all of this followers and made off with all the goods that had been seized there. He caused fear in everyone by plundering those he

---

13. Freyne, "The Galileans in the Light of Josephus' *Vita*," 412.

14. Citing John Hanson's translations from Horsley and Hanson, *Bandits, Prophets, and Messiahs*, 112.

encountered in his craving for power and in his zealous pursuit of royal rank. (*Ant.* 17.271–272)

If these parallel reports about Judas were completely isolated and unique we might suppose that Judas was simply an ambitious regional strongman opportunistically seizing the chaotic situation after the death of Herod to set himself up as king in Sepphoris. Josephus, however, clearly understands Judas and his followers as a phenomenon parallel to at least two other movements. And suddenly, in reports of these disturbances in Galilee, Perea, and Judea respectively, he uses the terminology of kingship. That is, he has already been describing revolt and rebellion in Jerusalem and elsewhere in the wake of Herod's death. Now he focuses on disturbances in which Judas "aspired to royal rank" (*basileious timēs*) or "attacked the others who vied for power" (*dynasteia*), Simon "assumed the diadem" and "was proclaimed as king" by his followers, and Athronges "aspired to a kingship" and for some time "was called a king" (*War* 2.56, 57, 61–62; *Ant.* 17.272, 273–274, 278–281). In *War* 2.55, moreover, he even provides a topical introduction: the opportunity induced many "to become king." Just as he has on occasion described some figures as "prophets" and others as "brigands" and yet others as "a special species of brigands," so now he has something more particular in view than just another *stasis* or *apostasis*. Thus from Josephus' procedure as a historian we have some reason to think that these are distinctive figures or movements and that there are some similarities between them.

The reports about Judas son of Ezechias, however, are much shorter than the others, hence much less is provided by way of particulars. Thus we must proceed cautiously in using information provided for the other popular kings in extrapolations for a picture of Judas. Josephus mentions that Athronges was a "mere shepherd" and Simon was a royal servant, meaning perhaps a lower level officer or a peasant or sharecropper on one of the royal estates (*War* 2.57, 60; *Ant.* 18.273, 278). Judas is identified only as "the son of Ezechias the brigand-chief." We have noted above that there is no reason to think that Ezechias was a Hasmonean noble, hence there is no basis for believing that his son was attempting to revive Hasmonean kingship. Moreover, it seems clear from Josephus' reports here and elsewhere that Judas son of Ezechias was not the same as Judas of Galilee, who is identified as a *sophistēs* and one of the principal leaders of the "fourth philosophy" that agitated against the census in 6 CE when Judea came directly under Roman rule (*War* 2.118). Thus there is no basis for scholarly speculation about a "messianic dynasty" continuing from Judas of Galilee in 6 CE to Menahem, a leader of the Sicarii in 66. We cannot simply assume from the general parallel with Simon and Athronges that Judas also was a commoner, although that seems most likely. It is possible that, as the son of a famous brigand-chief, Judas was already recognized as a popular leader even before his "ambition for royal rank" in 4 BCE.

In the introductory generalization in the *War*, Josephus writes that these movements occurred in various places in the countryside, and his accounts of those headed by Simon and Athronges confirm our impression that they were based in the peasantry (*War* 2.55, 57, 65; *Ant.* 17.273–285). Is Judas' movement an exception? The extremely cursory report in *War* 2.56 has "in Sepphoris," while the somewhat longer *Ant.* 17.271 indicates more clearly that Judas "gathered together a large number" of men "around Sepphoris," in which he raided the royal palace and then "made off" back into the countryside from which they had come. That the Roman retaliation involved burning the city and enslaving its inhabitants (*War* 2.68) does not necessarily mean that the Sepphorites themselves were involved in Judas' movement or the attack on the royal palace. But it is at least conceivable that some of the Sepphorites in 4 BCE, like many of the Jerusalemites, were ready to strike out against Herodian-Roman rule, even though they were directly or indirectly dependent on it economically. It is inherently more likely, however, that Judas' movement, like the others, was based in the countryside, as Josephus' framing and one account indicate. In that case, the large number of men that he gathered together may have been "desperate" (*Ant.* 17.271) because of the heavy economic pressures that Herod had placed on the peasantry in order to underwrite his many grandiose building and cultural projects, as well as his elaborate Hellenistic administration, the Galilean center of which was Sepphoris.

We can assume from the general context and the specific targets of their attack that these movements were rebellions against Herodian-Roman rule. Judas and company in particular attacked the royal palace in Sepphoris not simply to obtain arms, but also to take (back) "all the property that has been seized there" (i.e., by Herodian officials; *Ant.* 17.271). This action is parallel to similar actions by Simon's movement, which burned the royal palace at Jericho and plundered "the things that had been seized there" and attacked other royal and aristocratic residences (*Ant.* 17.274). The scope and importance of these movements are indicated by the size of the military forces that the Romans mobilized to reconquer the countryside and by the brutal punitive measures they took in retaliation, such as the burning of Sepphoris and enslavement of its people (*Ant.* 17.286–295).

Freyne suggested that "in realistic terms Judas son of Ezechias would have had to represent himself as carrying forward some recognizable tradition of kingship."[15] So long as we think only in terms of recent, established rulers in Palestine, without considering possibilities either in the "little tradition" or in biblical narratives themselves, then the two options would appear to be the Herodian or the Hasmonean (although the latter house was primarily high priestly rather than kingship). Freyne thus argues that since the rebellion of Judas is against Herodian kingship, it must be an attempt to restore the Hasmonean kingship. His argument goes something like this: Judas was in Sepphoris; Sepphoris was a Hasmonean stronghold; therefore . . . the underlying assumption is that Judas is a surviving member of a Hasmonean "noble" or "landowner" family. That is not impossible, but it is highly unlikely. And the argument is farfetched. As Freyne himself points out, some of the Hasmonean officers went over to the rival Hasmonean side and were killed by the Romans, others were drowned in the Lake in a resurgent popular uprising, and Herod had most of those remaining killed when he finally had a firm grip on power in Jerusalem. Moreover, Judas would have to have been skillful indeed to emerge from the tightly repressive Herodian security apparatus that included informers and secret police to have survived, particularly in and around Sepphoris, which was the center of Herodian rule in Galilee.

Procedurally, however, since we have the movements of Athronges and Simon (and later that of Simon bar Giora and perhaps Simeon bar Kokhba) as well as that of Judas to explain in terms of their similar forms and characteristics, it would be better to treat them together rather than separately with regard to being informed by a "recognizable tradition of kingship." Moreover, even though they have left few if any records, in contrast to the literate elite, common people do generate and sustain cultural traditions. In this case, the Judean "biblical" tradition, and probably Israelite popular tradition as well, provided yet another and highly recognizable tradition of kingship, that exemplified by Saul, David, Jeroboam, and Jehu, among others. Judas's movement, like those of Athronges and Simon, etc., were probably informed in some way by this tradition of popular kingship, which may have revived among the people precisely because the Hasmonean and/or Herodian kingship was illegitimate and oppressive (e.g., Ps Sol

---

15. Horsley, *Galilee*, 215.

17:5–8; many passages in the Dead Sea Scrolls; and the general opposition to Herod).[16]

To draw any connections between Judas and his movement and Jesus of Nazareth would be purely speculative. But as we become more concrete in our approach to the historical context of Jesus and his followers, it is surely at least interesting that the movement and revolt led by Judas was taking place in the immediate environs of Sepphoris and Nazareth within a few years of Jesus' birth. Here was a mass movement among Galilean peasants from villages around Sepphoris taking common action under the leadership of a popular figure they recognized as king. This occurrence of a concrete movement that took the social form of popular kingship (messianic pretender) here in Galilee as well as in Judea and Perea is all the more significant as we realize that there is little evidence of "messianic expectations" in Palestinian Jewish literature prior to the time of Jesus. The movement, moreover, was brutally suppressed and Sepphoris, the principal administrative city in Galilee, just a few miles from Nazareth, had been sacked and some of its people enslaved by a conquering Roman army that swept through the region, surely leaving vivid memories among the Galilean people in the area.

THE URBAN POOR IN TIBERIAS

Josephus' accounts of events in Tiberias in 66–67 provide us with at least a fragmentary picture of the behavior of the urban poor in an anarchic time of revolutionary excitement. The principal conflict in the city was between "the respectable men" headed by Julius Capellus who remained loyal to Rome and Agrippa II, on the one hand, and "the most insignificant persons," on the other, who were ready for war (*Life* 32–35). The conflict thus fell clearly along the main line of political-economic division within the city.[17] "The respectable men," who are elsewhere also clearly the (ten)

16. See further, Horsley, "Popular Messianic Movements," 473–83.

17. Although polarized thus, however, the situation both in Tiberias and in Galilee as a whole was more complex. Cohen imposes a simplistic scheme of two parties, "war" and "peace," on the particular topics he treats, including Tiberias, removing any motivation for more precise analysis of a given situation. For example, he does not differentiate between the council (*boulē*) and the principal men (*Josephus*, 217). But *Life* 167–168// *War* 2.638–641 and *Life* 381, concerning an appeal to Agrippa, do not necessarily mean that the whole council was pro-Roman; in 381 Josephus writes that *hoi prōtoi ton ek tēs boulēs* had invited the king to take over the city. Actions taken by the principal factions in

principal men of the city (*Life* 64–65, 69), are the holders of wealth and power, judging from their names and positions, such as the Roman-sounding Julius Capellus himself, two men named Herod, and Comsus the son of Compsus whose brother Crispus, the former perfect under Agrippa I, was busy "on his estates across the Jordan" (*Life* 33). The other faction consisted "of sailors and the destitute (*tōn aporōn*)" (*Life* 66). Since their leader, Jesus son of Sapphias, is elsewhere identified as the *archon* of the city by Josephus (*Life* 66, 271), it has been speculated that the office was elective or that he became a "demagogue."

The terms in which urban life in Palestine are often discussed, as "Greek/Hellenistic" or "Jewish," are vague, even vacuous and indeterminate. In order to take advantage of the fragments of information provided by Josephus, we must move to particular characteristics of Tiberias assessed against what is known of ancient urban life in general and Palestine in particular. Tiberias was founded as his capital by Herod's son, the Tetrarch Antipas. However much traditional Greek "city" terminology may have been utilized in the foundation and/or Josephus' description, Tiberias was a royal administrative city with a mixed population ruled by Herodian officials, some of them probably Judean (and some) with Roman names.

Judging from the way in which Roman imperial officials addressed their formal correspondence, a Greek *polis* would have consisted of "*archōn(ai), boulē*, and *dēmos*,"[18] and influence and actual power gradually came to be held by the *dekaprōtoi* within the *dēmos* or *boulē*. Tiberias seems to fit precisely this picture, as Josephus summons *tēn Tiberieōn boulēn kai tous prōtous tou dēmou*, and later attends a meeting at which the *archōn* Jesus presides (*Life* 64, 271, 278, 296, 300). However, it would be highly unusual in Roman times for the *archōn* to have been so "revolutionary" (see further below); Josephus may reflect the "raised eyebrows" among proper Judeans and Greeks alike that the "citizens" of Tiberias were derived from such humble circumstances, some perhaps as not even having been "free"; and the confident assertions in scholarly reconstructions that "there was a *boulē* of 600" in Tiberias is based on a text in which Josephus has typically exaggerated the numbers (how many boats had he commandeered from

---

Tiberias, moreover, must be understood in the historical context that involved not simply Roman imperial rule, but other political-economic-religious-ethnic relationships, such as with Galilean peasants, cities of the Decapolis, the Roman client ruler Agrippa under whose rule they had recently been placed, and the rivalry with Sepphoris.

18. Abbott and Johnson, *Municipal Administration in the Roman Empire*, e.g., ##35, 36, 68, 71, 75, 76, 80, 82, etc.).

the Tarichaeans in order to ship the 2,600 Tiberians he supposedly arrested back to Tarichaeae? *War* 2.641). Thus perhaps we should not lay too much stock simply in the standard terminology used by Josephus. As Tcherikover pointed out in his analysis of Josephus' accounts pertaining to Jerusalem, "Our chief literary source is remarkably unclear and inaccurate when he uses political-legal terminology."[19]

There are a number of other indications that Tiberias was not a typical Hellenistic city, but a royal administrative city with a mixed population, some descendants of the Galilean villages that had been forcibly bought into the city (Josephus, *Ant.* 18.36–38). A proper Greek city had its own territory, under its own jurisdiction. But Tiberias is described in passing as the center of a toparchy of a Herodian kingdom, hence must not have held jurisdiction over a territory of its own (*War* 2.252).[20] A Greek city would have had its own coinage dated according to the era of the city. But coins from Tiberias are Antipas' coins dated by the year of his rule, and it is not until Trajan that it had its own coinage dated by the city's era.[21] Tiberias clearly had a stadium, which served as a gathering place (*War* 2.618; *Life* 92, 331). But important political assemblies were apparently held in the *proseuchē*, "a huge building, capable of accommodating a large crowd" (*Life* 277). This "house of prayer" appears to have been much larger than the later Galilean synagogue-buildings uncovered by archaeologists. The most important building in Tiberias, however, must have been the royal palace, which was lavishly decorated and furnished in a style that observed no scruples about Judean religious sensitivities (*Life* 65). Surely under Antipas and perhaps later as well under Agrippa I, the royal court and administration dominated the city's life. The very names mentioned by Josephus indicate that those who were the wealthy and powerful "leading men" of the city had themselves been, or were descended from, prominent members of Antipas' or Agrippa's administration (*Life* 32–33). And in his comments about the founding of Tiberias, Josephus explains that one of the two principal types of settlers brought in were government "magistrates" (*Ant.* 18.37).[22]

19. Tcherikover, "Was Jerusalem a Polis?," 63.

20. Jones, *Cities of the Eastern Roman Provinces*, 276.

21. See, e.g., Meshorer, *Jewish Coins of the Second Temple Period*, 74–75; Kindler, *The Coins of Tiberias*, #2.

22. Freyne introduces his "ousted Hasmonean nobles" theory again in this connection. He identifies these "notables or nobles" with both *hoi prōtoi tōn galilaion* in Mark 6:21 and those around Arbela who gave Herod so much trouble (sixty years earlier!), hence they are now being taken into Tiberias so that Antipas can control them.

The picture we receive of Tiberias is thus not that of a typical Greek city, but of a royal administrative city with a mixed population, some of which were (descendants of) former Galilean villagers, and a "prayer-house" at which public political discussions were held. The city may have been dominated less by the royal court and administration once it lost its position as capital of Galilee–Perea to Sepphoris in mid-first century, although it was still the center of a toparchy. The language of the royal administration was likely Greek,[23] even though apparently only a small percentage of the inhabitants of the city were "Greek." Josephus gives some indication that at least certain prominent Tiberians resented both their loss of prominence in Galilee to their rival city, Sepphoris, and their recent transfer to the jurisdiction of Agrippa II. It may or may not be significant that Josephus places the articulation of the jealousy of Sepphoris in the mouth of another (rival) intellectual who had aspirations toward more sophisticated Greek literary culture (Justus of Tiberias, who later became a secretary-historian for Agrippa II). In any case, at the outbreak of the Great Revolt, the principal men who dominated political-cultural life in Tiberias had their political-economic base in the royal administrative character and function of the city.

Thus it is not surprising that these leading men of the city, with Herodian or Roman names, staunchly resisted the instruction of the Jerusalem government to destroy the royal palace with its animal representations in a style prohibited by the Torah (*Life* 65). Neither Hasmonean nor Herodian rulers had observed the prohibitions against such representations (e.g., *Ant.* 12.230; 14.34; 19.357), and one would not expect their officers and associates to have been concerned. In this case the royal palace represented the principal heritage of the city whose very foundation had been centered around it.

The faction of the sailors and destitute headed by Jesus, however, required no urging to implement the instruction from Jerusalem, but burned and looted the royal palace in collaboration with certain Galileans, and then killed all the Greek residents of Tiberias as well (*Life* 66–67).[24] Freyne,

23. But had all those settlers brought in from Antipas' Galilean territory learned their Greek as a second language?—leaving open the question of precisely what their "native" language may have been.

24. Cohen presents an incredible picture of the parties, principal figures, and events in Tiberias, with Josephus as leader of both the destruction of the royal palace and the massacre of the Greeks and "the respectable" elite engaged shoulder to shoulder in pillage with the sailors, paupers, and peasants (*Josephus*, 118). It is unclear why a modern

who is at pains to insist that there was no revolutionary impulse in Galilee, curiously finds that this was an "obvious act of zealotism" perpetrated by "a pocket of zealotism in Tiberias and its region," and inspired by "Zealot ideals" emanating from Jerusalem.[25] Since it is now being recognized that there was no historical reality behind that modern concept that has confused this and other issues, we must inquire more precisely into Josephus' reports. The Jerusalem government that sent Josephus with the instruction was certainly not the rebel coalition that drove out the Romans in the summer of 66, but the "moderate" and "counter-revolutionary" junta comprised of high priests and leading Pharisees who moved to the fore later that year in an attempt to control the rebellion and reach a negotiated settlement with the Romans—while pretending, insofar as possible, to be making preparations for defense. Whatever the purposes of the *koinon* in Jerusalem, if there was a "halakhic" motivation behind the instruction to destroy the palace, it was located in Jerusalem and not among the "sailors and poor" of Tiberias, who were highly unlikely to have been well-versed in halakhic debates.[26] It is highly questionable to draw conclusions about the motives of the Tiberian poor from the supposed motives of the Jerusalem *koinon* which are themselves utterly unclear given the lack of evidence.

It is perhaps more justifiable, but still utterly hypothetical, to generalize from other incidents in Galilee. For example, when two of Agrippa's gentile nobles from Trachonitis deserted to Galilee with their horses, arms, and money, "the people" (Josephus calls them "Judeans") would have forced them to be circumcised. Judging from Josephus' report, there was some sense among the people that the presence of these uncircumcised nobles was threatening their struggle against the Romans (*Life* 112–114, 149–154). The incident appears to illustrate a sensitivity among the people (Galilean Israelites), undoubtedly intensified by the circumstances, about circumcision as a symbol of their solidarity as a people against outsiders. They had already come into armed conflict with the Greeks in the cities around the periphery of Galilee. But this case may also express a class conflict, the suspicion in which the people would have held nobles, particularly foreign nobles of the king to whom those around Tarichaeae had recently been subjected. The incident thus indicates a sensitivity among the people

---

historian should label as "criminals" those who implemented what had been commissioned by the Jerusalem assembly led by the priestly aristocracy.

25. Horsley, *Galilee*, 234–35, 311–12.

26. Freyne, *Galilee*, chap. 8.

about their sense of identity as a people, although it is unclear how it illustrates anything about halakhic rigor. But there is no reason to find any direct connection between "the Jews" who pressed the issue of the gentile nobles' circumcision (apparently at Tarichaeae) and the Tiberian faction of the sailors and poor who set fire to the royal palace.[27]

There is a more direct link between another incident that happened supposedly in Tarichaeae and the Tiberian poor (on the following see *Life* 126–135; *War* 2.595–607). After some young men had ambushed the king's finance officer, Ptolemy, or his wife and brought the plunder to Josephus in Tarichaeae, Josephus secretly consigned the spoil to two "friends" of the king to be returned. Not trusting "their general" (who all but boasts of his utter duplicity and secret agenda), the young men agitated in the villages around Tarichaeae and Tiberias that Josephus was intending to betray the countryside (*chōra*; *Life* 129) to the Romans. At the eventual confrontation in the hippodrome in Tarichaeae, says Josephus, the principal instigator of the angry mob was Jesus son of Sapphias, the *archōn* of Tiberias. Supposedly he used the Torah as a rallying symbol, claiming that Josephus was about to betray it. That does not indicate anything about halakhah, but it does suggest that loyalty to the Torah as the embodiment of the independence and the traditional way of life (not merely "religion") of the people was a central issue in the revolt for Galilean villagers. In this incident, like the one involving the gentile nobles, class conflict is clearly again central. The people suspected, rightly so as it turned out, that Josephus' real loyalties were to the king, his officer, and ultimately the Roman overlords. The link with the Tiberian party of the poor, of course, is Jesus himself, who was supposedly its leader as well as the *archōn*, and we could hypothesize that the Torah, particularly as a symbol *and embodiment* of the traditional ideals and way of life of the people had come to the fore in the circumstances of the revolt and the excitement of sudden independence from Roman rule.

We have at least some sense of the political-economic circumstances and relations of the destitute class of Tiberias itself. A number of factors indicate that the poor of Tiberias could well have harbored some latent hostilities towards the king and the royal palace as a symbol of their circumstances that may have motivated their attack. Hobsbawm has pointed out that the people of a royal city, most of whom are dependent economically on the business of the court and administration, will usually be loyal to the

---

27. Cf. Freyne, *Galilee*, 312: "the same zealot fanatics." Also unclear is precisely what evidence would point to "rigorist sectarian attitudes shared by the people at large."

king as a symbol of their own identity and involvement. But Tiberias had no long-standing heritage as a royal city. It was a new foundation, not even two generations old in 66 CE, and had been the "royal city" proper for only about fifteen years under Antipas and then briefly and in qualified fashion under Agrippa I. Moreover, although the "magistrates" brought to live in the city were apparently already connected with the royal administration, the other settlers apparently had no such link. Indeed, even if we somewhat discount the tone of Josephus' caustic account of the founding, some coercion was involved in bringing some of those subject to the king into the city. Some "were even poor men who were brought in to join the others from any and all places of origin" (*Ant.* 18.37). Thus many of the residents of the city had started poor and remained poor.[28] Since the city was founded on the site of ancient Israelite tombs, furthermore, it was suspect on the basis of Judean tradition and sensitivities, which may have placed sensitive Galilean settlers in a continuing situation of conflicting loyalties. It stands to reason that these people who were brought in as settlers were also the ones who were required to build the royal palace, with its lavish decorations and ostentatious wealth, While the return of the administrative apparatus of the capital to Sepphoris meant a loss of prestige as well as political-economic standing for the principal families and professional intellectuals or bureaucrats such as Justus, it may well have meant unemployment for some of the already marginal and "destitute." There were clearly multiple bases for possible hostility among the poor directed against the royal palace.

If or insofar as the faction (*stasis*) of the sailors and destitute of Tiberias had a social form, it was defined by the structure and circumstances of the situation. It is highly unlikely that it had any organization, although there may have been other leaders besides Jesus. This "party" of the poor apparently persisted in its rebellious stance through all attempts of Josephus to control the various factions in Galilee and in particular through the several attempts made by "the respectable" principal men of Tiberias itself to induce Agrippa II to take control of the city. When the Romans advanced through Galilee in the summer of 67 subduing the rebellion in systematic fashion, Jesus and his followers made a valiant attempt to resist the inexorable Roman reconquest, while the *protoi* negotiated submission. In a daring guerrilla attack they managed to capture some horses from

---

28. It is unclear what might have constituted "the opportunities of the hellenistic city environment" of which these poor could have availed themselves in order to achieve "social mobility." See Freyne, *Galilee*, 236.

Vespasian's forces. But they apparently could not control the city, which was surrendered by the other faction, whereupon they fled to Tarichaeae where they continued their daring resistance (*War* 3.443–470). One of Josephus' sharp criticisms of Justus may indicate that the "185 fellow-citizens" slain in the internal Tiberian civil strife consisted largely of some of these "sailors and poor." And it would seem likely that many among the "2000 Tiberians found at the siege of Jerusalem" (surely an exaggerated figure) were former followers of Jesus son of Sapphias who, once resistance at Tiberias and Tarichaeae was futile, fled with other Galileans to Jerusalem to continue the resistance (*Life* 353–354).

5

Archaeology and the Villages of Upper Galilee
A Dialogue with Archaeologists

IT WAS WITH CONSIDERABLE excitement and anticipation that many textual scholars greeted the undertaking by a team of archaeologists to excavate villages in Upper Galilee. Finally some archaeologists were focusing not on another ruling city or one of its major monuments, but on places where ordinary people lived in locations directly relevant to the roots of both the Christian Gospels and Rabbinic literature. Text-oriented scholars can learn a great deal from the reports of those excavations that pertain to their labors. These reports on Upper Galilean villages also pose a number of questions that may provide a basis for ongoing dialogue between textual studies and archaeology of the Galilee.

Some of those questions are rooted in the shifting "paradigms" in the study of early Judaism and Christianity. Both textual scholars and archaeologists depend upon the assumptions and conceptual apparatus of their fields.[1] The determining influence of the standard academic assumptions and conceptual apparatus is all the more powerful when interwoven with religious communities for which certain literature and/or sites are special. For example, both Jewish- and Christian-oriented studies often assume that there was a unitary or essential "Judaism" with certain characteristics, and

---

1. Cf. Kuhn, *The Structure of Scientific Revolutions*.

that Galilee was basically "Jewish" in early Roman times.² Such assumptions influence not only the interpretation of textual and material remains, but also the way in which they were "read" prior to the application of standard critical tools and analyses. Thus, as we increasingly recognize the considerable diversity of "Judaism" and the differences in social location and interests among the different social strata, groups, and movements, both those concentrating on textual remains and those excavating the material remains of ancient Palestine must often adjust our assumptions and concepts.

Similarly, both text specialists and archaeologists are faced with the need to question their operative models of social (political–economic–religious) relations or to construct more critically models appropriate to the sources being examined, making needed adjustments even in the process of that examination. This is true at several interrelated levels, from the household (which in a traditional agrarian society almost certainly included crafts), to the regional political-economic structure (which in a traditional agrarian society almost certainly did not mean a basically market economy), to the imperial political-economic arrangements (which probably had indirect as well as direct impact on village and household). It would be unfair for biblical scholars to criticize archaeological reports published years earlier for not anticipating their own later appropriation of social-scientific methods and cross-cultural studies. The point is to ask how archaeologists and historians in dialogue can now build on the archaeologists' results in moving toward a critical reconstruction of the social world of Upper Galilee.

To facilitate dialogue with colleagues who have been more exclusively oriented to texts, archaeologists will need to clarify their approaches and procedures. They also will need to explain how particular artifacts provide evidence for certain dimensions of historical life. Pottery provides evidence of chronology. But does it also provide evidence of trade? Coins provide evidence of chronology only if the stratigraphy can be controlled. But what are the complexities and contingencies that we need to consider when attempting to use coins as evidence of trade? It is obviously prohibitive in cost and time to excavate a very large portion of a given site. But how wide a sampling and how representative a sounding are necessary for how extensive a generalization?

As a way of organizing this discussion, I shall follow the archaeologists' own steps in interpretation of their findings in the "conclusions" of

---

2. E.g., Freyne, *Galilee*; Kee, "Early Christianity in the Galilee"; E. M. Meyers, "Roman Sepphoris."

Archaeology and the Villages of Upper Galilee

the book on Meiron,[3] the most completely excavated Upper Galilean village; I shall also include other pertinent material from the Meiron book as well as material from their reports on Gush Halav, Khirbet Shema and en-Nabratein.[4] My questions and comments can then also be framed as an exercise in tracing the history of these villages in Upper Galilee. As preliminary steps toward examining the conclusions about the principal strata at Meiron and the nearby villages, I have questions about the reading and use of literary sources and about how we locate Meiron "on the map."

"READING" AND THE USE OF LITERARY SOURCES

The excavators gather and discuss literary references as a most helpful introduction to the history of the principal site to be explored. To focus only on their discussion of the rabbinic references to Meiron:

> It is thus quite clear that by the time of Stratum III, Meiron's literary pedigree is amply documented. The supposed presence of Simeon bar Yochai there, and the visitation by Rabbi Judah the Prince, redactor of the Mishnah, lend even further importance to the site as a center of learning. The association of Meiron with the burial place of bar Yochai and his son Eliezer and none less than Hillel the Elder, together with an array of other rabbinic personalities, shows how the importance of Meiron grew through the ages as later generations sought to place their stamp of legitimacy on many sacred places in the Holy Land . . .[5]

Indeed, the rather meager collections of literary sources for Meiron in the rabbinic sources, as for many other important Jewish sites, once again underscores the necessity of examining the data of material culture to understand better the world of the sages.[6]

Rather elaborate claims are made on the basis of texts that appear to have been taken at face value. Among the citations of rabbinic references to Meiron, the one given to *benei Meiron*, in the Babylonian Talmud

---

3. E. M. Meyers, Strange, and C. L. Meyers, *Excavations at Ancient Meiron*.

4. E. M. Meyers et al., "Preliminary Report on the 1977 and 1978 Seasons at Gush Halav"; E. M. Meyers, Kraabel, and Strange, *Ancient Synagogue Excavations*; E. M. Meyers, Strange, and C. L. Meyers, "Preliminary Report on the 1980 Excavations at en-Nabratein, Israel"; and E. M. Meyers, Strange, and C. L. Meyers, "Second Preliminary Report on the 1981 Excavations at en-Nabratein, Israel."

5. E. M. Meyers, Strange, C. L. Meyers, *Excavations at Ancient Meiron*, 4.

6. E. M. Meyers, Strange, C. L. Meyers, *Excavations at Ancient Meiron*, 4–5.

commenting on Mishnah Rosh Hashanah 1:2, has a problematic textual history. It is clear even from the rabbinic opinions cited that the Mishnah had referred to *noumeron* (Greek loan word for a military unit), not *bene meron*.[7] This makes us wonder when the other rabbinic references can be dated. Such problematic or post-Mishnaic rabbinic texts hardly provide a "literary pedigree" for Meiron of Stratum III (135–250 CE). No text suggests that Meiron was important "as a center of learning." Meyers, Strange, and Meyers have surely indicated how one should (more critically) approach the later rabbinic and other references to Meiron in their comment about later generations seeking to place their stamp of legitimacy on certain holy places. The opening sentence of their next paragraph then states frankly the serious lack of rabbinic sources for particular sites. It is unclear then how "the literary record" can be claimed to agree that ca. 250–365 was the height of Meiron's culture and that there were only a few squatters thereafter. Moreover, if Meiron was not "a center of learning"; then how would the data of material culture in Meiron lead to better understanding of the world of the sages? Perhaps indirectly. Archaeological reports on sites in Upper Galilee are often heavily dependent on a few literary references for establishing a basic orientation for evaluation of the material remains unearthed. Fuller dialogue with scholars trained in critical evaluation of the pertinent texts could contribute to such basic orientation.

PUTTING MEIRON AND OTHER VILLAGES "ON THE MAP"

After discussing Meiron as a holy site of pilgrimage since the later Middle Ages, the authors attempt "to reconstruct the road system in Upper Galilee" and Meiron's central location in it—on the basis of some of those late-medieval pilgrimage reports. They conclude that we can "infer that Meiron lay on a major east-west route through upper Galilee."[8] That inference, however, has been escalated into the claim of "its pivotal place in Galilee where it straddles a major ancient crossroads and constitutes the very heart of Jewish Galilee in all its conservatism."[9] In the conclusions, this supposed system of roads undergirds what is understood as a commercialized

---

7. Foerster, "Excavations at Ancient Meron," 263.
8. E. M. Meyers, Strange, C. L. Meyers, *Excavations at Ancient Meiron*, 6.
9. E. M. Meyers, Strange, C. L. Meyers, *Excavations at Ancient Meiron*, 4.

economy in which barrels of olive oil are being transported by donkey cart to Tyre to be exchanged for grain.[10]

Recent archaeological work on the ancient Roman road system in Palestine suggests that such a claim for a "major" route through Meiron and a road "system" in Upper Galilee is inflated beyond the evidence.[11] The main military and trade route across Palestine was through the Great Plain, whose terminus at the Mediterranean was Caesarea—once it was built by Herod—which decreased the importance of Acco-Ptolemais. The principal route across Galilee was between Sepphoris and Tiberias; north and south it was between Tiberias and Caesarea Philippi. By comparison, whatever route went through Meiron or Gush Halav was not major, either for the Roman administration or for interregional trade. Even the road reconstructed by Meyers, Strange, and Meyers does not show Meiron straddling "a major crossroads." It would seem important to keep some sort of broader regional and comparative perspective when evaluating finds in the villages of Upper Galilee.

STRATUM I: (LATE-) HELLENISTIC (= STRATUM IV AT GUSH HALAV)

The substantial number of Hasmonean coins, in addition to some significant Hellenistic Tyrian mints, indicate that by the early second century BCE[12] Galilee and Meiron in particular were falling more and more within the orbit of Judean influence. "The Hasmonean coins came from all over the site, suggesting not so much a small circumscribed settlement as a persistent and growing one ... As the century progressed, possible garrisons of the Jewish army were attached to the small community at Meiron."[13] Since some archaeologists avoid making any connections with literary sources, it is most welcome that Meyers, Strange, and their collaborators give periodic attention to passing references in both Josephus and rabbinic literature. It would seem, however, that a broader approach to this literature would help produce a broader orientation to the general area in

---

10. E. M. Meyers, Strange, C. L. Meyers, *Excavations at Ancient Meiron*, 157–58.

11. Esp. Isaac and Roll, *Roman Roads in Judaea I*.

12. It is clear from the context that the early first century BCE is meant. In the early second century, the Seleucids were firmly in control of Galilee and the Zadokite high priesthood still well entrenched in Jerusalem.

13. E. M. Meyers, Strange, C. L. Meyers, *Excavations at Ancient Meiron*, 155.

which they have consciously attempted to implement a regional archaeological study. They draw on both Josephus and a few rabbinic references to identify the site for both Meiron and Gush Halav. Josephus, however, provides a great deal of information both about one of the sites (Gush Halav) and about social–political–economic relations in Upper Galilee generally, although he must be read extremely critically on the Galilee he attempted to dominate in 66–67. In many cases we can draw important historical conclusions with a critical use of his accounts, partly by correlating them with passing references in rabbinic literature. Moreover, direct information on Gush Halav may well be indirectly pertinent to the neighboring sites (Meiron or Khirbet Shema').

We have compelling reasons to doubt Josephus' reports that he fortified all those places in Galilee, including both "Mero/Ameroth" and "Gischala." But he also reports that John of Gischala built up the walls of his native place and that Titus directed his troops to pull down some of the walls of Gischala after the village had surrendered in 67 (*War* 4.117). When these references are combined with a critical reading of m. Arachin 9:6, a second-century CE projection onto the time of Joshua of the "old" fortresses of the Hasmoneans and/or Herodians prior to the wars of 4 BCE and/or 66–67 CE,[14] we have a fairly solid indication that Gush Halav was the site of a Hasmonean–Herodian fortress (cf. Jotapata and Sepphoris). That implies also that whatever Hasmonean (or Herodian) military garrison was in the area was located at Gush Halav, and not Meiron. Given "the significant quantities of Chalcolithic, Early Bronze, and Middle Bronze pottery, . . . significant quantities of Iron II material"; . . . "several nearly complete bowls [from the Persian period]," and the Hellenistic and Hasmonean coins and ceramics found there, Gush Halav had been a well-established settlement for centuries before the Hasmonean regime took over at the very end of the second century BCE.[15] Recognition of the presence of a Hasmonean military fortress at Gush Halav also gives us a more realistic, concrete sense of precisely how "the Hasmoneans" (Jannaeus) were attempting to "reintegrate distant segments of the population into the

---

14. Miller, *Studies in the History and Tradition of Sepphoris*.

15. Judging from the Early Bronze, Iron II, Persian, and Hellenistic pottery that turned up in unstratified fills there, so also had the village of Nabratein to the southeast been occupied for centuries prior to the Hasmonean takeover (E. M. Meyers, Strange, C. L. Meyers, *Excavations at Ancient Meiron*, 5, 11–13; E. M. Meyers, Strange, C. L. Meyers, "Second Preliminary Report on the 1981 Excavations at en-Nabratein, Israel," 35–36).

religious and political life of their kingdom."[16] It also reminds us that Galilee generally had not been under Jerusalem rule for eight centuries prior to 104 BCE. During those centuries Judaean institutions and traditions had developed (and changed) dramatically, with the "second temple" having replaced Solomon's and the Torah having been shaped after the exile of the Judaean ruling aristocracy. Assuming (amidst the paucity of evidence) that the inhabitants of those upper Galilean villages were descendants of former northern Israelites, we are left to inquire more precisely what divergences may have developed between Judaean and Galilean traditions and by what means and in what ways the inhabitants would have been exposed to the Judaean traditions. The distinction commonly made by anthropologists and historical sociologists between the "great tradition" (official and often written as well as oral) and "little tradition" (popular, oral, and often varying locally) may be of some help to both archaeologists and textual scholars in exploring this issue.[17]

STRATUM II: 50 BCE–135 CE, EARLY ROMAN

> By the mid first century B.C.E., or the beginning of the Early Roman Stratum II, there is convincing archaeological evidence both stratigraphic and numismatic that the smallish Jewish community of Meiron was expanding... There is still virtually no archaeological evidence for Meiron or its environs being involved in either the first or second Jewish wars with Rome. Still Josephus' treatment of the Meiron area may reflect some local nationalism and growth. Further a single specimen of the first war was recovered, an unusual discovery outside the largely southern locale of the Revolt.[18]

These generalizations would appear to outrun or misconstrue the evidence available. Can one really conclude so confidently that Meiron was "smallish" yet "expanding" without more complete probes into a wider sample of the site? The same question applies to the claim that there was "growth" in Gush Halav in the first century "beyond the time of John of Giscala."[19]

---

16. E. M. Meyers, Strange, C. L. Meyers, and R. S. Hanson, "Preliminary Report on the 1977 and 1978 Seasons at Gush Halav," 36.

17. Scott, "Protest and Profanation."

18. E. M. Meyers, Strange, C. L. Meyers, *Excavations at Ancient Meiron*, 155–56.

19. E. M. Meyers, Strange, C. L. Meyers, and R. S. Hanson, "Preliminary Report on the 1977 and 1978 Seasons at Gush Halav," 36.

It is difficult to understand how coins, even "rare numismatic specimens," necessarily indicate "economic vitality" in a village; even more difficult to understand is how coins of Nero and the client king Agrippa II indicate "involvement in the national life of the Jewish population of Palestine."[20]

Josephus' accounts of John of Gischala and his followers from the villages of Upper Galilee may well reflect "growth" insofar as several hundred refugees from the Tyrian frontier villages joined in the unrest (*War* 2.588). "Nationalism," however, is one of those anachronistic concepts increasingly being applied to the Jewish revolt of 66-70, inappropriately so.[21] As is clear from Josephus' extensive accounts, the revolt in 66-70 generally involved popular groups along with some basically lower priestly elements in Jerusalem in conflict with their own priestly and Herodian aristocracy as well as the Romans. A critical reading of Josephus' accounts concerning Galilee indicates localized popular rebellion or resistance against the Herodian or Roman governing elite in Tiberias or Sepphoris. Even allowing for Josephus' blatant defaming of his rival for power, John of Gischala, Upper Galilee was clearly a scene of unrest. Josephus' report that there was little resistance to Roman reconquest, on the one hand, while John and many others fled to Jerusalem to continue resistance, on the other, seems highly credible. That provides an appropriate local context for the one coin of the first war recovered at Meiron. It also might provide a context for whatever led Meyers et al. to posit a gap in occupation on the basis of only one probe, 2m to the sides of the lower synagogue at Gush Halav.[22] That is, with "the possibility... [of] occupation on the upper tell during this period and even elsewhere at the lower site," evidence for disruption in a limited area of that lower site would seem rather to point to a limited disruption such as may have ensued with the Roman retaking of the town, with destruction of some of the wall, etc. The Roman retaking of the town in 67 also provides a possible context for the "bronze finger ring engraved 'DOMITILA' in Greek" found at Gush Halav,[23] the most famous "Domitillas" having been the three generations in the Flavian family, with the "granddaughter" born prior to Vespasian's ascension in 69. The latter's son Titus and the Roman

20. E. M. Meyers, Strange, C. L. Meyers, *Excavations at Ancient Meiron*, 155-56.

21. Cf. A. D. Smith, *Theories of Nationalism*

22. E. M. Meyers, Strange, C. L. Meyers, and R. S. Hanson, "Preliminary Report on the 1977 and 1978 Seasons at Gush Halav," 36

23. E. M. Meyers, Strange, C. L. Meyers, and R. S. Hanson, "Preliminary Report on the 1977 and 1978 Seasons at Gush Halav," 55.

army that retook Gush Halav and/or the garrison that remains there would have been acquainted with a "DOMITILA."

> The period between these wars, however, appears to have been quite pivotal from several points of view. As the neutron activation analysis of certain Meiron and related materials suggests, the village after 70 C.E. was absorbing a number of new inhabitants coming from the south ... Perhaps it is this influx of new blood from Judea which enables the village to develop its distinctive character and its special sense of community. It was during this era that the priestly clan of Yehoiariv relocated in Meiron, perhaps lending a certain status to this village, in contrast with many of its neighbors, bereft of such "official' contact with nationalist hopes or institutions.[24]

The nonarchaeologist is left wondering just what neutron activation analysis can indicate. Presumably it can indicate the locus in which pottery is made, if an appropriate control group of pottery is available. So, presumably, one can conclude that some of the pottery found in Meiron was manufactured at a Judaean site. That still leaves the question of how it came to Galilee. Adan-Bayewitz interprets the distribution of pottery made at one site but found in others as evidence for trade in pottery, not migration of people.[25] Beyond these ceramic finds, is there any evidence for "a number of new inhabitants coming from the south"?[26] What sort of archaeological evidence suggests the "distinctive character" and "special sense of community" in Meiron? One would think that in a "conservative" peasant village a big influx of newcomers would have posed a severe problem of adjustment and assimilation, one way or another.

That would only have been further exacerbated for a village of provincial peasants if a large number of the newcomers had been high-ranking priests from the capital city. According to Josephus, the villagers of Upper Galilee had staunchly resisted his attempts to assert the authority of the provisional high priestly government in 66–67. The assertion that the priestly clan of Yehoiariv, which "formerly served in the temple administration," was "reconstituted" at Meiron after 70 places a great deal of credibility

24. E. M. Meyers, Strange, C. L. Meyers, *Excavations at Ancient Meiron*, 156; cf. p. 3.
25. Adan-Bayewitz, *Common Pottery in Roman Galilee*.
26. Admitting the lack of archaeological evidence for migration to Galilee for Judaea, E. M. Meyers elsewhere ("The Cultural Setting of Galilee," 701) refers rather vaguely to "the lists of priestly courses, Josephus, and the rabbinic literature" as "the evidence from literary sources," but without any specification of particular passages. Josephus is an unlikely source for such evidence.

in later Jewish traditions about the locations of the priestly courses after the destruction of the temple.[27] The priestly *mishmarot* and their places of residence were a popular theme in the medieval liturgical poems called *piyyutim*.[28] An earlier reference to the courses and their towns appears in an inscription from Caesarea dated to the end of the third or to the early fourth century.[29] A passage in the Palestinian Talmud connects Yehoiariv specifically with Meron:

> Rabbi Levi said, "Yehoiariv is a (name of a) man. Meron is a city. *Mesarebay* means He (God) delivered (*mesar*) His house (*bayta'*, i.e., temple) to His enemies." Rabbi Berekiah said, "(*Yehoiariv* means) God (*yah*) contended (*heriv*) with his children because they rebelled (*maru*) and defied (*seravu*) Him." (y. Ta'anit 4, 68d)

Levi was active in the second half of the third century, Berakhiah in the late fourth century. Can we project the reconstitution of Yehoiariv in Meiron after the revolt of 66–70 on the basis of these traditions, or is sometime after the Bar Kokhba revolt more realistic? We might also ask what particular finds are in mind when Meyers, Strange, and Meyers claim for the clan of Yehoiariv that "archaeologically speaking their impact is readily discernible in the growth and building activity of the community attested in Stratum III."[30] If, as the excavators admit, "stratigraphically speaking, a pre-70 C.E. community cannot be isolated from a post-70 C.E. community," then what archaeological evidence did they find in Strata I and II to lead them to claim a growth in the community's size or "a slow and gradual intensification of the Jewish character of Meiron"?[31] Were the finds from the earlier strata any less "aniconic" than those of Stratum IV? What exactly were "the persistent reminders" from Stratum II that "despite Meiron's more priestly character" its material culture fits "within the mainstream of everyday life of first century Palestine . . . strongly influenced . . . by outside influences, notably Hellenism."[32]

---

27. E. M. Meyers, Strange, C. L. Meyers, *Excavations at Ancient Meiron*, 3, 156.
28. Miller, *Studies in the History and Traditions of Sepphoris*, 122–27.
29. Avi-Yonah, "The Caesarea Inscription of the Twenty-Four Priestly Courses."
30. E. M. Meyers, Strange, C. L. Meyers, *Excavations at Ancient Meiron*, 3.
31. E. M. Meyers, Strange, C. L. Meyers, *Excavations at Ancient Meiron*, 156.
32. E. M. Meyers, Strange, C. L. Meyers, *Excavations at Ancient Meiron*, 156–57.

ARCHAEOLOGY AND THE VILLAGES OF UPPER GALILEE
STRATUM III: 135–250 CE, MIDDLE ROMAN (=GAP AT GUSH HALAV?)

> Stratum III represents a period of stabilization of village life as well as beginnings of an attempt to lay out the framework of a town plan on the model of the Roman grid . . . Village life was clearly expanding . . . In MI the large domestic-industrial complex . . . was off to a vigorous start . . . The ceramic and numismatic profiles form a picture of a burgeoning population engaged in a number of trades and occupations . . . It is surely Tyre which received barrels of olive oil from Meiron and its adjacent communities, a commodity which was exchanged for other goods . . . It was Meiron's legendary olive oil production within its agriculturally-based economy that was the cornerstone of the local diet as well as the basis of its commercial relations with other areas . . . In return for its rich and perhaps overabundant supply of olives, Meiron no doubt received in return wheat or some other grains as well as money.[33]

As already noted, a dramatic expansion and rebuilding would not likely lead to stabilization, but rather to disruption of the more traditional life of the indigenous population. The hypothesis of a Roman-style town plan is based on only one "planned insula laid over Stratum II remains." Can a town-wide grand plan be projected on this limited basis? Foerster is highly skeptical about "trying to impose Roman concepts of urban town-planning on a small settlement."[34] It is unclear how a decreasing number of coins somehow indicates a burgeoning population. A parallel hypothesis of "expansion and modest wealth" for the village of Nabratein is more credibly based on the finds in a recently built villa that coincides with the building of a synagogue there.[35] But of course that evidence might indicate not so much expansion of population as the emergence of a modestly wealthy social stratum, which may have spearheaded the mobilization of labor and economic resources for such major building projects as a village and a synagogue. Presumably the better indicators of population growth—an increase in space occupied or the density of occupation—were beyond the scope of a limited excavation. The hypothesis that "the expansion of Jewish communal life at Meiron in Stratum III can be related . . . to the transfer of

---

33. E. M. Meyers, Strange, C. L. Meyers, *Excavations at Ancient Meiron*, 157.

34. Foerster, "Excavations at Ancient Meron," 266.

35. E. M. Meyers, Strange, C. L. Meyers, "Preliminary Report on the 1980 Excavations at en-Nabratein, Israel," 14.

the Sanhedrin to Tiberias around 230 C.E." involves both a (standard but now questioned) synthetic construction of the continuity and authority of the Sanhedrin in Jewish history and an assumption of rabbinic influence on local life that is not born out by rabbinic literature itself.[36]

More questionable is the apparent industrial–commercial model applied to the material remains of Meiron. This would appear to have determined both the assessment of buildings and artifacts and the interpretation of the findings in general. It also raises questions about the procedure of basing ever broader and more speculative hypotheses upon earlier conjectures. The escalation toward the "large domestic–industrial complex" and a commercial economy with the vicinity of Meiron as the center of the entire olive oil industry in Roman Palestine" begins from speculation about two distinctive items found in Room E of the main house in Field I.[37] The initial speculation about the first, a "most striking remnant of ancient technology"—a rounded stone installation 0.75m north–south and 1.2m east–west and 0.56m high topped by a semicircular stone with a finished inside and top surface, with a 0.51m square trimmed block inside the stone circle, along with a cooking pot—is cautious and tentative: "the function of this installation can only be conjectured."[38] Further speculation focuses on the second item, "a bronze plane or scraper with an iron handle," found in the debris on the floor: "This suggested that wood-working activities were carried out here, perhaps the manufacture of wooden containers or barrels for the thriving Galilean olive and olive oil industry centered around ancient Meiron. A stone workbench along Wall 2006 would have provided an auxiliary work surface. Room E, it appears, might be called a cooperage."[39] Next comes a jump from a scraping tool to an industry: "All together, the layout of the main building, with living quarters and workshops identified, and the existence of attached buildings has led the Expedition to refer to the MI insula as a domestic-industrial complex."[40] By the conclusion, however, the excavators not only jump from a *conjecture* that the function of the installation was barrel-making to a workshop that "*might be* called a cooperage," but they make an even greater leap, claiming that "the existence of a *possible* cooperage or barrel producing shop in MI enables us to

---

36. Goodman, *State and Society in Roman Galilee.*
37. E. M. Meyers, Strange, C. L. Meyers, *Excavations at Ancient Meiron*, 157.
38. E. M. Meyers, Strange, C. L. Meyers, *Excavations at Ancient Meiron*, 36–37.
39. E. M. Meyers, Strange, C. L. Meyers, *Excavations at Ancient Meiron*, 37.
40. E. M. Meyers, Strange, C. L. Meyers, *Excavations at Ancient Meiron*, 38.

hypothesize that transport of olive oil at some times was effected in wooden barrels carried in mule-drawn or donkey-drawn carts."[41] "Certain local crafts and industries, particularly with respect to olive production, would be expected," they claim, citing finally "the authority and force of the literary notices which identify the vicinity of Meiron as the center of the entire olive oil industry in Roman Palestine."[42]

There appear to be a number of problems both with such assessments of their findings and with their broader commercial interpretation, the least of which is the failure of any olive press to appear in the digs at Meiron.[43] Foerster is skeptical about the evaluation of Room E as a commercial and crafts workshop, suggesting instead that it is another "open courtyard connected with the K–L courtyard," containing an oven, a grinding stone, and other domestic objects. He believes, further, that the bronze scraping tool, which could not sustain much of a cutting edge, could not have been used effectively in woodworking.[44] Any traditional village household would presumably have done its own crafts, and most selling portrayed in passing in rabbinic literature apparently took place in a domestic house. It is difficult to understand what would be the criteria for what Meyers, Strange, and Meyers call "structural evidence of crafts in Room E" i.e., what would distinguish a "domestic-industrial complex" from a regular domestic complex.[45] The jump from a potential woodworking tool to barrels for oil would be credible only if there were evidence that barrels were used for storage or shipment of oil in ancient Palestine. Presumably rabbinic literature would have been concerned about purity issues with respect to such vessels, making the presence or absence of such a topic in rabbinic literature an appropriate test. Furthermore, the rabbinic

---

41. E. M. Meyers, Strange, C. L. Meyers, *Excavations at Ancient Meiron*, 157–58 (my emphasis).

42. E. M. Meyers, Strange, C. L. Meyers, *Excavations at Ancient Meiron*, 157.

43. Frankel, "Some Oil Presses from Western Galilee," 65–68.

44. Foerster, "Excavations at Ancient Meron," 266–67.

45. E. M. Meyers, Strange, C. L. Meyers, *Excavations at Ancient Meiron*, 37. In the interest of maintaining communications with other academic fields, it would perhaps be better to avoid idiosyncratic usage of a term used elsewhere in academic discourse to distinguish modern industrialized societies from ancient or medieval or modern "pre-industrial" (agrarian or horticultural) societies. Certainly local crafts "would be expected" in the villages of Upper Galilee as elsewhere, but not industries.

references cited[46] mention only the legendary quality of the oil in Meiron, Teqoʻa and Khirbet Shemaʻ, not its quantity.

Most problematic, surely, is the projection of a commercial model onto artifacts, houses, and olive production—a projection paralleled in the interpretation of the incidence of Tyrian coins found at these Upper Galilean villages.[47] As explained more fully elsewhere,[48] it seems highly unlikely that one can move directly from the incidence of Tyrian coinage to trade with Tyre. That Meiron and other Upper Galilean villages were trading their oil for grains in the way that Meyers, Strange, and Meyers imagine seems highly unlikely, given the high cost of overland transport. In Upper Galilean villages, as generally in the Roman empire, self-sufficiency was the fundamental principle of the economy.[49] Upper Galilean villagers would have produced a surplus of oil beyond their own needs; such was demanded, of course, by the Roman (and Herodian) government as taxes or tribute, as Meyers, Strange, and Meyers recognize.[50] Given its legendary quality, it is conceivable that some oil was transported—despite the high cost—to Tyre and elsewhere. But exchange of oil for grain would not have been the basis of the village economy. Rather, as elsewhere in agrarian societies, each household produced most of what it consumed and consumed much of what it produced.[51] Beyond the possible export of produce taken in taxes, trade would likely have been primarily in luxury goods for the local or regional elite (below).

Meyers' attempts to delineate the distinctive features of the (conservative) culture of the Upper Galilean villages have been complicated by his attempts to make the supposedly extensive trade with Tyre fit into an otherwise intelligible pattern.[52] Once we recognize that the supposed trade with Tyre results from the commercial model imposed onto the ancient situation, the hypothesis of regionalism in Galilee becomes all the more convincing.

46. E. M. Meyers, Strange, C. L. Meyers, *Excavations at Ancient Meiron*, 3n23.

47. E. M. Meyers, "Introduction" 1–4.

48. Horsley, "The Historical Jesus and Archaeology in the Galilee," 105–6.

49. Finley, *The Ancient Economy*, 93–149; Jones, *The Roman Economy*, 29–60; Garnsey and Saller, *The Roman Society*, 42–46.

50. E. M. Meyers, Strange, C. L. Meyers, *Excavations at Ancient Meiron*, 157.

51. Wolf, *Peasants*.

52. E. M. Meyers, "Galilean Regionalism as a Factor in Historical Reconstruction"; E. M. Meyers, "The Cultural Setting of Galilee"; and E. M. Meyers, "Galilean Regionalism: A Reappraisal."

STRATUM IV: 250–365 CE, LATE ROMAN (=VIA AT GUSH HALAV)

> The beginning of Stratum IV signals the heyday of the Meiron community . . . symbolized in the construction of the basilical synagogue on the highest point of the hill . . . The repertoire of finewares from the Patrician House reveals a family and culture with access to the very best domestic products available in the markets of the day . . . Other factors, particularly in Stratum IV, point to the piety, or the general religious character, of the Meiron population. [Besides] the general prominence of the synagogue . . . the discovery of a *miqveh* built slightly earlier than Stratum IV . . . leads to the supposition that Stratum IV inhabitants . . . would also have had such an installation for their use in matters of personal purity . . . The medical report on the bones recovered in the tomb indicates that endog[a]my or marriage among kin was a major cause of disease at Meiron . . . The simplest historical interpretation . . . is that such selectivity derives from a sense of religious self-consciousness . . . Finally, a sense of religious conservatism emerges from an analysis of the food remains and inscribed jars of Room F in the Patrician House.[53]

The "conclusions" section on Stratum IV leaves more issues unaddressed than addressed, particularly when the findings are compared with those of earlier strata. The Patrician House and Lintel House are not all that large and ostentatious. However, they do reveal significant fine-wares, attesting a certain amount of trade with the outside in luxury goods for the local elite—what we would expect in such a regional agrarian economy. Such fineware was not unprecedented in Upper Galilean villages, as can be seen from the first century BCE–CE sherd inscribed with *arist.* in Greek found at Gush Halav.[54] The amount of finewares in Stratum IV, however, was apparently significantly more than in earlier strata. Together with the appearance of a few larger houses and the construction of an impressive basilica-style synagogue, this indicates a striking increase in resources mobilized with focus on these buildings and the families who occupied these houses. Does such evidence point to certain interrelated developments in the third century, such as an increasing social differentiation between emerging wealthy

---

53. E. M. Meyers, Strange, C. L. Meyers, *Excavations at Ancient Meiron*, 157–58.

54. E. M. Meyers, Strange, C. L. Meyers, and R. S. Hanson, "Preliminary Report on the 1977 and 1978 Seasons at Gush Halav," 56.

families and others, a larger group of families with means, an ability of the powerful to mobilize the considerable resources of labor and materials and support to build such an imposing edifice as the synagogue building (as well as their own more spacious houses)?

The cavity identified as a miqveh also raises more questions than are addressed. Foerster points out that it must have been an extremely tiny installation, requiring unusual size or agility to enter and exit.[55] The presence of numerous *miqvaot* in the areas excavated from the same period at Sepphoris poses a curious contrast to their absence in the excavated areas of Meiron.[56] How would the lack of concern for ritual purity in Stratum IV at Meiron square with the hypothesis of the priestly course of Yehoiariv having settled there well over a century previously? Another key discovery taken as evidence for a conservative religious (priestly?) piety at Meiron is interpreted differently by Foerster, who writes: "There is nothing unusual in the assemblage found in this room [F], which was most probably a storage place for some of the valuables of the house including foodstuffs." He takes the "inscription" with its impossible *alep* rather as a simple decoration "very like the typical late Roman and Byzantine patterns made with a comb-like tool with five teeth before firing," as illustrated by two pottery lids found in the same Patrician House.[57]

The evidence from the excavated tomb also raises more questions than are addressed by the report on Meiron. There would appear to be a serious ambiguity or discrepancy in the major hypotheses presented in the conclusions. On the one hand, the authors want to have a burgeoning population expanded especially by extensive immigration from Judaea, including the priestly clan of Yehoiariv, with stabilization and solidarity in the Meiron community. On the other hand, the most compelling way to explain the tomb spanning Strata II through IV that appears to be of one family, and that endogamous, is out of conservative religious orientation. There are obvious historical-cultural factors that would have made it most difficult for provincial Galilean peasants to assimilate, or assimilate to, the incoming Judaeans or Jerusalem priestly families, with all the attendant issues of status and power. Besides which, the conservative Galilean families with their own indigenous regional customs, and the conservative Judaean and Jerusalem priestly families, with their highly

55. Foerster, "Excavations at Ancient Meron," 267.
56. E. M. Meyers, Netzer, and C. L. Meyers, *Sepphoris*, 27–29.
57. Foerster, "Excavations at Ancient Meron," 268.

self-conscious purity codes and special customs, would have encountered numerous obstacles to solidarity in the newly expanded community. If endogamy is a reasonably credible hypothesis to account for the data in the tomb, then perhaps it would fit better with a hypothesis of conflict within the village of Meiron that would likely have resulted from the hypothesized influx of a priestly clan and other Judaeans sometime in the course of the second century.

UPPER GALILEAN REGIONALISM

While the excavations of the villages and assessment of the findings were underway, Meyers presented the double hypothesis that Upper Galilee displays a distinctive regional culture and that this culture was conservatively Jewish.[58] Simply on the basis of the topography of the region and the fact that it was not included in the Roman "urbanization" of Palestine, it seems highly credible that its culture was both regional and less impacted by Roman-Hellenistic culture than that of Lower Galilee. Meyers' case for Upper Galilean regionalism on the basis of material culture, however, appears questionable on two counts.

First, it is unclear when and in what way Upper Galilean village culture was "Jewish." As noted above, Meyers, Strange, and Meyers comment that by the early first century BCE Galilee and Meiron "were falling more and more within the orbit of Jewish influence," i.e., that the Hasmoneans took control of the area.[59] Galilee was then directly under Jerusalem rule for only a century (the first two-thirds of which were filled with extreme turmoil!) before the Romans installed their client ruler Antipas (4 BCE), who built his capital city over a cemetery and adorned his palace in violation of the ancestral laws of the Judaeans (*Ant.* 18.38; *Life* 65). Meyers (1976: 101) claims that "On the basis of material culture alone, it would appear that Upper Galilean village life was firmly rooted, with its own distinctive elements, by the time the Second Temple was destroyed."[60] In the subsequent reports on excavations of the villages of Upper Galilee, however, one can

---

58. E. M. Meyers, "Galilean Regionalism as a Factor in Historical Reconstruction"; E. M. Meyers, "The Cultural Setting of Galilee"; and E. M. Meyers, "Galilean Regionalism: A Reappraisal."

59. E. M. Meyers, Strange, C. L. Meyers, *Excavations at Ancient Meiron*, 155.

60. E. M. Meyers, "Galilean Regionalism as a Factor in Historical Reconstruction," 101.

find little by way of material culture distinctive to Upper Galilee or distinctively "Jewish" prior to 70 CE. Meyers' argument that "Josephus pictures Galilee as consisting mainly of Torah-true Jews"[61] is based solely on a 1973 dissertation that preceded much of the development of a critical reading of Josephus' histories.[62]

For the middle and late Roman periods, Meyers lays great emphasis on the importance of the influx of Judaeans into Upper Galilee after the destruction of Jerusalem. But in that connection he gives two diametrically opposed explanations of ostensibly distinctive regional elements in Upper Galilean material culture. On the one hand, a very strong influence by "the already established community . . . would explain why 'northern' ceramic forms come to predominate early in the second century."[63] On the other hand, the resettled Judaeans, once they had gained an economic base in the Upper Galilean villages, were supposedly responsible for the building of the synagogues of late antiquity and for the fragments of "Jewish art."[64] If we are persuaded about the influx of Judaeans, which rests only on weak literary evidence in the first place, then the "Jewish" material culture appears to be an eclectic amalgam of indigenous pottery types and imported building styles and decorative elements.

Second, it is unclear just how different the material culture of Upper Galilean villages is from that of Lower Galilee, particularly that of Lower Galilean villages. Upper Galilee is judged "Jewish" and "conservative" on the basis of third- and fourth-century evidence from villages. Lower Galilee is judged to be more cosmopolitan and Roman-Hellenized on the basis of evidence introduced in connection with Jesus–Nazareth–Sepphoris in the first century CE or evidence largely from sites such as Beth Shearim, Hammat-Tiberias, and Magdala, i.e., cities or large towns near cities-and in the case of Beth Shearim not even clearly considered part of Galilee in the first century and certainly not typical.[65] But can we assume that Lower

---

61. E. M. Meyers, "Galilean Regionalism as a Factor in Historical Reconstruction," 93; and E. M. Meyers, "The Cultural Setting of Galilee," 693, 701.

62. E.g., Cohen, *Josephus in Galilee and Rome*; Rajak, *Josephus*; Bilde, *Flavius Josephus*. Freyne's parallel argument (*Galilee*) that Galileans in the early Roman period were solidly loyal to temple and Torah was based on later rabbinic references, many of which appear to suggest just the opposite. His work also preceded the development of more critical methods of reading rabbinic texts by Neusner and others.

63. E. M. Meyers, "The Cultural Setting of Galilee," 700

64. E. M. Meyers, "Galilean Regionalism as a Factor in Historical Reconstruction," 99.

65. Cf. E. M. Meyers and Strange, *Archaeology, the Rabbis, and Early Christianity*, 44.

Galilean villages simply assimilated Roman-Hellenistic cultural influences rather than reacted against them?

Moreover, on second look some of the Upper Galilean material culture may appear not all that different from the corresponding Lower Galilean culture. (a) Inscriptional evidence as presented may have been misleading. Inscriptions in Greek are indeed all but lacking in Upper Galilee. But a large proportion of the Greek inscriptions in Lower Galilee are clustered in sites around the Sea of Galilee; and, far more important, it seems inappropriate to include as evidence typical for Lower Galilee inscriptions from Beth Shearim, which became the burial place of choice for wealthy diaspora Jews. (b) The bulk of ceramics in any region would likely be locally produced. This makes all the more striking the recent recognition that a significant proportion of certain cooking wares in both Lower Galilee (including Sepphoris and Tiberias) and Upper Galilee (and even the Golan) were produced at Kefar Hananya, on the border between the two regions.[66] (c) As Meyers acknowledged,[67] evidence of architectural types among synagogue buildings does not vary by region, but across and within regions (the broadhouse building at Khirbet Shema' being only a kilometer from the basilical building at Meiron). (d) The "Jewish art" in Upper Galilee, which Meyers calls "conservative,"[68] does not appear all that different from the corresponding art in Lower Galilean sites. Vale's count of particular representations indicates an equally high occurrence of geometric (80%), vegetable (50%), floral (40%), and circle surround (40%) motifs (and the almost total lack of Torah shrines) in both Upper and Lower Galilean synagogues.[69] These similarities would appear to balance or outweigh the differences: menorah (55/30%, Upper/Lower), animal (30/80%), fowl and human (both 12/40%). The evidence for variation in material culture between Upper and Lower Galilee thus boils down to a

---

66. Adan-Bayewitz, *Common Pottery in Roman Galilee*. Moreover, Meyers' grand claims for the significance of the incidence of Tyrian coins in Upper Galilean villages ("Introduction," 1–4) quickly become less persuasive when one notes the similar percentage of Tyrian coins in a horde at Magdala, cited by his collaborator (Hanson, *Tyrian Influence in the Upper Galilee*, 53, 69n5).

67. E. M. Meyers, "Galilean Regionalism as a Factor in Historical Reconstruction," 99.

68. E. M. Meyers, "Galilean Regionalism as a Factor in Historical Reconstruction," 99.

69. Vale, "Literary Sources in Archaeological Description." Moreover, if the eagle is a distinctively Upper Galilean motif within Galilee (E. M. Meyers, "Galilean Regionalism as a Factor in Historical Reconstruction," 99), it is surely not a distinctively Jewish motif, since it is prominent in pagan temples in the wider area, such as the one at nearby Kedesh (Fischer, Ovadiah, and Roll, "The Roman Temple at Kedesh").

less striking language difference than claimed (no Greek compared with some Greek) and to far less of a difference in synagogue art, with more menorahs and less animal, fowl, and human representation in the north. Is it possible that the variations in culture between villages and cities or towns within Lower Galilee were as significant as those between Upper and Lower Galilean villages?

ON PROCEEDING MORE RELATIONALLY AND SYSTEMATICALLY

Having long since outrun my own historical competence by the time of late antiquity, I wish only to reflect somewhat on how we might be able to ask questions and address issues across some of the categories into which archaeologists, like textually or historically oriented scholars, divide up the material to be analyzed and evaluated. Some examples: What might bones have to do with trade? As discussed above, the Meiron excavators worked with a market model of the economy in Meiron and Upper Galilee generally, suggesting that the superabundant olive oil was traded, primarily in Tyre, for grains and money. They then report, as part of their probing attempt to explain the sudden abandonment of the site in the late fourth century, that analysis of the bones in the Meiron tomb indicates an overall iron and protein deficiency, a deficiency that would not have existed "if fish were a regular part of the diet."[70] That suggests that there was not an active trade with Magdala, Capernaum, or Tiberias for fish. It might also be pertinent to the question of trade to ask what kinds of pottery were not found at Meiron, Gush Halav, and Khirbet Shemaʿ in comparison with coastal sites, particularly cities where the well-to-do were likely importing heavy and valuable goods via the sea lanes. Were amphorae associated with fine wines found in Upper Galilean villages, indicating trade for oil or other products? If not, does their absence suggest anything about trading patterns? The use of certain types of pottery might also be pertinent to the question of trade and "industry" (crafts). What was the usual container for olive oil in Palestine? Were amphorae used, and were those among the pottery made in the region, or brought in from some distance?

I return, finally, to the correlation between material and literary sources for the reconstruction of social life in antiquity. One of the ways

70. E. M. Meyers, Strange, C. L. Meyers, *Excavations at Ancient Meiron*, 161.

Archaeology and the Villages of Upper Galilee

in which the work of Meyers, Strange, Meyers and their collaborators is an important breakthrough in archeological approach is their broader long-range strategy of analyzing not just a site, but a site as part of a region. If an individual archaeological site is to be considered as part of a region, then literary sources should be approached similarly. That is, instead of looking only for the references to Meiron in an analysis of Meiron, or Gush Halav in an analysis of Gush Halav, the literary sources available—primarily Josephus for Strata I and II and rabbinic literature for Strata III and IV should be read as they treat the whole region.

But of course that moves us back to how we should be assessing our literary sources anyhow, i.e., by reading them in both their literary and historical-social context. For example, besides Josephus' sketch of the involvement of the Gischalans and other Upper Galilean villagers in localized insurrections in 66–67, he points to certain long-range hostilities between Upper Galileans and Tyrians, particularly in Kedesh, hostilities related to a certain class conflict in nearby Tyrian territory, manifest in the Tyrian refugees who joined the Upper Galileans in the social turmoil of 66–67. Josephus also mentions the "imperial stores of grain" in Upper Galilee that John of Gischala wanted to raid (while Josephus had his own designs on the granaries). Not only would this confirm the archaeologists' suggestion that Upper Galilean villagers paid their imperial taxes in kind (grain as well as oil), but it indicates that the Upper Galileans raised their own grain (with "surplus" for taxes)—further confirmation that a commercial model of the Upper Galilean political economy is inappropriate.

This regional approach to the literary sources and their correlation with the material remains also reminds us to deal more fully with what some of those references are in the sources, e.g., what it may have meant in political-economic terms, that the principal Upper Galilean villages were a tetrakomia, at least for a certain period. The political-economic status of villages and the changes therein would appear to be highly pertinent to the assessment of the findings of these important excavations. While many scholars trained primarily in analysis of literary sources are finally recognizing the importance of archaeological findings, some archaeologists have recently recognized that literary and archaeological evidence can be correlated only by means of some (re-)construction of the social world from which they originated.[71] Both may soon realize that any evidence must be

---

71. Strange, "Some Implications of Archaeology for New Testament Study," 24–30.

interpreted in the context of the dominant historical political-economic system in ancient Roman Palestine, for which comparative sociological analyses of traditional agrarian societies are more appropriate than early modern market models.[72]

---

72. Lenski, *Power and Privilege*; Kautsky, *The Politics of Aristocratic Empires*, with appropriate adaptations.

6

Archaeology of Galilee and the Historical Context of Jesus

MUCH OF THE RECENT debate about the historical Jesus hinges on assessment of the cultural ethos of Galilee. As recently as 1980—prior both to recent archaeological explorations and to the application of comparative sociological analysis to ancient Palestine—Sean Freyne could still paint a picture of Galilee reminiscent of the Galilean idyll of Ernest Renan. Freyne concluded that the social world of Galilee consisted primarily of peasant villages, with cities lying on the perimeter.

> Their life style and occupation did not bring them into any kind of meaningful contact with the real agents for social change . . . Horizons were limited because the rhythm of life was determined by the seasons, and so there was no sense of unrest or frustration.[1]

Even after reviewing the intervening archaeological explorations in Galilee, he reaffirmed basically the same sketch of "an essentially rural Galilee."[2]

Almost simultaneously in understandable excitement over recent archaeological explorations at Sepphoris, other interpreters sketched an opposing picture. Lower Galilee, at least, was highly urbanized, as much

1. Freyne, *Galilee*, 195.
2. Freyne, *Galilee, Jesus, and the Gospels*, 145.

so as anywhere else in the Roman empire![3] Scholars eager for evidence to support their interpretation of Jesus as a sage, even a Cynic or Cynic-like sage, quickly appropriated the newly discovered Galilee.[4] Ironically, what had been almost a passing comment by archaeologist Eric Meyers a decade previously, that "the great urban centers" had mediated a "cosmopolitan atmosphere" to the villages of Lower Galilee,[5] became the basis for positing a highly Hellenized culture, even Cynic philosophy, as the context in which Jesus taught an unconventional wisdom. The timing of the discovery of a cosmopolitan Galilee as a context for Jesus the sage could not have been better. Jesus scholars had only recently determined that the supposedly "eschatological" or "apocalyptic" Jesus of modern scholarly construction was a secondary stratum in the Jesus-tradition.[6] Suddenly the previous historical basis for understanding Jesus, the Israelite (biblical) tradition which he appeared to presuppose, was viewed as a secondary layer of interpretation to the Cynic-like sage who spoke in sapiential aphorisms.

In contrast to previous treatments of Jesus, at least these recent studies were taking note of archaeological reports. Few studies in the 1980s had yet done so. Sanders made no use of archaeology;[7] even the issue of social conflict had not led researchers into archaeology.[8] The dialogue, however, has barely begun. And some ironies are immediately evident, such as textual scholars borrowing archaeological reports which are, in turn, based primarily on previous textual studies. For example, Crossan makes the link crucial to his case between pan-Mediterranean culture and Jesus by means of a reconstruction of the social world of Galilee derived from recent archaeological reports. The key points in the latter, however, are in turn taken by "archaeologists" from texts or scholarly analysis of texts. Most of the information about Sepphoris taken to indicate that it had courts, a fortress, a palace, two markets, archives, a royal bank, and an arsenal were taken from Josephus or late rabbinic literature.[9] Crossan's final step, implicitly

---

3. Overman, "Who Were the First Urban Christians?"; Edwards, "First Century Urban/Rural Relations in Lower Galilee."

4. Mack, "The Kingdom That Didn't Come"; Crossan, *The Historical Jesus*.

5. E. M. Meyers, "The Cultural Setting of Galilee," 697–98.

6. Borg, "A Temperate Case for a Non-eschatological Jesus"; Kloppenborg, *The Formation of Q*; Mack, "The Kingdom That Didn't Come."

7. Sanders, *Jesus and Judaism*.

8. Such as Horsley, *Jesus and the Spiral of Violence*; Oakman (*Jesus and the Economic Questions of His Day*), on the other hand, draws more substantively on archaeology.

9. Overman, "Who Were the First Urban Christians?," 164.

linking Jesus with the cosmopolitan cultural currents supposedly dominant in Sepphoris, derives ultimately from an argument by Goodman based on inferences from literary sources.[10] The argument might be susceptible to the charge of circularity except that, to double the irony, Goodman's inferences from literary sources pertain to *Jewish Aramaic culture* two centuries later!

While the dialogue has barely begun, both archaeologists and text-oriented scholars may benefit from common problems and adjustments that will be necessary in adjusting to new evidence and new questions. For example, both are struggling with conceptual categories heavily influenced by theology. Understandably, given the standard conceptual apparatus of scholarly training, archaeologists' interpretation of material remains is dominated by the same dichotomies of essentialist categories (e.g., "Jewish" vs "Hellenistic") that often still dominate interpretations of texts. Archaeologists as well as textual scholars, moreover, are recognizing that the significance attributed to a particular text-fragment or material artifact depends upon the interpreter's picture of the social world of ancient Palestine. Both may therefore have an interest in critical approaches to the reconstruction of the social world that constituted the historical context of both texts and material culture.[11] Given the general paucity of evidence for Roman Galilee, comparative material and comparative sociological and anthropological studies may be of considerable mutual interest for further historical inquiry into life in ancient Galilee.[12]

ESSENTIALIST CONCEPTS VERSUS ARCHAEOLOGICAL AND LITERARY EVIDENCE

Both the "cosmopolitan/Hellenistic" Galilee and the "Jewish" Galilee may be more the product of the essentialist habits of the modern scholarly mind than of archaeological and literary evidence. On the basis of synthetic

---

10. See Edwards, "First Century Urban/Rural Relations in Lower Galilee."

11. "Settlement" archaeologists, some of whom were mentioned appreciatively by Strange ("New Developments in Greco-Roman Archaeology in Palestine," 85), increasingly emphasized that political-economic structures and political changes shape social and settlement patterns (Trigger, *A History of Archaeological Thought*, 284). More recently, archaeologists such as Renfrew stress the importance of social organization and power relations, while pointing out that for literate societies (such as ancient Roman Palestine) literary sources can answer many of the social questions (Renfrew and Bahn, *Archaeology*, 153, 162).

12. Horsley, *Sociology and the Jesus Movement*; Horsley, *Galilee*.

modern constructs given artifacts are identified as "Hellenistic" or "Jewish." Then on the basis of a few such artifacts, a site is declared to have a certain cultural identity or character. A critical examination of recent archaeological reports will indicate how inadequate and inappropriate the standard essentialist categories are to the material and literary evidence.

Claims of an urbanized and cosmopolitan Galilee seem to derive from Meyers' characterization of the "great urban centers" of Lower Galilee in contrast to the "regionalism" of the villages of Upper Galilee. Sepphoris and Tiberias (and even Tarichaeae/Magdala) are identified as Hellenistic cities primarily on the basis of Josephus' reports about them (or other towns!) that one or another had a *boulē*, an *ekklēsia*, a *stadion*, or a *hippodrome*, typical institutions of a Hellenistic polis. Tcherikover demonstrated some time ago, however, than we cannot conclude that Jerusalem was a Hellenistic *polis* on the basis of the terminology used by Josephus, who, in communicating with his readers, is casting in typical Hellenistic terms what were still very different and distinctive Jerusalem institutions. It is unwarranted, therefore, to conclude that Sepphoris, as rebuilt by Antipas after 4 BCE, or Tiberias, the new city founded by Antipas less than two decades later, were typical Hellenistic *poleis*, with all the attendant Hellenistic or Roman-Hellenistic cultural elements.

A highly influential insertion at least into the American discussion has been the grand estimates of the population of these cities: 30,000 for Sepphoris, nearly as high for Tiberias and Tarichaeae, and even 12,000 to 15,000 for Capernaum.[13] These appear to be grossly inflated figures. In estimating population in the late Roman-Byzantine period, the time of maximum density, Broshi indicates that Diocaesarea/Sepphoris and Tiberias were medium-sized cities of 60 and 40 hectares respectively (compared with Caesarea at 95 or Aelia Capitolina at 120).[14] If the density of the Galilean cities was comparable to that of Pompeii at 125–156 per hectare rather than the unusually high density of Ostia at 435,[15] then the population of each would have been below 10,000 in late antiquity, and correspondingly much less at the time of their initial (re-)building under Antipas. Recent estimates for Capernaum have returned to the more sober earlier figure of somewhat over a thousand.[16] There are thus no firmer bases for the claims

---

13. E.g., Meyers and Strange, *Archaeology, the Rabbis, and Early Christianity*.
14. Broshi, "The Population of Western Palestine in the Roman-Byzantine Period."
15. Reed, "The Population of Capernaum."
16. Cf. Reed, "The Population of Capernaum."

of the scope of "urbanization" in Galilee at the time of Jesus than there are for its characterization as Hellenistic and cosmopolitan.

However, if the recent portrayals of the Galilean cities as Hellenistic *poleis* are not credible, would the standard conceptual obverse of a heavily "Jewish" cultural ethos be any more credible? Meyers's more recent portrayals of Sepphoris "in the light of new archaeological evidence and recent research" appear almost to refute his earlier picture of the "great urban centers" of Lower Galilee and their "cosmopolitan atmosphere." While continuing to rely on essentialist categories, he now claims that "there can be little doubt that the overwhelming majority or virtually all of the inhabitants of Sepphoris in the first century CE were Jewish."[17] Meyers attempts to demonstrate that "the archaeological record thus far revealed supports the picture of Sepphoris presented by Josephus and some of the rabbinic literature, i.e., that Sepphoris from the first century CE onwards was a city inhabited by many well-to-do, aristocratic Jews of a priestly background."[18] However, Josephus presents no such picture of Sepphoris in the first century CE, and Meyers can produce little archaeological evidence for his claim prior to the Middle and Late Roman periods. Other archaeologists are finding that generally speaking "ethnicity is difficult to recognize from the archaeological record."[19] A critical review of the limited literary evidence previously adduced on this question suggests, in fact, that there is little or no evidence to warrant such an essentialist claim for Sepphoris in the first century (the time of Jesus).

The claim that "Sepphoris was apparently the home town of many priests, some of whom even served as high priests in the Jerusalem Temple" rests almost completely on late rabbinic evidence.[20] Earlier scholars proceeded in a rather trusting and synthetic manner. Two examples are specially relevant to the question of priestly presence in Sepphoris. (1) Relying first on the lists of the twenty-four priestly courses (and their locations in Galilee) in medieval liturgical poems known as *piyyutim*, then taking somewhat at face value the late version of a tradition in the eighth century Kohelet Rabbah (the earlier parallel in y. Kilayim 9, 32b lacks the

---

17. E. M. Meyers, "Roman Sepphoris," 324; E. M. Meyers, Netzer, and C. L. Meyers, *Sepphoris*, 12.

18. E. M. Meyers, "Roman Sepphoris," 322; E. M. Meyers, Netzer, and C. L. Meyers, *Sepphoris*, 10.

19. Renfrew and Bahn, *Archaeology*, 169.

20. E. M. Meyers, Netzer, and C. L. Meyers, *Sepphoris*, 10.

crucial "sons of Yedayah"!), earlier reconstructions assumed early dates for the presence of the Jedaiah priestly clan in Sepphoris. (2) It is even claimed, on the basis of t. Yoma 1.4; y. Yoma 1, 38d; b. Yoma 12b; and Josephus (*Ant.* 17.166), that one priestly family in Sepphoris was so prominent that shortly before his death Herod had bestowed the high priesthood on two of its members.[21]

Stuart Miller, however, has recently pioneered a more critical examination of these and other rabbinic traditions regarding priestly presence in Sepphoris. On (1) he demonstrates that only the tradition in y. Ta'anit 4, 68d can be used to locate the *mishmar* of Yedayah in Sepphoris, sometime in the fourth century, which fits with the dating of the fragmentary inscription of the priestly courses found at Caesarea.[22] On (2) he finds no evidence in the rabbinic traditions that Joseph ben Elim had any special social or political standing among the priestly aristocracy.[23] If we follow Miller's critical assessment of rabbinic traditions, then there is no rabbinic memory of priestly presence in Sepphoris until the latter half of the second century. As to the first century CE or earlier, we can only speculate that the Hasmoneans might have stationed some priests in Sepphoris in the role of "magistrates" in "civil" and administrative affairs. But what would have happened to those priestly families under Herod and particularly in the Josephus-reported destruction and enslavement of 4 BCE? It seems unlikely that Antipas would have had much of an interest in bringing priests to Sepphoris and probably he had no authority to do so. The late rabbinic evidence available suggests that Judean priests probably settled in Sepphoris only after the destruction of the temple, even more likely after the Bar Kokhba Revolt. They apparently had achieved some prominence in the city by the third and fourth centuries.

---

21. E.g., Stern, *Greek and Latin Authors*, 1:272 n2. Stern and others, trusting these rabbinic traditions as good evidence for the prominence of the Sepphorean Joseph ben Elem (who served as high priest for an hour!) at the time of Herod, then draw the conclusion that, because Josephus (in *Ant.* 17.166) describes Joseph as his 'relative,' the high priest Matthias was also from Galilee. Sean Freyne (*Galilee*, 165, 285) takes the implications a logical step further, citing Joseph ben Elem as an example of "priestly aristocratic landowners in Sepphoris," a step which Meyers appears to follow.

22. Miller, *Studies in the History and Tradition of Sepphoris*, 120–27. It is puzzling that Meyers ("Roman Sepphoris," 326 n27) does not follow this study that he calls "the definitive treatment." On the fragmentary inscription, see Avi-Yonah, "The Caesarea Inscription."

23. *Studies in the History and Tradition of Sepphoris*, 62–88.

Further clarification of the archaeological evidence and perhaps some reconceptualization of our categories of interpretation, however, may be necessary in order to assess the implications of recent archaeological findings at Sepphoris. Meyers asserts that "the considerable first-century remains that have been uncovered . . . point to a Torah-true population, judging by the number of ritual baths (*miqva'ot*) in houses and by the strict practice of burial outside the city precincts."[24] This places a great deal of weight on both (a small number of) ritual baths and burial customs. Was burial outside a city distinctive to Judean customs or, more particularly, distinctive to the Torah? Moreover, one wonders just how a chamber with a stepped entrance is deemed a *miqveh* or is determined to be a distinctively Jewish/Judean bath. An earlier assessment was less certain: "Although the identity of these pools as ritual baths seems likely, the identity of their users is far more speculative."[25] Were both the *miqvaot* and the burial customs particular marks of Torah-observance in the first century?

As Meyers himself points out, most of the archaeological evidence found at Sepphoris comes from the Middle and Late Roman strata. By the end of the second century numbers of Judeans had moved to Sepphoris, Tiberias, and smaller Galilean towns. In addition to priestly families, many rabbis who had gone to Yavneh after the destruction of Jerusalem relocated in Galilee and established academies at Usha, Beth Shearim, Sepphoris, and (eventually) Tiberias. The activity of Judah the Prince, including the redaction of the Mishnah, took place in the midst of a thriving multicultural urban center around 200 CE. The mixture of pagan and Jewish culture that Meyers describes in middle–late Roman times had clearly emerged by that time.[26] It is unclear, therefore, how a concept such as "Torah-true" is appropriate to the supposedly Jewish residents of the Western residential area of Sepphoris, given the artifacts unearthed there. Meyers assumes that the introduction of ritual baths in nearly every complex where early Roman houses were further developed means the residents were Jewish. Yet "the several bronze figurines [and] hundreds of second-third century decorated disc lamps, many with presumably pagan symbols, . . . found in this same area suggest a high degree of Hellenization among the Jewish residents . . . [and an] upper class lifestyle."[27] Is it possible that upper class Jewish families

24. E. M. Meyers, "Roman Sepphoris," 325.
25. E. M. Meyers, Netzer, C. L. Meyers, "Sepphoris—Ornament of Galilee," 18.
26. E. M. Meyers, "Roman Sepphoris," 329.
27. E. M. Meyers, "Roman Sepphoris," 329.

of third century Sepphoris may have been, at least in their own minds, simultaneously "Torah-true" (or "Mishnah-true," i.e. in their rites of purity) and "Hellenized" in the decor and implements of their houses?

Interpretation of the archaeological findings depends at least partly on how we pose questions to the data. In the case of the western residential area of Sepphoris in the third century it seems inappropriate to perpetuate the standard essentialist concepts "Jewish" and "pagan" on the basis of a particular privileged set of literary remains (Torah or Mishnah) and then proceed to apply those concepts to material remains. The same principle, however, would apply to late second temple times, when there is even less evidence, literary or material, for the residents of Sepphoris and their cultural ethos. Given its role as an urban administrative center or capital usually for regimes based elsewhere, it would appear far more important to trace the shifting political history of Sepphoris than to categorize evidence according to essentialist categories. For the regime using Sepphoris as its administrative base in Galilee would surely have determined the cultural ethos of the city.[28]

THE SHIFTING POLITICAL HISTORY OF SEPPHORIS

As symbolized and embodied in its prominent fortress, which persisted in some form virtually into modern times, Sepphoris had long functioned as a militarily fortified administrative base for whatever regime dominated Galilee. In approaching this question, therefore, it is important to consider the broader historical background of shifts in imperial control of Galilee, from the Persian, through the Ptolemaic and Seleucid, to the Roman empire, with a brief interlude of Hasmonean rule in the early first century BCE. Presumably each successive regime that used Sepphoris as an administrative base would have influenced the ethos of the town in some way, if only through the principal administrative officers it stationed there during its period of domination.

Settled already during seventh–sixth centuries and the Persian period, Sepphoris had almost certainly become a fortified administrative town

---

28. With regard to Sepphoris and other sites in Galilee in particular, recent rigorous attention to strata in archaeological digs should be matched by more rigorous attention to historical changes, particularly changes of rulers, who apparently had such an important role in shaping the urban ethos as well as in sponsoring major buildings.

under the Ptolemies and Seleucids.[29] The Hasmoneans probably inherited it as an already defensible fortress, as indicated in Josephus' report of Ptolemy Lathyrus' unsuccessful attack shortly after Alexander Janneus became king-high priest (*Ant.* 13.388). One would presume that, during the centuries of Jerusalem's reconstitution as the capital of the Judean temple-state, Sepphoris had been a Persian and then a Greek-speaking Hellenistic town prior to the Hasmonean take-over in 104 BCE.

The Hasmonean regime controlled Sepphoris for only two generations before the Romans took control of Palestine and then installed Herod as their client ruler. The Hasmoneans clearly kept a garrison in Sepphoris as well as in certain other strongholds in Galilee, presumably to maintain order and assure the payment of taxes (*Ant.* 14.413–414; *War* 1.303). That meant, presumably, that at the very least they installed trusted Judeans as the officers at the head of the administrative apparatus there. Since the Hasmoneans were involved for much of this time with further expansion of their rule and/ or virtual civil war with their subjects or rival factions, however, they seem unlikely to have devoted much energy to the thorough implantation of Judean culture in a recently secured district administrative town such as Sepphoris. In this connection one wants to know more about the "Greek words in Hebrew letters in Sepphoris as early as the Hasmonean period" which apparently "refer to titles or data that may be associated with officials or official functions of the city."[30] The Hasmonean regime was otherwise characterized by increasing Hellenistic influence, particularly under Alexander Jannaeus. These Greek words for administrative officers and functions in Hebrew letters suggest that while Hebrew became the official administrative language of the city, Greek terms and culture continued to thrive in the town.

Herod not only replaced the Hasmonean garrison at Sepphoris but would have systematically rooted out the remaining Hasmonean officers in Sepphoris just as he eliminated Hasmonean family and high officers in the rest of the realm. Given his practices elsewhere of sponsoring Hellenistic-style building projects and administration, it seems unlikely that he would have fostered a distinctively Judean administration and culture (religion) in Sepphoris.[31] Josephus' sole reference suggests only the military and

---

29. E. M. Meyers, Netzer, and C. L. Meyers, *Sepphoris*, 10.

30. E. M. Meyers, "Roman Sepphoris," 330.

31. Since it is not at all clear that a "synagogue" was found at Masada, one can hardly argue that Herod may have "supported synagogue Judaism privately" (vs. E. M. Meyers

political-economic administrative presence entailed in "the royal (fortress-palace)" along with the arms and goods stored there, in connection with the popular insurrection after the death of Herod (*Ant.* 17.271; *War* 2.56). Given the circumstances of the Hasmoneans during their brief control of Sepphoris and the characteristic Hellenistic-Roman orientation of Herod, it seems unlikely that a (distinctively) Judean culture would have become well-established during the hundred years of Jerusalem's control of the town. It would be most significant as well as surprising, therefore, were some clear indications of Judean culture to be found in further excavations at Sepphoris.

It is unclear precisely why the Romans would have "burned the city and enslaved its inhabitants" in 4 BCE (*War* 2.68; *Ant.* 17.289; was it simply in punitive retaliation for the revolt in the area? Or were Judas and his forces still in the town?).[32] Then, when Antipas took over his tetrarchy as Roman client ruler, says Josephus, he "fortified Sepphoris to be the ornament (*proschēma*) of all Galilee and called it Autokratoris, ("Imperial/Capital [City]," *Ant.* 18.27). The standard historical interpretation that Antipas thus "rebuilt" the city as his capital appears to be confirmed by the findings of the University of South Florida investigations. In excavations of building after building, they discovered the founding on bedrock in the early Roman period.[33] Meyers et al., however, claim to have found "no trace of violent destruction in the Herodian period" and emphasize the continuity of structures and culture.[34] The respective dating of the theatre illustrates the different interpretations given to the rebuilding of the city by Antipas, with Strange et al. opting for the time of Antipas, while Meyers et al. prefer a later date.

Antipas is often described in New Testament studies as a "Jewish king," his aniconic coins often being cited as evidence. It seems doubtful that Judeans would have viewed him so. Certainly the priestly aristocrat Josephus and/or the Jerusalem priestly (provisional) government at the beginning of the great Revolt in 66 did not view him as particularly loyal to "the laws of the Judeans" (to use Josephus' standard phrase). In building his

---

and Strange, *Archaeology, the Rabbis, and Early Christianity*, 24).

32. It is unclear why Meyers ("Roman Sepphoris," 323) says that Judas' attack on the royal palace/fortress "failed."

33. Strange, "Six Campaigns at Sepphoris."

34. E. M. Meyers, "Roman Sepphoris," 323; E. M. Meyers, Netzer, and C. L. Meyers, *Sepphoris*, 11.

second capital, Tiberias, he had both desecrated a cemetery and decorated his royal palace in violation of the law and ancestral tradition of the Judeans (*Ant.* 18.38; *Life* 64-65).

It would seem rather that Antipas would have established Roman (Hellenistic) style capitals at both Sepphoris and Tiberias, befitting the background and position of a Roman client ruler in the East who had been raised in Rome (*Ant.* 17.20) and both socialized and competed with other such Roman client rulers. "Herod Antipas' reconstruction of Sepphoris marked its transition from a Greek city to a Roman one," as Longstaff put it.[35] After deposing Antipas in 39 CE, moreover, the Romans took direct control of Sepphoris as their administrative capital in (western) Galilee. The theatre at Sepphoris, the founding of which Strange and Longstaff attribute to Antipas himself, exemplifies the Roman political-cultural style that would have come to dominance in Sepphoris under Antipas and the Romans, if not already under Herod the Great. The Latin names of the "Herodian" officers who still comprised the "principal men" in Tiberias in 66 also fit such a picture, and it is easy to imagine a similar set of names among the elite in Sepphoris as well, descendants of those brought in by Antipas to staff his royal administration, including bank and archives (*Life* 38).[36] Finally, Sepphoris' staunchly pro-Roman stance throughout the revolt in 66-67 and refusal to aid the Judeans' cause in any way (*Life* 30, 38, 104, 124, 232, 346-348, 373, 394-395) fits the "Roman" reading of the rebuilt Sepphoris, while insufficiently explained as mere "political" disagreements with supposedly "fellow-Jews."

Strange has recently suggested the concept of "Roman urban overlay" for the way in which Antipas rebuilt the city of Sepphoris. Once the Romans had conquered Palestine, Roman client rulers "imposed a distinctive *urban overlay*" upon a base of local Jewish culture.[37] "This 'urban overlay' . . . bore the major institutions, ideas, and symbols of Roman culture in Judea. The local Jewish culture, on the other hand, bore its own institutions, ideas, and symbols" (without significant disruption by the overlay).[38] This overlay was a "successful graft onto the local culture" because "as a matter

---

35. Longstaff, "Nazareth and Sepphoris," 12.

36. If Sepphoris was burned and its inhabitants enslaved in 4 BCE, as Josephus reports, then there would have been some discontinuity of inhabitants between the Judeans established there under the Hasmoneans (and Herod?) and the new Sepphorites brought in by Antipas.

37. Strange, "Some Implications of Archaeology for New Testament Studies," 32.

38. Strange, "Some Implications of Archaeology for New Testament Studies," 32.

of fact, the Jewish culture was already rural and urban and to some extent Hellenized, and therefore prepared for Roman dominance."[39] The symbols of specifically Roman culture, sometimes on a co-opted Hellenistic base, included "baths, hippodromes, theatres, amphitheaters or circuses, odeons, nymphaea, figured wall paintings, statues, triumphal movements, temples, etc. . . ."[40] "Symbols of the Jewish foundation include the Second Temple, synagogues or places of assembly, art forms with Jewish symbols (menorah, ethrog, lulab), and tombs."[41] The excavations at Sepphoris should provide a test case "for distinguishing local institutions and symbols from their Roman counterparts in the archaeological record."[42]

The rebuilt Sepphoris would likely have symbolized Roman dominance as the fortified capital of the client ruler Antipas and/or of the later Roman administration. Strange's development of this scheme, however, requires serious qualification, particularly in connection with how the dominant "overlay" stood in relation to the dominated society and its culture. To say that the relation of particular Jewish cultural symbols would have varied independently simply takes them out of the overall context of cultural subordination.[43] To say that Jewish culture was already urban as well as rural and therefore prepared for Roman domination[44] appears to be untrue of pre-Herodian Galilee in particular and does not appear to take into account the repeated and widespread resistance to Roman domination in "early Roman" Palestine in general (in 40–37 and 4 BCE and 66–70 CE, to mention only the major instances). To say that the idea "city" was not a foreign idea, but "expressed what the locals had in mind" and that "the citizens of the city . . . gave expression to their idea of a city by planning the city, building it, and living in it"[45] does not appear to take into account the degree to which rulers such as Antipas determined the building projects such as Sepphoris and Tiberias.

The foundation of Tiberias (within two decades of the rebuilding of Sepphoris, if Antipas was responsible) dramatically illustrates just how unurbanized Galilee was at the beginning of the first century CE. That there

39. Strange, "Some Implications of Archaeology for New Testament Studies," 32.
40. Strange, "Some Implications of Archaeology for New Testament Studies," 33.
41. Strange, "Some Implications of Archaeology for New Testament Studies," 33.
42. Strange, "Some Implications of Archaeology for New Testament Studies," 35.
43. Strange, "Some Implications of Archaeology for New Testament Studies," 38.
44. Strange, "Some Implications of Archaeology for New Testament Studies," 32.
45. Strange, "Some Implications of Archaeology for New Testament Studies," 34.

was a popular insurrection around Sepphoris parallel to those in Judea and Perea after Herod's death is a vivid reminder that Galilee, like those other areas, was not exactly "prepared for Roman dominance." If the most prominent inhabitants of the newly founded Tiberias or the reestablished Sepphoris were Herodian officials from Sebaste or Caesarea, Strange would have a point. If they were previous residents of Sepphoris or Jerusalemites, the new "Roman urban overlay" would have been at least somewhat strange. In any case, the building of Tiberias was sponsored by a Roman client ruler and would have been designed by his men, with little attention to the concerns of Jerusalem priestly circles or the Galilean villagers (*Life* 64–65). If Josephus' account of the building of Tiberias (*Ant.* 18:36–38) is any indication, the vast majority of the new residents would have had little to do with the planning, let alone the conception of the city-building.

Strange seems to have two incompatible concepts of the relations between the Roman overlay and indigenous "Jewish" culture. He thinks of Antipas making a synthesis of foreign innovation and local tradition, on the one hand.[46] Yet then he contends that "the local Jewish culture bore its own institutions, ideas, and symbols" without much disruption, on the other.[47] The latter does not appear to take into account striking examples of how the very "Jewish symbols" he mentions had already been dramatically affected by the influences of Hellenistic-Roman culture and political domination. The most obvious example is the "Second Temple" which had been massively reconstructed by Herod and in which there were prayers for Rome and the emperor led by high priests who were now the creatures of the Rome's client king or governor.[48] There is little or no evidence of synagogue buildings in first-century Galilee,[49] unless we mean the *proseuche* in Tiberias, a city built as another example of the "Roman urban overlay." As Strange himself comments, "Jewish architecture is difficult to pinpoint in the first century."[50] Perhaps that would be rooted in the fact that it was the rulers who determined major building projects, and they were pressing precisely the "Roman urban overlay."

---

46. Strange, "Some Implications of Archaeology for New Testament Studies," 35.
47. Strange, "Some Implications of Archaeology for New Testament Studies," 32.
48. Strange, "Archaeology and the Religion of Judaism," 650–55.
49. Flesher, "Palestinian Synagogues before 70 C.E."; Foerster, "Notes on Recent Excavations at Capernaum."
50. Strange, "Some Implications of Archaeology for New Testament Studies," 39.

The major problem with Strange's suggestion of a "Roman urban overlay" in Sepphoris at the time of Antipas (and Jesus), however, is that the principal "symbols" of the Roman overlay are yet to be found in Sepphoris itself. One can construct his picture of the Roman overlay only by combining evidence from several sites elsewhere in Herodian and subsequent Roman Palestine. Thus, although one could argue that the theatre in Sepphoris, supposedly built by Antipas, would provide an early example of Roman institutions imposed on Palestine, there is as yet no further evidence of a more complete Roman urban overlay in early first century Sepphoris. It seems highly likely that Sepphoris became ever more Romanized in the course of the late first and second centuries, with the establishment of direct Roman rule after the death of Agrippa I and the reconstitution of the city as Diocaesarea, as part of the general Roman policy of "urbanization" of Palestine under Hadrian and after.[51] The fuller "Romanization" of Sepphoris and Tiberias in the course of the second and third centuries, however, should not be projected back into the time of Antipas and Jesus.

HOW "HELLENIZED AND "COSMOPOLITAN" WAS GALILEE AT THE TIME OF JESUS?

That Sepphoris may have maintained certain traits of Hellenistic culture from the Ptolemaic and Seleucid periods and had been somewhat "Romanized" under Herod and/ or Antipas does not mean that it was all that "cosmopolitan" at the time of Jesus. Sepphoris may have been more cosmopolitan than Tiberias, for which the literary evidence is more plentiful. But Tiberias was apparently not all that cosmopolitan, judging from Josephus' accounts of both the founding of the city and the turmoil of 66-67 CE. Antipas had built the city without scruples about violating the cemetery on the site and decorated his royal palace with features objectionable to the later provisional high priestly regime in Jerusalem (*Ant.* 18:36; *Life* 64-65). The principal public building, moreover, was the "stadium." Yet there was also a huge *proseuche* (synagogue-building) where a large public assembly could be held. Among the residents fifty years after the founding of the city were some "Greeks." Yet they were not a substantial enough group to hold their own in 66 CE against the resentful popular party led by Jesus son of Sapphias (*Life* 66-67). The ten "principal men" (many with Latin names) and the historian Justus (Josephus' rival) who dominated affairs politically and

---

51. Avi-Yonah, *The Jews under Roman and Byzantine Rule*.

economically may have had some cosmopolitan pretensions. They resisted the instructions of the provisional high priestly government in Jerusalem to destroy the royal palace because of the objectional representations in its decor. Yet they were apparently officers of the Herodian toparchy administration (of Agrippa II), and could barely hold their own against the "riff-raff" who must have been descendants of the lowly people brought in by force at the city's founding, according to the aristocratic priest and historian Josephus. If those "Greeks" and Herodian officials cultivated a degree of cosmopolitan culture, then it was apparently a thin veneer.

Sepphoris may have been somewhat more "cosmopolitan" than Tiberias. Yet its cultured elite would presumably have been a similarly small percentage of the inhabitants, and it was quickly displaced in prominence by the new capital Tiberias, losing the archives and the royal bank as well as the important patronage of Antipas. Given the lack of literary or archaeological evidence for Sepphoris, we can only speculate whether through or underneath its elite there were carriers of cosmopolitan culture in the city.

Comparison with other cities in Palestine may help place in perspective the limited degree to which Sepphoris and Tiberias ever became cosmopolitan Roman-Hellenistic cities, let alone had already become so in the early first century. In neither city apparently has there been found the imported marble columns which are ubiquitous in the cities of Caesarea and Scythopolis, just south of Galilee. Similarly, no examples of imperial art have been found in the Galilean cities, while numerous examples were unearthed at Caesarea and Scythopolis. Or, to return to the institutions characteristic of Hellenistic cities, to date excavations of Sepphoris (and Tiberias) have not found evidence of a gymnasium, a hippodrome, an odeon, or a nymphaeum.

URBAN-RURAL RELATIONS IN GALILEE

The case for a cosmopolitan Lower Galilee in which a Cynic(-like) Jesus would fit also depends on the assumption of continuity of culture between city and country/villages. Roman-Hellenistic cultural influence is supposed to have emanated from city to villages in such a way that villagers were acculturated.[52] The assumption of cultural continuity in turn rests on the assumption of economic reciprocity between city and villages (or even villages' dependency on city). "People from the surrounding area probably

52. E.g., E. M. Meyers, "The Cultural Setting of Galilee," 698.

also flocked to Sepphoris on such occasions [as when the theatre was functioning], either to attend the theatre or to hawk their wares."[53] Neither assumption, however, is warranted by archaeological or literary evidence.

Cultural interaction between Galilean villagers and Sepphoris was probably far less frequent than recently imagined (apparently on a modern urbanized industrialized social model). It seems rather unlikely that many peasants would have "attended the theatre" in Sepphoris. Boatwright's study of "Theatres in the Roman Empire" finds that outside of Rome theatres were normally used only five to twenty-five times per year.[54] Moreover, they were used predominantly for political-cultural affairs, what Varro, in the first century BCE, or Robert Bellah and Ernst Barker in the twentieth, would call ceremonies of "civil religion." The audience or participants would have been primarily the residents of Sepphoris, many of whom were economically and politically dependent, directly or indirectly, on the administrative apparatus centered there. The seating capacity, moreover, would have accommodated only the adult population of Sepphoris.

Villages, on the other hand, were semi-autonomous corporate communities with their own social forms and traditional customs. Since peasants generally do not leave written records of their culture, we have no direct information—unless of course archaeologists unearth some. Yet it is perhaps noteworthy that the Mishnah makes clear distinctions between the respective regional customs of Judea, Perea, and Galilee, and even occasionally notes particular local customs within Galilee. The synoptic Gospels indicate that there was a clear difference between the Galilean and the Jerusalem dialects linguistically (in Aramaic?), a point now confirmed by modern study of distinctive regional variations in ancient Hebrew.[55] The fragmentary evidence available thus point to local-regional culture in towns and villages that would have been different from the nascent "Roman urban overlay" in Sepphoris and Tiberias.

The recent emphasis on the urbanization of Galilee in the first century (and after) assumes a high volume of "trade" between villages and city and an economic dependency of villages on the city for markets and services and protection.[56] Arguments for an extensive urban–rural trading network are

---

53. E. M. Meyers, "Roman Sepphoris," 333.

54. Boatwright, "Theaters in the Roman Empire."

55. Rendsburg, "The Galilean Background of Mishnaic Hebrew."

56. E.g., Edwards, First Century Urban/Rural Relations in Lower Galilee"; Adan-Bayewitz and Perlman, "The Local Trade of Sepphoris."

based almost exclusively on Adan-Bayewitz's ground breaking demonstration, through electron-activation analysis, that pottery made in the village of Kefar Hananya, between Upper and Lower Galilee, is found at sites up to about 25 kilometers away, the quantities varying inversely with the distance from the site of manufacture (1993). There is no evidence, however, that Kefar Hananya pottery was "marketed" by middlemen in "central market places" in Sepphoris and Tiberias. Adan-Bayewitz's own evidence virtually disproves such an imposition of an early-modern market model: (1) the appearance of the pottery varies inversely with distance from Kefar Hananya itself, not Sepphoris or Tiberias. (2) His rabbinic evidence suggests that the potters themselves delivered their wares on order or demand.[57] Even if there were considerable 'trade' in pottery, there are no grounds for extrapolating from trade in pottery to a generalized system of commercial (and cultural) interaction. Including trade in staple foods. Pottery production was unusual, dependent on a supply of clay, and its distribution apparently involved limited contact between producer and consumer-user. Archaeological evidence, primarily the distribution of pottery, cannot be claimed as evidence for an urban-rural trading network that supposedly provided the basis of cultural continuity between city and countryside. As Adan-Bayewitz points out himself at the outset of his presentation, "manufacture and trade in the Roman world were primarily local. Self-sufficiency in basic products was a fundamental principle of the ancient economy."[58]

Far from suggesting cultural continuity, the literary evidence for Galilee at the time of Jesus indicates sustained tension and even overt conflict between cities and the Galilean peasantry. Readers of Josephus' *Life* are familiar with his frequent description of extreme hostility between the Galileans and Sepphoris and (the elite of) Tiberias. Most striking, even allowing for exaggeration by Josephus, was the vehement hostility of "the Galileans" to Sepphoris at the time of the revolt in 66–67. Despite the implication in Josephus' first comment about it (*Life* 30), this conflict cannot be dismissed as due only to the pro-Roman stance of Sepphoris in 66. It was part of a general and long-standing resentment by the Galilean villagers of the cities from which they were ruled (e.g., *Life* 373–375). Intense Galilean hostility to Sepphoris went back at least as far as Herod the Great. Judging from Josephus' accounts (*War* 2.56; *Ant.* 17.271), the attack on the royal fortress led by Judas son of Ezechias after the death of Herod in 4

---

57. Adan-Bayewitz, *Common Pottery in Roman Galilee*, 229–30.
58. Adan-Bayewitz, *Common Pottery in Roman Galilee*, 19

BCE was a popular insurrection, apparently by peasants in the surrounding area. Far from a cultural continuity between cities and villages, the available evidence suggests a considerable degree of hostility to the cities among the Galilean villagers.

THE HISTORICAL CONTEXT OF JESUS' MINISTRY

Critical review of recent reports on archaeological explorations in Galilee thus indicate that archaeological evidence, even when combined with literary evidence, cannot deliver either a solidly Jewish (Judean) Galilee or a cosmopolitan Hellenistic Galilee as a cultural context for the ministry of Jesus. Indeed, the archaeological evidence and the construction of a historical context for Jesus resist comprehension according to such standard essentialist scholarly categories. The survey of the political history and the urban–rural relations necessary to accommodate archaeological as well as literary evidence, however, points to a historical structural conflict between the cities established by the rulers of Galilee and the Galilean people, the vast majority of whom lived in village communities.

That conflict, in fact, was becoming more intense precisely during Jesus' lifetime. Although we do not (yet) know the extent to which a "Roman urban overlay" was constructed by Antipas, it is clear that this Herodian whom the Romans placed over Galilee and Perea in 4 BCE engaged in major "development" projects. Although there is some dispute about the date of the theatre, it is clear that major rebuilding took place in Sepphoris in the early first century. As Josephus says, the rebuilt fortress city was his "ornament of all Galilee." Although Tiberias has not been extensively excavated yet, it is clear that Antipas founded this city as a second capital for his realm, complete with stadium and royal palace. Suddenly, within two decades, there were two "cities" in Lower Galilee, one or both visible to many villagers and within a half-day's walk. Such major "development" projects take resources, they have a cost. In a traditional agrarian economy, that cost is borne by the peasant producers, either in taxed goods or in direct labor on the construction. Wages for the latter, of course, were funded from the former. Herod had apparently already taxed the goods and endurance of the people, numbers of whom revolted at news of the tyrant's death. With the rebuilding of one city and the founding of a second, then, Antipas made a sudden new economic as well as cultural impact on the Galileans.

Archaeology of Galilee and the Historical Context of Jesus

It is sociologically naive simply to assume that cultural influences flow from city to village. Any influence from Sepphoris or Tiberias to Galilean villagers would have been mediated through the structure of political-economic relations between rulers and ruled, urbanites and villagers. Far from villages having been "satellite" or "dependent" on the cities, however, the dependency worked the other way. Cities obtained their revenues from the villages, precisely because villages and towns were politically subject to regimes based in the cities.

Economically, dependency was of city upon villages. As generally in antiquity, a city such as Sepphoris lived from the products taken from the villagers in the form of taxes, rents, or interest on loans by the rulers or landlords resident in the city.[59] Under Antipas, as under Herod, the principal form of Sepphoris' and Tiberias' income would have been tax revenues. As Josephus writes quite bluntly, in bestowing a tetrarchy upon Antipas, Augustus was providing his client ruler with a yearly revenue of two hundred talents from Galilee and Perea (*War* 2.95; *Ant.* 17.318). Influence of cities on the Galilean people would also have depended on how the people reacted. Here the available literary evidence, as noted above, indicates a decidedly hostile reaction. Although Galilean villagers may not have interacted frequently with the cities, they had clear images of what went on in the rulers' quarters. The synoptic Gospels provide a window or two onto some of those images: "great banquets" and rulers' birthday celebrations, at which popular prophets could be beheaded for a royal whim (Luke/Q 14:15-24; Mark 6:17-28); "look, those who put on fine clothing and live in luxury are in royal palaces" (Luke/Q 7:25). According to numerous Gospel traditions, moreover, Jesus addresses precisely the kinds of conditions that would have resulted from the sudden impact of intensified "urbanization" of Galilee on a peasantry that in normal times was economically marginal at best: indebtedness, hunger, and disintegration of fundamental social forms of family and village community (Luke/Q 6:27-38; 11:2-4; 12:22-31).

If assessed according to the structure and historical dynamics of urban-rural, ruler-ruled conflict in late second temple Palestine—instead of in the old essentialist categories of "Jewish" versus "Hellenistic"—recent archaeological evidence may point to a context in which Jesus' ministry and the movement(s) formed in response can be understood. In recent years scholarship on Jesus has been more willing to take seriously the portrayals in both the Christian Gospels and Josephus' histories of the conflict

---

59 Finley, *The Ancient Economy*; Garnsey and Saller, *The Roman Empire*.

between popular movements or leaders and the ruling institutions and officers in Jerusalem. Recent archaeological excavations in Galilee may now provide more windows onto the similar structural conflict between city and villages, rulers and ruled, as it intensified in the Galilean context precisely in the generation of Jesus and his followers.

Acknowledgments

THE AUTHOR AND PUBLISHER gratefully acknowledge the journals and publishers where the chapters in this volume first appeared.

Chapter 1 first appeared as "Expansion of Hasmonean Rule in Idumea and Galilee." In *Second Temple Studies III*, edited by Philip R. Davies and John Halligan, 134–65. JSOTSup 340. London: Sheffield Academic, 2002.

Chapter 2 first appeared as "Conquest and Social Conflict in Galilee." In *Recruitment, Conquest, and Conflict: Strategies in Judaism, Early Christianity, and the Greco-Roman World*, edited by Peder Borgen, Vernon K. Robbins, and David Gowler, 129–68. Emory Studies in Early Christianity 6. Atlanta: Scholars, 1998.

Chapter 3 first appeared as "Power Vacuum and Power Struggle." In *The First Jewish Revolt: Archaeology, History, and Ideology*, edited by Andrea Berlin and Andrew Overman, 87–109. London: Routledge, 2002.

Chapter 4 first appeared as "Bandits, Messiahs, and Longshoremen." In *SBL Seminar Papers 1988*, edited by David J. Lull, 183–99. Atlanta: Scholars, 1988.

Chapter 5 first appeared as "Archaeology and the Villages of Upper Galilee: A Dialogue with Archaeologists." *BASOR* 297 (1995) 5–16.

Chapter 6 first appeared as "Archaeology of Galilee and the Historical Context of Jesus." *Neotestamentica* 29 (1995) 211–29.

Bibliography

Abbott, Frank F., and Allan C. Johnson. *Municipal Administration in the Roman Empire.* Princeton: Princeton University Press, 1926.
Adams, Robert McC. "Anthropological Perspectives on Ancient Trade." *Current Anthropology* 15 (1974) 239–58.
Adan-Bayewitz, David. *Common Pottery in Roman Galilee: A Study of Local Trade.* Bar-Ilan Studies in NearEastern Languages and Culture. Ramat Gan: Bar Ilan University, 1993.
Adan-Bayewitz, David, and I. Perlman. "The Local Trade of Sepphoris in the Roman Period." *IEJ* 40 (1990) 153–72.
Appelbaum, Shimon. "The Hasmoneans—Logistics, Taxation, and Constitution." In *Judaea in Hellenistic and Roman Times: Historical and Archaeological Essays,* 9–29. SJLA 40. Leiden: Brill, 1989.
Avi-Yonah, Michael. "The Caesarea Inscription of the Twenty-Four Priestly Courses." In *The Teacher's Yoke: Studies in Memory of Henry Trantham,* eds. E. Jerry Vardaman et al., 46–57. Waco, TX: Baylor University Press, 1964.
———. *The Jews under Roman and Byzantine Rule.* New York: Schocken, 1976.
Banks, Robert. *Jesus and the Law in the Synoptic Tradition.* SNTSMS 28. Cambridge: Cambridge University Press, 1975.
Bar-Kochva, Bezalel. *Judas Maccabaeus: The Jewish Struggle against the Seleucids.* Cambridge: Cambridge University Press, 1989.
Bilde, Per. *Flavius Josephus between Jerusalem and Rome: His Life, His Works, and Their Importance.* Journal for the Study of the Pseudepigrapha 2. Sheffield: JSOT Press, 1988.
Blok, Anton. "The Peasant and the Brigand: Social Banditry Reconsidered." *Comparative Studies in Society and History* 14 (1972) 494–503.
Boatwright, Mary T. "Theatres in the Roman Empire." *BA* 53 (1990) 184–92.
Booth, Roger P. *Jesus and the Laws of Purity: Tradition History and Legal History in Mark 7.* Journal for the Study of the New Testament Supplements 13. Sheffield: JSOT Press, 1986.
Borg, Marcus J. "A Temperate Case for a Non-eschatological Jesus." *Forum* 2/3 (1986) 81–102.
Broshi, Magen. "The Population of Western Palestine in the Roman-Byzantine Period." *BASOR* 236 (1979) 1–10.

Bibliography

Bull, Robert J., and G. Ernest Wright. "Newly Discovered Temples on Mt. Gerizim in Jordan." *Harvard Theological Review* 58 (1965) 234–37.
Carney, T. F. *The Shape of the Past: Models and Antiquity*. Lawrence: Coronado, 1975.
Carr, David M. *Writing on the Tablet of the Heart: Origins of Scripture and Literature*. Oxford: Oxford University Press, 2005.
Chancey, Mark A.. "The Ethnicities of Galileans." In *Galilee in the Late Second Temple and Mishnaic Periods*, edited by David A. Fiensy and James Riley Strange, 1:112–28. 2 vols. Minneapolis: Fortress, 2015.
———. *The Myth of a Gentile Galilee*. SNTSMS 118. Cambridge: Cambridge University Press, 2002.
Chaney, Marvin L. *Peasants, Prophets, and Political Economy: The Hebrew Bible in Social Perspective*. Eugene, OR: Cascade Books, 2017.
Charlesworth, James H., ed. *The Messiah: Developments in Earliest Judaism and Christianity*. Minneapolis: Fortress, 1992.
Cohen, Shaye J. D. *Josephus in Galilee and Rome: His Vita and as a Historian*. Columbia Studies in the Classical Tradition 8. Leiden: Brill, 1979.
———. *From the Maccabees to the Mishnah*. Library of Early Christianity 7. Philadelphia: Westminster, 1987.
———. "The Place of the Rabbi in Jewish Society of the Second Century." In *The Galilee in Late Antiquity*, edited by Lee I. Levine, 157–63. New York: Jewish Theological Seminary, 1992.
Coote, Robert B. *In Defense of Revolution: The Elohist History*. Minneapolis: Fortress, 1991.
Crossan, John Dominic. *The Historical Jesus: The Life of a Mediterranean Jewish Peasant*. San Francisco: HarperCollins, 1991.
Davies, Philip R. "Hasidim in the Maccabean Period." *JJS* 28 (1977) 127–40.
De Ste Croix, G. E. M. *The Class Struggle in the Ancient Greek World*. Ithaca, NY: Cornell, 1981.
Edwards, Douglas. "First Century Urban/Rural Relations in Lower Galilee: Exploring the Archaeological and Literary Evidence." In *Society of Biblical Literature 1988 Seminar Papers*, edited by David J. Lull, 169–82. Atlanta: Scholars, 1988.
Elliott, John H. "Social Scientific Criticism of the New Testament and Its Social World: More on Methods and Models." *Semeia* 35 (1986) 1–35.
Finley, M. I. *The Ancient Economy*. Berkeley: University of California Press, 1973.
Fischer, Moshe, Asher Ovadiah, and Israel Roll. "The Roman Temple at Kedesh, Upper Galilee: A Preliminary Study." *Tel Aviv* 11 (1984) 146–72.
Flesher, Paul V. M. "Palestinian Synagogues before 70 C.E.: A Review of the Evidence." In *Studies in the Ethnography and Literature of Judaism*, edited by Jacob Neusner, Ernst Frerichs, 67–81. Approaches to Ancient Judaism 6. Brown Judaic Studies 192. Atlanta: Scholars, 1989.
Foerster, Gideon. "Excavations at Ancient Meron." *IEJ* 37 (1987) 262–69.
———. "Notes on Recent Excavations a Capernaum." In *Ancient Synagogues Revealed*, edited by Lee I. Levine, 207–11. Jerusalem: Israel Exploration Society, 1981.
Frankel, R. "Some Oil Presses from Western Galilee." *BASOR* 286 (1992) 39–71.
Freyne, Sean. "Bandits in Galilee: A Contribution to the Study of Social Conditions in First Century Palestine." In *The Social World of Formative Christianity and Judaism: Essays in Tribute of Howard Clark Kee*, edited by Jacob Neusner et al., 50–68. Philadelphia: Fortress, 1988.

———. "Hellenistic/Roman Galilee." In *Anchor Bible Dictionary*, edited by David Noel Freedman, 1:895–899. New York: Doubleday, 1992.

———. *Galilee: From Alexander the Great to Hadrian, 323 B.C.E. to 135 C.E.: A Study of Second Temple Judaism*. Wilmington, DE: Glazier, 1980a.

———. *Galilee, Jesus, and the Gospels*. Philadelphia: Fortress, 1988.

———. "The Galileans in the Light of Josephus' *Vita*." *NTS* 26 (1980) 397–413.

Garnsey, Peter, and Richard Saller. *The Roman Empire: Economy, Society, and Culture*. Berkeley: University of California, 1987.

Giddens, Anthony. *The Nation-State and Violence*. Berkeley: University of California, 1989.

Goodman, Martin. "The First Jewish Revolt: Social Conflict and the Problem of Debt." *JJS* 33 (1982) 417–27.

———. *The Ruling Class of Judaea: The Origin of the Jewish Revolt Against Rome, A.D. 66–70*. Cambridge: Cambridge University Press, 1987.

———. *State and Society in Roman Galilee, A.D, 132–212*. Totowa, NJ: Rowan & Allanheld, 1983.

Grabbe, Lester L. *Judaism from Cyrus to Hadrian*. Vol. 2. Minneapolis: Fortress, 1992.

Gutmann, Joseph, ed. *The Synagogue: Studies in Origins, Archaeology and Architecture*. New York: Ktav, 1915.

Hanson, John S. "Diadem: Insignia of Popular Messiahs in Josephus." Unpublished paper.

Hanson, R. S. *Tyrian Influence in the Upper Galilee*. Cambridge, MA: American Schools of Oriental Research, 1980.

Harper, G. M. "Village Administration in the Roman Province of Syria." *Yale Classical Studies* 1 (1928) 105–68.

Hayes, John H., and Jeffrey Kwan1991 "The Final Years of Samaria." *Biblica* 72 (1991) 153–81. Reprinted in John H. Hayes, *Interpreting Ancient Israelite History, Prophecy, and Law*, edited by Brad E. Kelle, 134–61. Eugene, OR: Cascade Books, 2013.

Hengel, Martin. *The Hellenization of Judaea in the first century after Christ*. Traanslated by John Bowden. Philadelphia: Trinity, 1989.

———. *Judaism and Hellenism*. 2 vols. Translated by John Bowden. Philadelphia: Fortress, 1974. Reprint, Eugene, OR: Wipf & Stock, 2003.

———. "Proseuche und Synagoge." In *The Synagogue: Studies in Origins, Archaeology and Architecture*, edited by Joseph Gutmann, 27–54. New York: Ktav, 1975.

Hobsbawm, Eric J. *Bandits*. 1st ed. New York: Dell, 1969.

———. *Bandits*. Rev. ed. New York: Pantheon, 1981.

———. *Primitive Rebels*. New York: Praeger, 1965.

Hoenig, Sidney. "The Ancient City-Square: The Forerunner of the Synagogue." In *ANRW* II.19.1 (1979) 448–75.

Horsley, Richard A. "Ancient Jewish Banditry and the Revolt against Rome, A.D. 66–70." *CBQ* 43 (1981) 409–32. Reprinted in *Politcs, Conflict, and Movements in First-Century Palestine*, edited by K. C. Hanson, 58–81. Eugene, OR: Cascade Books, 2023.

———. *Archaeology, History, and Society: The Social Context of Jesus and the Rabbis*. Valley Forge, PA: Trinity, 1996.

———. "Bandits, Messiahs, and Longshoremen: Popular Unrest in Galilee around the Time of Jesus." In *Society of Biblical Literature 1988 Seminar Papers*, edited by David J. Lull, 183–99. Atlanta: Scholars, 1988.

———. "Can Study of the Historical Jesus Escape Its Typographical Captivity?" *Journal for the Study of the Historical Jesus* 19 (2021) 265–329.

Bibliography

———. "Contesting Authority: Popular versus Scribal Tradition in Continuing Performance." In *Text and Tradition in Performance and Writing*, 99–122. Biblical Performance Criticism Series 9. Eugene, OR: Cascade Books, 2013.

———. *Galilee: History, Politics, and People*. Valley Forge, PA: Trinity, 1995.

———. "High Priests and the Politics of Roman Palestine." *JSJ* 17 (1986) 23–55. Reprinted in *Politcs, Conflict, and Movements in First-Century Palestine*, edited by K. C. Hanson, 1–29. Eugene, OR: Cascade Books, 2023.

———. "Historical Jesus and Archaeology in the Galilee: Questions from Historical Jesus Research to Archaeologists." In *Society of Biblical Literature 1994 Seminar Papers*, edited by E. H. Lovering, 91–135. Atlanta: Scholars, 1994.

———. *Jesus and Empire: The Kingdom of God and the New World Disorder*. Minneapolis: Fortress, 2003.

———. *Jesus and the Politics of Roman Palestine*. 2014. Revised with a new preface. Center and Library for the Bible and Social Justice Series. Eugene, OR: Cascade Books, 2021.

———. *Jesus and the Spiral of Violence: Popular Jewish Resistance in Roman Palestine*. San Francisco: Harper & Row, 1987. Reprint, Minneapolis: Fortress, 1993.

———. *Jesus in Context: Power, People, and Performance*. Minneapolis: Fortress, 2008.

———. "Josephus and the Bandits." *JJS* 10 (1979) 37–63. Reprinted in *Politcs, Conflict, and Movements in First-Century Palestine*, edited by K. C. Hanson, 33–57. Eugene, OR: Cascade Books, 2023.

———. "'Like One of the Prophets of Old': Two Types of Popular Prophets at the Time of Jesus." *CBQ* 47 (1985) 435–63. Reprinted in *Politcs, Conflict, and Movements in First-Century Palestine*, edited by K. C. Hanson, 113–41. Eugene, OR: Cascade Books, 2023.

———. "Menahem in Jerusalem: A Brief Messianic Episode among the Sicarii—not 'Zealot Messianism.'" *Novum Testamentum* 27 (1985) 334–48. Reprinted in *Politcs, Conflict, and Movements in First-Century Palestine*, edited by K. C. Hanson, 192–204. Eugene, OR: Cascade Books, 2023.

———. *The Pharisees and the Politics of Roman Palestine*. Eugene, OR: Cascade Books, forthcoming.

———. *The Pharisees and the Temple-State of Judea*. Eugene, OR: Cascade Books, 2022.

———. *Politics, Conflict, and Movements in First-Century Palestine*. Edited by K. C. Hanson. Eugene, OR: Cascade Books, 2023.

———. "Popular Messianic Movements around the Time of Jesus." *CBQ* 46 (1984) 471–95.

———. "Popular Prophetic Movements at the Time of Jesus: Their Principle Features and Social Origins." *Journal for the Study of the New Testament* 26 (1986) 3–27. Reprinted in *Politcs, Conflict, and Movements in First-Century Palestine*, edited by K. C. Hanson, 142–63. Eugene, OR: Cascade Books, 2023.

———. *The Prophet Jesus and the Renewal of Israel: Moving beyond a Diversionary Debate*. Grand Rapids: Eerdmans, 2012.

———. "Q and Jesus: Assumptions, Approaches, and Analyses." *Semeia* 55 (1991) 175–209.

———. "Questions about Redactional Strata and the Social Relations Reflected in Q." In *1989 Society of Biblical Literature Seminar Papers*, edited by David J. Lull, 186–203. Atlanta: Scholars, 1989.

———. *Revolt of the Scribes: Resistance and Apocalyptic Origins*. Minneapolis: Fortress, 2010.

———. *Scribes, Visionaries, and the Politics of Second Temple Judea*. Louisville: Westminster John Knox, 2007.

———. "The Sicarii: Ancient Jewish Terrorists." *Journal of Religion* 59 (1979) 435–58. Reprinted in *Politcs, Conflict, and Movements in First-Century Palestine*, edited by K. C. Hanson, 167–91. Eugene, OR: Cascade Books, 2023.

———. *Sociology and the Jesus Movement*. New York: Crossroad, 1989.

———. *Text and Tradition in Performance and Writing*, 99–122. Biblical Performance Criticism Series 9. Eugene, OR: Cascade Books, 2013.

———. "The Zealots: Their Origin, Relationships and Importance in the Jewish Revolt." *NovT* 2 (1986) 159–92.

Horsley, Richard A., with John S. Hanson. *Bandits, Prophets, and Messiahs: Popular Movements in the Time of Jesus*. New Voices in Biblical Studies. 1985. Reprinted with a new preface, Valley Forge, PA: Trinity, 1999.

Horsley, Richard A., and Patrick Tiller. "Ben Sira and the Sociology of the Second Temple." In *Second Temple Studies III: Studies in Politics, Class, and Material Culture*, edited by Philip R. Davies and John M. Halligan, 74–107. Journal for the Study of the Old Testament Supplements 340. Sheffield: Sheffield Academic, 2002.

Isaac, Benjamin. "Bandits in Judaea and Arabia." *Harvard Studies in Classical Philology* 88 (1984) 171–203.

Isaac, Benjamin, and Israel Roll, I. *Roman Roads in Judaea I: The Legio-Scythopolis Road*. BAR International Series 141. Oxford: B.A.R., 1982.

Jalabert, Louis, and René Mouterde, eds. *Inscriptions Grecques et Latines de la Syrie*. Vol. 5. Bibliothèque archéologique et historique. Paris: Geuthner, 1929.

Jensen, Morten Hørning. "The Political History in Galilee from the 1st Century BCE to the End of the 2nd Century CE." In *Galilee in the Late Second Temple and Mishnaic Period*, vol. 1: *Life, Culture, and Society*, edited by David A. Fiensy and James Riley Strange, 51–77. Minneapolis: Fortress, 2014.

———. "Purity and Politics in Herod Antipas's Galilee: The Case for Religious Motivation." *Journal for the Study of the Historical Jesus* 11 (2013) 3–34.

Jones, A. H. M. *The Cities of the Eastern Roman Provinces*. 2nd ed. Oxford: Clarendon, 1971.

———. *The Roman Economy: Studies in Ancient Economy and Administrative History*. Oxford: Blackwell, 1974.

———. "The Urbanization of Palestine." *Journal of Roman Studies* 21 (1931) 78–85.

Jossa, Giorgio. "Josephus' Actions in the Galilee during the Jewish War." In *Josephus and the History of the Graeco-Roman Period*, edited by Fausto Parente and Joseph Sievers, 265–78. SPB 41. Leiden: Brill, 1994.

Kasher, Aryeh. *Jews, Idumaeans, and Ancient Arabs: Relations of the Jews in Eretz-Israel with the Nations of the Frontier and the Desert during the Hellenistic and Roman Era*. Texts and Studies in Ancient Judaism 18. Tubingen: Mohr Siebeck, 1988.

Kautsky, John. *The Politics of Aristocratic Empires*. 1982. Reprinted with a new introduction, New Brunswick, NJ: Transaction, 1997.

Kee, Howard Clark. "Early Christianity in the Galilee: Reassessing the Evidence from the Gospels." In *The Galilee in Late Antiquity*, ed. Lee I. Levine, 3–22. New York: Jewish Theological Seminary, 1992.

———. "The Transformation of the Synagogue after 70 CE: Its Import for Early Christianity." *NTS* 36 (1990) 1–24.

Kindler, Arie. *The Coins of Tiberias*. Tiberias: Hamei Tiberia, 1961.

Kloppenborg, John S. *The Formation of Q*. Studies in Antiquity and Christianity. Philadelphia: Fortress, 1987.

Bibliography

Kuhn, Thomas S. *The Structure of Scientific Revolutions*. 2nd ed. Chicago: University of Chicago Press, 1970.

Lenski, Gerhard. *Power and Privilege: A Theory of Social Stratification*. New York: McGraw, 1966. 2nd ed., Chapel Hill: University of North Carolina Press, 1982.

Levine, Lee I. , ed. *The Galilee in Late Antiquity*. New York: Jewish Theological Seminary, 1992.

———. "The Jewish Patriarch (Nasi) in Third Century Palestine." In *ANRW* II.19.2 (1979) 619–88.

———. *The Rabbinic Class of Roman Palestine*. New York: Jewish Theological Seminary, 1989.

Longstaff, Thomas R. W. "Nazareth and Sepphoris: Insights into Christian Origins." *Anglican Theological Review* 11 (1990) 8–15.

Mack, Burton L. "The Kingdom that Didn't Come: A Social History of the Q Tradents." In *Society of Biblical Literature 1988 Seminar Papers*, edited by David J. Lull, 608–35. Atlanta: Scholars, 1988.

———. *A Myth of Innocence: Mark and Christian Origins*. Philadelphia: Fortress, 1988.

———. *Wisdom and the Hebrew Epic: Ben Sira's Hymn in Praise of the Fathers*. Chicago Studies in the History of Judaism. Chicago: University of Chicago Press, 1985.

Mendels, Doron. *The Land of Israel as a Political Concept in Hasmonean Literature: Recourse to History in Second Century B.C. Claims to the Holy Land*. Texts und Studien in Ancient Judaism 15. Tübingen: Mohr Siebeck, 1987.

Meshorer, Ya'akov. *City-Coins of Eretz-Israel and the Decapolis in the Roman Period*. Jerusalem: Israel Museum, 1985.

———. *Jewish Coins of the Second Temple Period*. Translated by I. H. Levine. Tel Aviv: Am Hassefer, 1967.

Meyers, Carol L. 1983 "Of Seasons and Soldiers: A Topological Appraisal of the Premonarchic Tribes of Galilee." *BASOR* 252 (1983) 47–59.

Meyers, Eric M. "The Cultural Setting of Galilee: The Case of Regionalism and Early Judaism." In *ANRW* II.19 (1979) 686–702.

———. "Galilean Regionalism as a Factor in Historical Reconstruction." *BASOR* 221 (1976) 93–101.

———. "Galilean Regionalism: A Reappraisal." In *Approaches to Ancient Judaism*, vol. 5, edited by William Scott Green, 115–31. Atlanta: Scholars, 1985.

———. "Introduction." In R. S. Hanson, *Tyrian Influence in the Upper Galilee*, 1–5. Cambridge, MA: American Society of Oriental Research, 1980.

———. "Roman Sepphoris in Light of New Archaeological Evidence and Recent Research." In *The Galilee in Late Antiquity*, edited by Lee I. Levine, 321–28. New York: Jewish Theological Seminary, 1992.

Meyers, Eric M., A. Thomas Kraabel, and James F. Strange. *Ancient Synagogue Excavations at Khirbet Shema', Upper Galilee, Israel, 1970–1972*. Durham, NC: Duke University Press, 1976.

Meyers, Eric M., Ehud Netzer, and Carol L. Meyers. *Sepphoris*. Winona Lake, IN: Eisenbrauns, 1992.

———. "Sepphoris—Ornament of All Galilee." *BA* 49 (1986) 4–19.

Meyers, Eric M., and James F. Strange. *Archaeology, the Rabbis, and Early Christianity*. Nashville: Abingdon, 1981.

Meyers, Eric M., James F. Strange, and Carol L. Meyers. *Excavations at Ancient Meiron*. Meiron Excavation Project 3. Cambridge, MA: ASOR, 1981a.

———. "Preliminary Report on the 1980 Excavations at en-Nabratein, Israel." *BASOR* 244 (1981b) 1–25.
———. "Second Preliminary Report on the 1981 Excavations at en-Nabratein, Israel." *BASOR* 246 (1982) 35–54.
Meyers, Eric M., James F. Strange, Carol L. Meyers, and R. S. Hanson. "Preliminary Report on the 1977 and 1978 Seasons at Gush Halav." *BASOR* 233 (1979) 33–58.
Miller, Stuart S. *Studies in the History and Traditions of Sepphoris.* SJLA 37. Leiden: Brill, 1984.
Moehring, H. R. Review of S. J. D. Cohen, *Josephus in Galilee and Rome.* JJS 31 (1980) 240–41.
Moxnes, Halvor. *The Economy of the Kingdom: Social Conflict and Economic Relations in Luke's Gospel.* Philadelphia: Fortress, 1988.
Neusner, Jacob. "The Demise of Normative Judaism." *Judaism* 15 (1966) 230–40.
———. "'First Cleanse the Inside': The Halakic Background of the Controversy Saying." *NTS* 22 (1976) 486–95.
———. *From Politics to Piety: The Emergence of Pharisaic Judaism.* Englewood Cliffs, NJ: Prentice-Hall, 1973.
———. *Judaism: The Evidence of the Mishnah.* Chicago: University of Chicago, 1981.
———. Review of Freyne, *Galilee. Journal of Religion* 62 (1982) 429–30.
Neusner, Jacob, et al., eds., *Judaisms and Their Messiahs at the Turn of the Christian Era.* Cambridge: Cambridge University Press, 1987.
Nock, Arthur Darby. *Conversion: The Old and the New in Religion from Alexander the Great to Augustine of Hippo.* London: Oxford University Press, 1933.
Oakman, Douglas E. *Jesus and the Economic Questions of His Day.* Studies in the Bible and Early Christianity 8. Lewiston, NY: Mellen, 1986..
Overman, J. Andrew. "Who Were the First Urban Christians?" In *Society of Biblical Literature 1988 Seminar Papers,* edited by David J. Lull, 160–68. Atlanta: Scholars, 1988.
Pritchard, James B. *Ancient Near Eastern Texts Relating to the Old Testament.* 3rd ed. Princeton: Princeton University Press, 1969.
Rajak, Tessa. *Josephus: The Historian and His Society.* Philadelphia: Fortress, 1983.
Rappaport, Uriel. "Where Was Josephus Lying—in His *Life* or in the *War?*" In *Josephus and the History of the Greco-Roman Period: Essays in Memory of Morton Smith,* edited by Fausto Parente and Joseph Sievers, 279–89. SPB 41. Leiden: Brill, 1994.
———. "Hellenistic Cities and the Judaization of Palestine in the Hasmonean Age." In *Doron: Studies in Classical Culture Presented to B. Z. Katz Benshalom,* edited by S. Perlman and B. Shimron, 214–30. Tel Aviv: Mif'al ha-Shikpul, 1967.
———. "Les Idumens en Egypte." *Revue de Philogie* 43 (1969) 73–82.
Reed, Jonathan L. "The Population of Capernaum." Claremont: IAC Occasional Papers, 1992.
Rendsburg, Gary A. "The Galilean Background of Mishnaic Hebrew." In *The Galilee in Late Antiquity,* edited by Lee I. Levine, 225–39. New York: Jewish Theological Society of America, 1992.
Renfrew, Colin, and Paul Bahn. *Archaeology: Theories, Methods and Practice.* New York: Thames & Hudson, 1991.
Safrai, S. "The Synagogue." In *The Jewish People in the First Century: Historical Geography, Political History, Social, Cultural and Religious Life and Institutions,* edited by

Bibliography

S. Safrai and M. Stern, vol. 2, 908–44. Compendia rerum Iudaicarum ad Novum Testamentum, Section 1. Assen: Van Gorcum, 1976.

Saldarini, Anthony J. "Johanan ben Zakkai's Escape from Jerusalem: Origin and Development of a Rabbinic Story." *JSJ* 6 (1975) 189–204.

———. *Pharisees, Scribes and Sadducees in Palestinian Society: A Sociological Approach.* Wilmington, DE: Glazier, 1988.

Sanders, E. P. *Jesus and Judaism.* Philadelphia: Fortress, 1985.

Schaefer, Peter. "Die Flucht Johanan b. Zakkai aus Jerusalem und die Gruendung des 'Lehrhauses' in Jabne." In *ANRW* II.19.2 (1979) 43–101.

Schultz, Siegfried. *Q: Die Spruchquelle der Evangelisten.* Zurich: Theologischer Verlag, 1972.

Schürer, Emil. *Geschichte des jüdischen Volkes im Zeitalter Jesu Christi.* 3rd / 4th ed. Leipzig: Hinrichs, 1901.

———. *The History of the Jewish People in the Age of Jesus Christ (175 B.C.–A.D. 135).* New rev. ed. by Geza Vermes, Fergus Millar, and Matthew Black. 3 vols. Edinburgh: T. & T. Clark, 1973–1987.

Schwartz, Stephen. "Israel and the Nations Roundabout: 1 Maccabees and the Hasmonean Expansion." *JJS* 2 (1991) 16–38.

———. "Josephus in Galilee: Rural Patronage and Social Breakdown." In *Josephus and the History of the Graeco-Roman Period: Essays in Memory of Morton Smith,* edited by Fausto Parente and Joseph Sievers, 290–307. SPB 41. Leiden: Brill, 1994.

Scott, James C. "Protest and Profanation: Agrarian Revolt and the Little Tradition [2 parts]." *Theory and Society* 4 (1977) 1–38, 211–46.

Shatzman, Israel. *The Armies of the Hasmoneans and Herod: From Hellenistic to Roman Frameworks.* Texte und Studien zum antiken Judentum 25. Tubingen: Mohr Siebeck, 1991.

Shaw, B. D. "Bandits in the Roman Empire." *Past & Present* 105 (1984) 3–52.

Sievers, Joseph. *The Hasmoneans and Their Supporters: From Mattathias to the Death of John Hyrcanus I.* South Florida Studies in the History of Judaism 6. Atlanta: Scholars, 1990.

Silberman, Neil Asher. *Between Past and Present: Archaeology, Ideology, and Nationalism in the Modern Middle East.* New York: Holt, 1989.

———. *Digging for God and Country: Exploration, Archeology, and the Secret Sruggle for the Holy Land, 1799–1917.* New York: Knopf, 1982.

Smallwood, E. Mary. "High Priests and Politics in Roman Palestine." *Journal of Theological Studies* 13 (1962) 14–34.

———. *The Jews under Roman Rule: From Pompey to Diocletian.* SJLA 20. Leiden: Brill, 1976.

Smith, Anthony D. *Theories of Nationalism.* 2nd ed. New York: Holmes & Meier, 1983.

Smith, Jonathan Z. *Drudgery Divine: On the Comparison of Early Christianities and the Religions of Late Antiquity.* Jordan Lectures in Comparative Religion 14. Chicago Studies in the History of Judaism. Chicago: University of Chicago, 1990.

Smith, Morton. "Zealots and Sicarii: Their Origins and Relation." *Harvard Theological Review* 64 (1971) 1–19.

Stager, Lawrence E. "The Song of Deborah: Why Some Tribes Answered the Call and Others Did Not." *Biblical Archaeology Review* 15 (1989) 1–11.

Stern, Menahem. "Aspects of Jewish Society: The Priesthood and Other Classes." In *The Jewish People in the First Century: Historical Geography, Political History, Social, Cultural, and Religious Life and Institutions,* edited by S. Safrai and M. Stern, vol.

2, 561–630. Compendia rerum Iudaicarum ad Novum Testamentum. Assen: Van Gorcum, 1976.

———. *Greek and Latin Authors on Jews and Judaism*. Vol. 1. 3 vols. Jerusalem: Israel Academy of Sciences and Humanities, 1974.

Strange, James F. "Archaeology and the Religion of Judaism in Palestine." In *ANRW* II.19.1, (1979) 646–85.

———. "The Capernaum and Herodium Publications." *BASOR* 226 (1977) 65–73.

———. "New Developments in Greco-Roman Archaeology in Palestine." *BA* 45 (1982) 85–88.

———. 1992a. "Six Campaigns at Sepphoris: The University of South Florida Excavations at Sepphoris, 1983–89." In *The Galilee in Late Antiquity*, ed. Lee I. Levine, 339–56. New York: Jewish Theological Seminary, 1992.

———. "Some Implications of Archaeology for New Testament Studies." In *What Has Archaeology to Do with Faith?*, edited by James H. Charlesworth and Walter P. Weaver, 23–59. Faith and Scholarship Colloquies. Philadelphia: Trinity, 1992.

Tadmor, Hayim. "Some Aspects of the History of Samaria during the Biblical Period." Jerusalem Cathedra 3 (1983) 1–11.

Tcherikover, V. A. "Was Jerusalem a Polis?" *IEJ* 14 (1964) 61–78.

Tcherikover, Victor A., Alexander Fuks, and Menahem Stern. *Corpus Papyrorum Judaicarum*. 3 vols. Cambridge: Harvard University Press, 1957–64.

Thackeray, H. St.J. *Josephus: The Man and the Historian*. Hilda Stich Stroock Lectures 1928. New York: Jewish Institute of Religion, 1929.

Theissen, Gerd. *The Gospels in Context: Social and Political History in the Synoptic Tradition*. Translated by Linda M. Maloney. Minneapolis: Fortress, 1991.

Tiller, Patrick A. "The Social Settings of the Components of 1 Enoch." In *After Apocalyptic: Rethinking Texts in Context*. Eugene, OR: Cascade Books, 2012.

Trigger, Bruce G. *A History of Archaeological Thought*. Cambridge: Cambridge University Press, 1989.

Ulrich, Eugene. *The Dead Sea Scrolls and the Origins of the Bible*. Studies in the Dead Sea Scrolls and Related Literature. Grand Rapids: Eerdmans, 1999.

Vale, Ruth. "Literary Sources in Archaeological Description: The Case of Galilee, Galilees, and Galileans." *JSJ* 18 (1987) 209–26.

Wellhausen, Julius. "Über den geschichtlichen Wert des zweiten Makkabäerbuches im Verhältnis zum ersten." *Nachbericht von der Gesellschaft der Wissenschaft zu Goettingen, Phil.-hist. Klasse*, 117–63. 1905.

Westerholm, Stephen. *Jesus and Scribal Authority*. Coniectanea biblica: New Testament Series 10. Lund: Gleerup, 1978.

Wild, Robert. "The Encounter between Pharisaic and Christian Judaism: Some Early Gospel Evidence." *Novum Testamentum* 27 (1985) 105–24.

Wolf, Eric R. *Peasants*. Foundations of Modern Anthropology Series. Englewood Cliffs, NJ: Prentice-Hall, 1966.

Wright, G. Ernest. *Shechem: The Biography of a Biblical City*. New York: McGraw-Hill, 1964.

Index

Alexander Jannaeus (Hasmonean king–high priest), 8, 12, 27, 33, 47, 55, 57–58, 70, 110, 135, 156, 181
archaeology of Galilee, 4, 21–24, 151–92
  essentialist categories, 175–78
  generalizations outrun evidence, 157–60, 165–66
  limitations of, 7–9, 22–24
  Sepphoris
    archeological evidence mostly late, 179
    evidence for priestly presence late, 177–78
    Hellenization among Jewish residents, 189
    Roman elements?, 183–86
  urban-rural relations, 187–92
    tension and conflict, 188–92
  use of literary evidence, 153–54, 155–57, 159–60
  villages in upper Galilee, 151–72
    industrial-commercial model projected onto, 161–64
    misreading of roads in, 154–55
    regional difference questionable, 167–70

banditry, social, 19, 128–31
bandits/brigands
  large gangs of in Great Revolt, 116–19
  escalated into revolt, 118–19, 130–31, 137–39

(standard) concepts and constructs problematic, 61–63, 151–52

(early) Christianity, concept of, 61–63
conflict between rulers and ruled, 12, 15–18, 19–21, 60, 80–85, 101–26, 127–50, 189–92
Costobar (Idumean officer of Herod), 39–40, 59
covenantal commandments
  as motives for Galileans, 85–91
    in burning of Antipas palace, 87
    in demand for circumcision of nobles, 88
    in peasant strike, 86–87
    in sabbath observance, 90
    in supplying oil to Caesarea Philippi, 88–89
    in Jesus' criticism of Pharisees and scribes, 93–99

Ezechias (bandit-chieftan in Galilee), 131–36

Freyne, Seán, 10–13, 21, 62, 65–66, 81, 83, 85, 128, 129, 131–33, 173

Gabara (town in Galilee), 111
Galileans, 2, 7–9
  and covenantal commandments, 85–91

Index

Galileans (continued)
    descendants of ancient northern Israelites, 52–53, 71–73
    loyal to covenant commandments, 13, 85–91
    Hasmonean take over of, 5–7, 28–29
    history different from Judeans, 102
    in Great Revolt, 112–16, 137–39
        distrust Josephus, 112–16, 148
        manipulated by Josephus, 112–15
        peasants hostile to urban elite, 112–16, 118–20
        (almost) a peasant revolt, 112–20
    no attachment to Jerusalem rule, 65–66, 81–85
    prior to Hasmonean take-over, 48–54, 71–73
    under Hasmonean rule, 47–59
    were they Jews/Judeans?, 28, 78
Galileans and the Torah/Law (see Galileans and the covenantal commandments)
Galilee
    as context for Jesus
    movement led by Judas son of Ezechias, 143
    neither cosmopolitan nor Jewish/Judean, 190–92
    cosmopolitan urbanized, 173–75
        not yet at time of Jesus, 186–87
    dynamics of Hasmonean rule in, 54–58
    Jerusalem rule in, 73–77
    take-over by Hasmoneans, 5–7, 64–73
    under Herod Antipas, etc. 77–79
    urban-rural relations, 187–90
        cultural interaction infrequent, 188
        tension and conflict, 189–92
    villages, 188
Gischala (village in Galilee)
    during Great Revolt, 111
    led by John, 111–12
Great Revolt, 4, 101–26
    complex set of conflicts, 101, 108–18
    high priests try to control, 104–6
    in Galilee, 108–18
    in Judea, 120–26
        three phases, 122–26
        mainly a peasant revolt, 125–26

Hasmonean(s) (high priests)
    conquest and rule of Idumeans, 35–45
    expansion of rule, 34–42
        a religious crusade or conversion?, 35–41
        in vacuum of imperial power, 41–42
    mercenary army, the basis of their power, 33, 35
    rise of, 30–33
    rule of the Galileans, 47–58
    dynamics of rule in Galilee, 54–59
    relations with Idumeans, 42–47, 58–59
    Roman confirmation of rule, 33–35
    take-over of Galilee, 5–7, 28–29, 64–73
Herod
    rule in Galilee, 75–76
Herod Antipas (ruler of Galilee), 77–78
    impact on Galileans, 102–3
high priests
    never completely accepted by all, 120–21
    no longer in control, 122
    predatory on the people, 121
    provisional government in Jerusalem, 103–6, 120–24
    try to control Great Revolt, 104–5, 107, 14–125
    reassert their rule in Galilee, 107
Hobsbawm, Eric, 19, 117, 119, 129–31, 135–36, 138, 148
(John) Hyrcanus (Hasmonean high priest)
    expansionist conquests, 41–42, 44–45

Idumeans
    Hasmonean conquest of, 5–6, 43–45
    relations with Hasmonean rulers, 42–47, 58–59

Israelite culture/tradition, 25
  in Galilee, 99–100
  "great" (elite) tradition, 102
  "little" (popular) tradition, 102
Israelites (northern), 11, 71–73

John of Gischala, 111–12, 118–19, 137
  rival of Josephus for control of Galilee, 112
Jonathan (first Hasmonean high priest), 31
(Flavius) Josephus
  agenda as historian, 103–5, 128
  as "general" controlling Galileans, 103–8
  manipulation of Galileans, 112–13
  military forces of, 105–7
  sent to control Galilee, 105–6
(early) Judaism
  concept of, 27–28, 61–63
  Christian construction of, 61–62
Judaization, 2–3, 11–12, 63–64, 73–77
Judea
  expansion of its rule, 27
  Great Revolt in, 120–26
Judean villagers, 6
Judas son of Ezechias, 139–43
  acclaimed king by followers, 142–43
  one of several popular messianic movements, 137–43

kings, popular, 20

Lenski, Gerhard, 4, 29, 93

Pharisees
  Jesus' criticism of, 93–99
  not leaders of synagogues/ assemblies, 91–92
  retainers of the high priests, 92–94
  role in Galilee?, 13–14, 57–58, 74, 76, 93

the poor in Tiberias, 20

religion
  embedded in political and economic activities, 100
retainers, 4, 92–93
Romans
  (re-)conquests, 102
  generating their own opposition, 116–17
rulers
  conflict with the people, 3, 15–18, 80, 102–26, 143–50

Sepphoris (city in Galilee)
  during Great Revolt, 108
  material evidence mostly late, 179
  Roman elements?, 183–86
  shifting political history, 180–86
sicarioi (scribal "terrorists"), 16, 123
Simon, consolidates Hasmonean rule, 32–33
(historical) sociological analysis, 3–4, 28–29
synagogues/ assemblies, 56, 91–92

temple state of Judea, 29–30
  part of an imperial system, 30
Tarichaeae (Magdala)
  allied with Josephus, 110–11
text-fragments as sources, 5
Tiberias (Herodian city in Galilee)
  conflicts during Great Revolt, 109–10
  Herodian elite in, 109–10, 143–46
  urban poor in, 143–50

"the Zealots" (modern scholarly construct), 129
Zealots (fugitive peasants in Jerusalem), 129